the
PERFECT
BLEND

100 blender recipes to energize & revitalize

tess masters

photography by anson smart

jacqui
small

contents

introduction: find your perfect blend 1

the recipes

INTRODUCTION

find your perfect blend

Hi, my name's still Tess, and I'm still a blendaholic and even more convinced that the blender's *the* greatest tool for making delicious, beautiful, healthy fast food. And, it's the power of plants to energize and revitalize, in endless blended combos, that gets me most excited. My readers, in emails by the truckload, have asked for recipes geared to specific health outcomes. They inspired me to choose my top twelve ways of looking at food, and to create recipes to help us achieve those goals.

I'm a cook, not a nutritionist, and because I enjoy virtually all plant-based foods, deciding which ones to feature posed a challenge. I went with ingredients I love and that help me stay in optimal health. Rather than serving up a comprehensive analysis of the nutritional properties and virtues of each of these hero foods, I've shared a few top-line takeaways – practical information on their health benefits, and how to prepare, blend and cook them for amazing textures and tastes. All my heroes boast more than one special power, and they work in combination, not just on their own. Many of them belong in multiple categories, or even in all twelve. The main food chart, on pages 2 and 3, serves as a guide, covering diverse nutrient-dense foods that create a balanced, healthy diet.

The variety of foods and exceptional recipes in this book aim to inspire us to eat well *and* have fun. As cooks, eaters and bodies, we're all unique, with different needs and preferences. This food is functional and geared towards flexibility, so you can tailor the recipes to your own taste and requirements.

The optional boosters listed for each recipe enhance flavour and/or nutrition. I've chosen them to work on their own or together, so you can supplement any base recipe with one, two or all three.

Grab your blender, choose your own adventure and discover what makes the perfect blend . . . for you.

	energy	immunity	detox	protein	weight loss	anti-inflammatory	fabulous fats	low carb	alkaline forming	probiotic promoting	well combined	feed the soul
almonds	•	•	•	•	•	•	•	•	•			•
apple	•	•	•	•	•	•	•		•	•		•
artichoke		•	•		•		•		•	•		•
asparagus	•		•			•	•	•	•	•		•
avocado	•	•	•	•	•	•	•	•	•	•	•	•
banana	•	•					•				•	•
beetroot			•			•	•		•			•
blueberries	•		•		•	•		•	•			•
broccoli	•	•	•		•	•	•	•	•			•
brussels sprouts		•	•		•	•	•		•			•
cabbage		•	•		•	•	•		•	•		•
carrots		•	•				•		•			•
cashew nuts	•			•					•			•
cauliflower		•	•			•			•			•
cayenne pepper		•	•		•	•	•	•	•	•	•	•
celery		•				•	•		•	•	•	•
chard		•	•	•	•	•	•	•	•	•	•	•
chia seeds	•	•	•	•	•	•	•		•			•
coconut	•	•	•	•	•	•	•		•			•
coriander		•				•	•		•		•	•
cranberries		•					•	•	•			•
courgette					•				•			•
cucumber			•			•	•		•			•
flaxseeds		•				•	•		•			•
garlic		•	•			•	•		•		•	•
ginger		•	•		•	•	•		•		•	•

	energy	immunity	detox	protein	weight loss	anti-inflammatory	fabulous fats	low carb	alkaline forming	probiotic promoting	well combined	feed the soul
grapefruit		•	•		•	•	•		•			•
hemp seeds	•			•	•		•	•	•			•
kale		•	•	•	•	•	•	•	•	•	•	•
lemon and lime		•	•		•	•	•		•		•	•
mango		•					•					•
mint			•				•	•	•		•	•
orange		•			•				•			•
pak choi			•	•		•	•	•	•	•	•	•
parsley			•			•		•	•			•
pineapple	•	•	•				•					•
pepper		•				•	•		•			•
pumpkin seeds	•			•			•	•				•
raspberries		•	•		•	•	•	•	•			•
rocket			•	•		•	•		•		•	•
sea vegetables		•	•	•		•	•	•	•	•		•
sesame seeds	•			•	•		•		•			•
shiitake mushrooms		•				•	•	•				•
spinach		•	•	•	•	•	•	•	•	•	•	•
spring greens		•	•	•		•	•	•	•	•	•	•
strawberries		•	•		•	•	•		•			•
sunflower seeds	•			•		•	•		•			•
sweet potato	•	•						•	•			•
tomato						•	•		•			•
turmeric		•	•			•	•		•			•
walnuts	•			•		•	•	•	•			•
watermelon		•			•				•			•

energy

energy

Simple carbs spike blood sugar, giving bursts of energetic bliss followed by dramatic dips and blasts of unhealthy inflammation and oxidation. Our magnificent machines run best on a foundation of complex, low-glycaemic carbohydrates, which break down more slowly for a sustained release of energy. To skip the unwanted aftermath – fatigue and stress – fill up with the best fuel.

bananas

A tasty treat of carbs, potassium, B vitamins, antioxidant vitamin C, manganese and copper, the trusty 'nana motors your carb-metabolizing machine, helping to build proteins, oxygenate the blood and support circulation, digestion and immunity. Delivering 27 g of carbs, half in natural sugars and one-fifth in resistant starch (RS), a ripe medium banana is a slimming satiator. RS makes you feel full, slows digestion, stabilizes blood sugar and revs up overall metabolism. An under-ripe 'nana, better yet, has twice as much RS! At either stage, bananas pack fibre for digestive cleansing. They also contain small amounts of fat, in the form of sterols, which are ace for the adrenals. Bananas service your spark plugs, too, with the amino acid tryptophan, elevating mood and staving off depression, while magnesium pulls back the throttle and calms the nervous system.

Great as a pick-me-up or workout boost in breakfasts, desserts and sandwiches, banana is magic in baked goods, as an egg replacer and high-fibre flavour enhancer. Fresh or frozen, it's an ideal sweetener for smoothies; not quite ripe, it ups the RS without a banana blast to the buds.

edamame

Loaded with complex carbs (and fibre to slow digestion), satiating fats, omega-3s and 9 g of muscle-building protein, 80 g (3 oz) of shelled soya beans (always buy non-GMO) is a pit stop that powers your ride with no lethargic lag. Edamame is premium fuel, with magnesium and B-complex vitamins for an oxygen-octane surge to your metabolism. To further oxygenate the blood, copper enhances iron absorption and phosphorous optimizes energy use.

The prep won't sap your strength, either – or burn up time. Banish the boiling; run frozen pods or beans under hot water and toss with natural salt for a satisfying snacketizer that replenishes lost electrolytes after a workout. For energy elation, throw shelled edamame into salads, soups and stews. These bouncing beans cram in the carbs, so pair with non-starchy veggies or sugar overload may slow you down. If you're suspicious of soya, see my tofu and tempeh riff (page 52). Key takeaway: in moderation, edamame is a healthy whole soya option.

pineapple

The prickly pineapple hides a soft, sweet centre, housing a horde of nutrients just raring to deploy! Manganese and thiamine (vitamin B_1) take point, upping enzyme activity for energy production and antioxidant defences. Iodine and manganese provide tactical support to the thyroid, regulating how fast fats and carbs are metabolized, helping us win the weight-loss war, too. Bromelain, the protein-digesting enzyme in pineapple, ups the energy ammo. It works like a personal assistant to the digestive tract, making sure that big protein molecules are broken apart optimally into the amino acids the body needs to support enzyme reactions, hormones, muscle development and lean body-mass formation. Bromelain also bolsters the ability of vitamin C to suppress coughs, loosen mucus, flush out toxins, reduce swelling and bloating and stimulate circulation, all for a deep-dive detox.

Fresh pineapple adds tang and aroma to sweet and savoury salads, drinks, salsas and gazpachos. Frozen, pineapple's great in granitas and ice creams, and makes a smoothie a sweet cream dream. The high vitamin C content in pineapple makes it an especially poor choice canned because it will leach more toxins (like BPA) from the container. The canned stuff looks fine on the supermarket shelf, where it should stay.

maça

This righteous root, aka Peruvian ginseng, pumps performance. Its steroid-like compounds help metabolize macronutrients to increase endurance and aid muscle and tissue recovery in your workout and beyond. It's also a top plant-based source of elusive and energizing vitamin B_{12}. To oxygenate and revitalize the adrenals and combat stress, maca provides an arsenal of antioxidants, vitamins, proteins and minerals like calcium, potassium and iron. It also supports healthy cortisol levels to reduce anxiety and depression, providing restful sleep. Or not: maca boosts libido and fertility, so you may be up all night, feeling grrrrreat!

Gelatinized maca powder is my pick over raw. Maca needs to be cooked because its starches are fibrous and largely indigestible. Heat does kill live enzymes and some nutrients, but it separates the root's starch, making beneficial alkaloids and other micronutrients easier to assimilate. This medicinal master is a potent player, so she's best in cameo roles. Adding 1 teaspoon up to 1 tablespoon of the powder gives a caramel note to smoothies and desserts. With compatriots like banana, cacao and coconut, maca conjures up magic; it's delish, too, with almond butter, yogurt and berries. Whatever your blend, enjoy it right away for balanced flavour – left to sit, maca gets bitter and assertive.

brown rice

Whole hulled rice supplies more sustenance than its refined white counterpart, and skips the energy-sapping slide. Brown rice is loaded with complex carbs and fibre, plus manganese to help burn those carbs (and protein) as fuel. Mitochondria, our cells' internal power plants, thrive on manganese, terminating free radicals produced in energy output before they can mess with our mojo. Brown rice also provides magnesium, a key mineral to turn off the body's stress response, a common cause of fatigue or 'burn out', to support sustained release of energy. As a fibre-rich alternative to white rice, brown rice fills you up. Like the noshable 'nana, it contains that all-important resistant starch (RS), boosting metabolism and burning fat.

water

To get fuel from food, our bodies need fluids. Via digestion and our blood, water transports all the nutrients we rely on, then flushes the wastes that cause fatigue. Even mild dehydration is a downer. So, load up on high-water-content foods like leafy greens, lettuces, cucumber, celery, radishes, tomatoes, peppers, cauliflower, broccoli, strawberries, grapefruit and melons, and be a lush with the liquids. Drink filtered water (see my filtration picks on page 211), or your body will be sifting out the unsavouries – and it's got better things to do.

more hero foods

- almonds
- apples
- avocado
- broccoli
- cashews
- cherries
- chia seeds
- coconut
- goji berries
- hemp seeds
- leafy greens (such as chard, kale, spinach)
- legumes (beans, lentils, peas)
- melons
- pistachios
- pumpkin seeds
- quinoa
- sprouts (such as alfalfa, broccoli, pea)
- sunflower seeds
- sweet potato
- walnuts

Zesty, sweet and loaded with nutrients and anti-inflammatory agents, this is my favourite workout drink. The coconut water replenishes electrolytes and the chia ups stamina and endurance. If your mix is frothy, don't be alarmed – the blended-pineapple suds settle with chilling.

glowing green chia

SERVES 2

240 ml (8½ fl oz) raw coconut water or filtered water

44 g (1½ oz) baby spinach

1 English cucumber, roughly chopped (do not peel)

320 g (11 ½ oz) ripe fresh pineapple, diced

1½ tsp finely grated lime zest, plus extra to taste

2 tbsp fresh lime juice, plus extra to taste

⅛ tsp ground turmeric

Pinch of natural salt (see page 139)

Alcohol-free liquid stevia (optional)

1 tbsp chia seeds (black or white), plus extra to taste

optional boosters

1 tbsp plain liquid chlorophyll

1 tbsp pure aloe vera juice

1 tsp wheatgrass powder (see page 171)

Throw all of the ingredients except the chia seeds, but including the boosters, into your blender and blast on high for 30–60 seconds until the ingredients are completely pulverized. Strain with a filtration bag, nut milk bag or fine-mesh sieve, and then whisk in the chia seeds. Transfer to a jar, seal tightly and chill in the fridge for 30–60 minutes. Enjoy cold.

NUTRITIONAL FACTS (PER SERVING)

calories 134 kcal | fat 1.9 g | saturated fat 0.2 g | sodium 174.4 mg | carbs 30.8 g | fibre 5.3 g | sugars 18.7 g | protein 3.4 g | calcium 104.6 mg | iron 2 mg

Power your engine with this supercharged chocolate shake. For a bigger energy boost, add the maca and chia, and for a wake-up, add the cayenne. Enjoy this one before the spring greens and pepper get pushy.

magic mojo

SERVES 2

480 ml (17 fl oz) unsweetened almond milk or hemp milk (strained if homemade)

4 tbsp espresso (2 shots), plus extra to taste

18 g (¾ oz) cacao powder or unsweetened cocoa powder

½ tsp probiotic powder (see page 154, optional)

30 g (1 oz) spring greens (stalks removed), chopped

60 g (2¼ oz) frozen raw cauliflower florets

65 g (2¼ oz) roasted almond butter

44 g (1½ oz) chopped pitted dates, soaked (see page 171)

1 tsp natural vanilla extract

1½ frozen bananas, plus extra to taste

optional boosters

1 tbsp maca powder (see page 7)

1 tbsp chia seeds (black or white)

Pinch of cayenne pepper

Throw all of the ingredients except the bananas and boosters into your blender, and blast on high for 30 seconds until well combined. Add the boosters and the frozen bananas and blast again on high for a further 30 seconds until smooth and creamy. Drink immediately before the spring greens get assertive and the chia seeds (if using) thicken the drink.

NUTRITIONAL FACTS (PER SERVING)

calories 526 kcal | fat 27.7 g | saturated fat 6.8 g | sodium 153.7 mg | carbs 62.1 g | fibre 11.3 g | sugars 40.1 g | protein 18.5 g | calcium 433.3 mg | iron 3.4 mg

The pleasure in every blissful bite is so worth the hour-of-prep pain. To simplify it all, make the cheeze, soured cream and beans a day ahead, then throw together the pico, guac and toppings right before serving. I load my nachos up with olives, jalapeño chillies and coriander. The base is so rich and cheezy, dairy devotees will dive into these with reckless abandon any way they can.

nosh-on-'em nachos

SERVES 6–8; BEANS MAKE 325 G (11½ OZ); PICO DE GALLO MAKES 265 G (9¼ OZ); GUACAMOLE MAKES 480 G (17 OZ)

beans
180 ml (6 fl oz) vegetable stock

2 tbsp tomato purée

½ tsp fresh lemon juice, plus extra to taste

¼ tsp ground cumin, plus extra to taste

¼ tsp chipotle powder, plus extra to taste

½ tsp Bragg Liquid Aminos, gluten-free soy sauce or tamari

½ tsp onion powder

½ tsp garlic powder

½ tsp natural salt (see page 139), plus extra to taste

1 (425 g/15 oz) can or 210 g (7 oz) cooked pinto beans, drained and rinsed

pico de gallo
360 g (12¾ oz) tomato, diced

50 g (1¾ oz) red onion, diced

7 g (¼ oz) finely chopped coriander leaves

1½ tbsp fresh lime juice, plus extra to taste

1 tbsp deseeded and finely chopped jalapeño chilli, plus extra to taste

1 tsp finely chopped garlic (about 1 clove, optional)

½ tsp natural salt (see page 139), plus extra to taste

Freshly ground black pepper

guacamole
2 avocados, stoned and peeled

80 g (3 oz) tomato, deseeded and diced

1 tbsp diced red onion, plus extra to taste

1 tsp finely chopped garlic (about 1 clove)

1 tsp deseeded and finely chopped green chilli, plus extra to taste

1 tbsp finely chopped coriander leaves

1½ tsp fresh lime or lemon juice, plus extra to taste

¼ tsp natural salt (see page 139), plus extra to taste

265 g (9¼ oz) organic or non-GMO white tortilla chips, plus extra to serve

240 ml (8½ fl oz) It's-Better-with-Cheeze Sauce (page 69)

240 ml (8½ fl oz) So Good! Soured Cream (page 183)

2 tbsp finely chopped salad onion (white and green parts)

optional boosters
34 g (1¼ oz) pitted black olives, sliced, plus extra to taste

29 g (1 oz) thinly sliced jalapeño chilli, plus extra to taste

2 tbsp finely chopped coriander, plus extra to taste

Preheat the oven to 190°C/ 375°F/Gas mark 5.

To prepare the beans, throw everything except the pinto beans into your blender and blast on high until well combined. Add the beans and process on medium speed for about 30 seconds until you reach a rustic consistency akin to refried beans. Add more vegetable stock if you prefer a looser bean mix. Set aside.

To make the pico de gallo, toss all of the ingredients together in a bowl and tweak the flavours to taste.

To make the guacamole, mash the ingredients together in a bowl to a rustic consistency and tweak the flavours to taste.

On a large ovenproof platter or in a baking dish, spread the bean purée in a flat circle. Cover with the corn chips and drizzle over the cheeze sauce. Bake for 5–7 minutes until hot. Remove from the oven. Top with the pico de gallo, guacamole and 80 ml (3 fl oz) of the soured cream. Top with the salad onion and the olive, chilli and coriander boosters. Serve immediately, and pass extra corn chips and the remaining soured cream around the table.

NUTRITIONAL FACTS (PER SERVING, BASED ON 6 SERVINGS)

calories 650 kcal | fat 27.1 g | saturated fat 4.2 g | sodium 1000.5 mg | carbs 53 g | fibre 11.5 g | sugars 5.3 g | protein 15.6 g | calcium 104.1 mg | iron 4.0 mg

This energizing green spin on a classic crowd-pleaser is rich, creamy and every bit as delicious as its conventional counterpart. Shredding the cavolo nero, a type of kale, is key to nipping any bitterness in the bud. Loaded with a variety of healthy carbohydrate and protein sources, rather than the usual cashews in a vegan Caesar, this is a light but satisfying meal. Hail to the kale!

NUTRITIONAL FACTS (PER SERVING, BASED ON 8 SERVINGS)

calories 456 kcal | fat 37 g | saturated fat 7.4 g | sodium 408 mg | carbs 19.8 g | fibre 8.4 g | sugars 3.3 g | protein 19.3 g | calcium 276.4 mg | iron 6 mg

kale! caesar

SERVES 8 AS A STARTER, 6 AS A MAIN; DRESSING MAKES 480 ML (17 FL OZ),
SEED CHEEZE MAKES 75 G (2³/4 OZ)

tempeh croûtons

2 tbsp coconut oil
(in liquid form), plus extra
as needed

227 g (8 oz) tempeh,
cut into very thin slices

seed cheeze

130 g (4¹/2 oz) hulled
raw sesame seeds

3 tbsp nutritional yeast flakes,
plus extra to taste

¹/2 tsp garlic powder, plus extra
to taste

¹/4 tsp natural salt (see page
139), plus extra to taste

dressing

120 ml (4 fl oz) filtered water

120 ml (4 fl oz) extra virgin
olive oil

4 tbsp fresh lemon juice, plus
extra to taste

40 g (1¹/2 oz) raw pine nuts,
soaked (see page 171)

40 g (1¹/2 oz) raw sunflower
seeds, soaked (see page 171)

1¹/2 tbsp white miso paste

1 tbsp capers, drained

1¹/2 tsp gluten-free vegan
Worcestershire sauce (see
page 210)

1¹/2 tsp Dijon mustard

2 tsp finely chopped garlic
(about 2 cloves)

¹/2 tsp natural salt (see page
139), plus extra to taste

¹/8 tsp freshly ground black
pepper

salad

500 g (1 lb 2 oz) romaine
hearts (about 5 hearts), cut
into ribbons

150 g (5¹/2 oz) cavolo nero
(1 large bunch, stalks
removed), cut into ribbons

320 g (11¹/2 oz) shelled raw
edamame

optional boosters

160 g (5³/4 oz) Brussels sprouts,
shaved

130 g (4¹/2 oz) raw sprouted
watermelon seeds

1 avocado, stoned, peeled
and sliced

To make the croûtons, heat the coconut oil in a very large frying pan over a medium heat and add the tempeh pieces, arranging them in one layer without crowding. You may have to do this in two batches. Fry for about 2 minutes until golden brown. Turn the pieces over and brown the other side for about 2 minutes. Remove from the pan and drain on kitchen paper, blotting with extra kitchen paper. Crumble into small pieces.

To make the seed cheeze, throw the seed cheeze ingredients into a food processor and process until the seeds have broken up and the texture resembles Parmesan cheese. Tweak the nutritional yeast, garlic powder and salt to taste.

To make the dressing, throw all of the dressing ingredients into your blender and blast on high for about 1 minute until smooth and creamy. Tweak the lemon juice and salt to taste.

In a large salad bowl, mix together the romaine lettuce, kale, edamame, the Brussels sprout and watermelon seed boosters and the dressing. Toss in the croûtons and three-quarters of the seed cheeze. Sprinkle with the remaining seed cheeze and top with slices of avocado.

haitian heaven

SERVES 6 AS A STARTER, 4 AS A MAIN

1 kabocha squash, cut into 8 pieces and deseeded

2.8 litres (5 pints) vegetable stock

2 tbsp grapeseed oil or extra virgin olive oil

150 g (5½ oz) yellow onion, diced

1 tbsp finely chopped garlic (about 3 cloves)

160 g (5¾ oz) carrot, diced

132 g (4½ oz) celery, diced

1 tbsp natural salt (see page 139), plus extra to taste

3 tbsp finely chopped fresh thyme, plus extra to taste

200 g (7 oz) green cabbage, shredded

100 g (3½ oz) leek (white part), chopped

135 g (4½ oz) turnip, peeled and diced

300 g (10½ oz) orange-flesh sweet potato, peeled and diced

150 g (5½ oz) potato, peeled and diced

140 g (5 oz) green pepper, deseeded and diced

2 tbsp onion powder

2 tbsp garlic powder

½ tsp freshly ground black pepper, plus extra to taste

¼ tsp chilli flakes, plus extra to taste

¼ tsp ground cloves

Pinch of cayenne pepper, plus extra to taste (optional)

1 tbsp coconut oil (in liquid form)

3 tbsp fresh lemon juice, plus extra to serve

14 g (½ oz) finely chopped coriander

optional boosters

1 avocado, stoned, peeled and sliced

55 g (2 oz) raw pecans or 70 g (2½ oz) cashews

20 g (¾ oz) salad onion (white and green parts), finely chopped

Throw the kabocha squash pieces into a large pot and cover with water. Bring to the boil over a high heat, then lower the heat to medium and simmer for about 30 minutes until the squash is fork tender. Allow to cool slightly, then scoop out the flesh and discard the skin. You should have about 850 g (1 lb 13 oz) of squash. Working in batches, throw the squash flesh into your blender with 720 ml (1¼ pints) of the vegetable stock and blast on high for about 30 seconds until puréed. Set aside.

In a large pot over a medium heat, warm the oil and sauté the onion, garlic, carrot, celery, 1 teaspoon of the salt and 2 tablespoons of the thyme for about 5 minutes until the vegetables begin to soften. Add the cabbage, leek, turnip, sweet potato, potato, pepper, onion powder, garlic powder, black pepper, chilli flakes, cloves, cayenne, the squash mixture, 1 teaspoon of the salt and the remaining stock. Cover, bring to the boil, then lower the heat to medium and cover partially. Cook at a high simmer for about 20 minutes until the vegetables are just tender. Allow to cool slightly. Stir in the coconut oil, lemon juice, coriander, remaining 1 teaspoon salt and the remaining tablespoon of thyme. Tweak the salt, thyme, chilli flakes, black pepper and cayenne to taste. Serve with a buffet of boosters, extra lemon juice and any other toppings you like.

This vegan version of the *soupe joumou* that Haitians devour on New Year's Day, and on Sundays all year, will rock your world. Chef Danielle Jean-François and her sister Michelle helped me tweak their grandma's recipe. Instead of using the traditional – and super-hot – habanero chillies, to keep the heat consistent we spiced things up with chilli flakes and some cayenne, then stirred in coconut oil in place of butter and soured cream. This soup's typically served with a ton of bread and butter and a buffet of toppings. Use the avocado, salad onion and nut boosters, or experiment with hot sauce, roasted aubergine, sautéed mushrooms or kale chips. However you serve it, one sensational spoonful will make you wonder how you've ever been happy without Haitian.

NUTRITIONAL FACTS (PER SERVING, BASED ON 6 SERVINGS)

calories 218 kcal | fat 7.5 g | saturated fat 2.7 g | sodium 931.2 mg |
carbs 37.4 g | fibre 7.3 g | sugars 7.5 g | protein 4.5 g |
calcium 136 mg | iron 2.5 mg

Since lasagne's ubiquitous, why cook up yet one more version if not to make it spectacular? I revel in the raves from everyone who's tried this healthier take on mamma's classic. (Check out the photo on page 132.) Meaty and cheezy, moist but not runny, the dish holds together beautifully – just let it cool for 15 minutes before cutting. Like most lasagnes, it's a 3-hour traipse through the Italian countryside. A perfect way to spend a lazy Sunday afternoon, so I'll mention one unlisted optional booster: the last glass of red from Saturday night to sip as you slave!

lick-your-plate lasagne

SERVES 8

5 tbsp extra virgin olive oil, plus extra as needed

704 g (1 lb 8 oz) baby spinach

750 g (1 lb 10 oz) Really Good Ricotta (page 133)

1 large aubergine, peeled lengthways every 12 mm (1/2 in), and then sliced into 5 mm (1/4 in) rounds

1 1/2 tsp natural salt (see page 139), plus extra to taste

1/4 tsp freshly ground black pepper, plus extra to taste

2 medium courgettes, sliced into 5 mm (1/4 in) rounds

1.75 kg (3 lb 14 oz) Terrific Tomato Sauce (page 189)

24 gluten-free vegan oven-ready lasagne sheets – about 1 1/2 (280 g/10 oz) packets

25 g (1 oz) finely chopped flat-leaf parsley leaves

optional boosters

1 tsp finely chopped fresh oregano

1 tsp finely chopped fresh thyme

1 tsp finely chopped fresh basil

Preheat the oven to 180°C/350°F/Gas mark 4. Grease a 23 x 33 cm (9 x 13 in) baking dish with olive oil.

In a large frying pan or pot over a medium-high heat, warm 2 tablespoons of the olive oil and sauté the spinach for 5–7 minutes until completely wilted. You may have to do this in batches. Allow to cool. Squeeze the liquid out of the spinach until it's as dry as possible. You should have about 220 g (7 3/4 oz) of spinach. Roughly chop the spinach, stir it into the ricotta and set aside. You should have about 960 g (2 lb 1 oz) of the spinach-ricotta mixture.

In a large bowl, toss the aubergine slices with 2 tablespoons of the olive oil, 1 teaspoon of the salt, pinch of the pepper, and the oregano, thyme and basil boosters. In another bowl, toss the courgette slices with the remaining 1 tablespoon of olive oil and salt and pepper.

Spread 250 g (9 oz) of the tomato sauce over the base of the baking dish. Then, lay one-third of the lasagne sheets in a single snug layer on top of the tomato sauce. Spoon half of the spinach-ricotta mixture over the pasta and spread evenly. Next, lay half of the aubergine rounds (so they are touching but not overlapping) in rows, filling the surface with one layer. Layer half of the courgette rounds on the aubergine. Top with 500 g (1 lb 2 oz) of the tomato sauce and spread evenly. Place another layer of lasagne sheets on top. Spoon 500 g (1 lb 2 oz) of the spinach-ricotta mix on top and layer on the remaining aubergine rounds, the remaining courgette rounds, 500 g (1 lb 2 oz) of the tomato sauce and the remaining lasagne sheets. Top with the remaining 500 g (1 lb 2 oz) of sauce. Cover with foil and bake for 1¼ hours or until the vegetables are cooked through. Remove from the oven and leave to rest for at least 15 minutes before slicing. Sprinkle with fresh parsley and cut into eight pieces.

NUTRITIONAL FACTS (PER SERVING)

calories 448 kcal | fat 21.7 g | saturated fat 3.2 g | sodium 1884 mg | carbs 53.3 g | fibre 11.1 g | sugars 14.7 g | protein 17.1 g | calcium 280.6 mg | iron 7 mg

In honour of a radical rice roaster, I've dubbed this 'the gem from Geoffrey'. Fragrant and loaded with flavour, this sensational side seduces your senses with every bite. For more ravishment yet, try the lentil, pine nut and lime zest boosters.

herbed roasted rice

SERVES 6–8; GREEN SAUCE MAKES 315 G (11 OZ)

green sauce

80 ml (2¾ fl oz) extra virgin olive oil

80 g (3 oz) coriander leaves

40 g (1½ oz) mint leaves

2 tbsp fresh oregano leaves

150 g (5½ oz) white onion, diced

1 tbsp finely chopped garlic (about 3 cloves)

2 tsp natural salt (see page 139)

1 tbsp deseeded and finely chopped jalapeño chilli, plus extra to taste

Pinch of chilli flakes, plus extra to taste

rice

3 tbsp grapeseed oil or extra virgin olive oil

1 tsp finely chopped garlic (about 1 clove)

Pinch of chilli flakes

570 g (1 lb 4 oz) brown basmati rice

1 tsp natural salt (see page 139), plus extra to taste

1 tbsp finely grated lime zest

1.4 litres (2½ pints) filtered water

20 g (¾ oz) coriander, finely chopped

40 g (1½ oz) salad onion (white and green parts), finely chopped

Freshly ground black pepper

optional boosters

240 g (8½ oz) cooked green lentils

70 g (2½ oz) dry-toasted pine nuts, plus extra to taste

1 tbsp finely grated lime zest, plus extra to taste

Preheat the oven to 200°C/400°F/Gas mark 6.

To make the green sauce, throw all of the sauce ingredients into the blender and blast on high for 30–60 seconds until smooth. You may need to add a tablespoon or so of filtered water to blend.

In a casserole dish over a high heat, warm the oil until hot and sauté the garlic, chilli flakes, rice and salt, stirring constantly, for about 5 minutes until fragrant. Add the lime zest and stir for a further 2 minutes until a mild citrus fragrance develops. Add the green sauce and the water and bring to the boil. Turn off the heat, place the lid on the pot and transfer to the oven for about 45 minutes until the water has been soaked up and the rice is cooked. Remove from the oven and stir the rice to allow the steam to escape. Allow the rice to stand, uncovered, for about 15 minutes to settle and finish cooking through. Fluff with a fork, then stir in the coriander, salad onion and boosters. Season with pepper and tweak the salt to taste.

NUTRITIONAL FACTS (PER SERVING, BASED ON 8 SERVINGS)

calories 407 kcal | fat 16.4 g | saturated fat 2.2 g | sodium 890.1 mg | carbs 59.3 g | fibre 4.1 g | sugars 1.7 g | protein 6.6 g | calcium 77 mg | iron 2.4 mg

Pistachios are a rich source of energy, offering high-quality carbohydrates, protein, heart-healthy monounsaturated fatty acids, antioxidants and minerals. My favourite way to eat them is in ice cream, every day of the week and twice on Sundays. But if you're going to indulge, why settle for a pallid pistachio punch? This dairy-free version, using a blend of pistachios and almond milk, delivers a full pistachio flavour, and thanks to coconut milk, a truly creamy texture. (You *will* need a high-speed blender and ice-cream maker.) The base recipe is righteous, but let the rosewater, vanilla and toasted coconut boosters take you off on an awesome adventure.

pistachio ice cream

MAKES 800 G (1 LB 12 OZ)

1 (398 ml/14 oz) can full-fat coconut milk (shake, then pour)

240 ml (8½ fl oz) unsweetened almond milk (strained if homemade)

198 g (7 oz) shelled, unsalted roasted pistachios

44 g (1½ oz) baby spinach

127 g (4½ oz) chopped pitted dates, soaked (see page 171)

½ tsp natural almond extract

⅛ tsp natural salt (see page 139)

optional boosters

¾ tsp pure rosewater (not rose syrup)

½ tsp natural vanilla extract

22 g (¾ oz) toasted shredded unsweetened coconut

Throw the coconut milk, almond milk, 130 g (4½ oz) of the pistachios, the spinach, dates, almond extract and salt into your high-speed blender, with the rosewater and vanilla boosters, and blast on high for about 1 minute until smooth and creamy. Pour the mixture into a bowl and chill in the fridge for at least 4 hours until really cold.

Churn the mixture in an ice-cream maker according to the manufacturer's instructions. Roughly chop the remaining pistachios and add them and the toasted coconut booster in the last 10 minutes of churning. Freeze for at least 12 hours before serving.

NUTRITIONAL FACTS (PER SERVING, BASED ON 6 SERVINGS)

calories 414 kcal | fat 30.3 g | saturated fat 13.9 g | sodium 72.4 mg | carbs 33.7 g | fibre 5.8 g | sugars 21.5 g | protein 9.7 g | calcium 87.7 mg | iron 4 mg

CHAPTER 2

immunity

immunity

Commanding an elite force of specialized cells, proteins, tissues and organs, the immune system rallies bone marrow, spleen, tonsils, thymus, lymph, blood, liver, gut, bowels and skin to fend off foreign threats to health. Battling viruses, bacteria, yeast, mould and fungus, as well as toxins, stress and other non-pathogen instigators of illness, the immune patrol triumphs with tactical support from allied foods.

shiitake mushrooms

The sumo wrestler of immunity foods, 'Shiitake-san' is bulked up with vitamins, minerals, phytonutrients and bioactive molecules that take tumours, bacteria, viruses (and, ironically, fungi) to the mat. Beta-glucan polysaccharides help direct proper immune responses to overpower inappropriate inflammation and excessive stress. With copper and iron to build red blood cells; zinc to build white ones; manganese, selenium and vitamin C to offset oxidation; and folate for cell division and manufacture of DNA, shiitakes muscle up for defence. As mushrooms absorb and concentrate compounds from whatever they grow in, go organic. Most of shiitake's nutrient and anti-inflammatory potential withstands both drying and cooking. To preserve nutrient density, cook lightly. Shiitakes bring their complex flavour to miso soup and tom kha (page 32), and are sensational sautéed. Add shiitake powder to stocks and sauces for an umami knockout.

garlic

The immunity sheriff, garlic cuts a wide swathe with its sulfur compounds – in particular, allicin, which digests into sulfenic acid, a free-radical crusher. Loaded with manganese, copper, selenium, calcium, and vitamins B_1, B_6 and C, plus essential enzymes, garlic backs up the lymph, liver and colon to run toxins out of town. With antibiotic and antiviral ammunition, this crusader banishes yeast, fungus, intestinal worms, heavy metals, plaque and mucus build-up. Garlic also supports digestive, respiratory, and cardiovascular health by policing

abnormal cells. The fiercest fighter in the allium clan is all about the iron, punching up production of proteins to smooth that metal's pathway to the blood. Allicin's a bit shy, and dissipates quickly, making it a poor choice in supplement form. To get the most bang for your buck and help it get cosy with raw garlic's alliinase enzymes, crush those cloves (if using enzyme-unfriendly acids such as citrus juice or vinegar, wait 5 minutes before adding them), then consume or cook fast.

sweet potatoes

Fending off bad guys 24/7, our skin provides a frontline defence in the immunity war. The health of the skin's connective tissue depends on vitamin A, and red-skinned, orange-flesh sweet potatoes are abundant in beta-carotene, that vitamin's precursor. High in vitamin C, too, this tuber also protects cellular structures and DNA from unhealthy inflammation and oxidation. Iron and potassium make it great for heart health as well. Sweet spuds are high in fructose, but deliver sweetness with considerably less sugar than fruits. Fructose, despite its bad press, is the most water-soluble simple sugar, making it an exceptional transport for B vitamins and antioxidants. Sweet potatoes' built-in blood-sugar moderators, in the form of fibre and B vitamins, make their simple carbs metabolize slowly, too. Roasting is righteous, but for the neatest nutrition steam, stew and stir-fry. While you're at it, get oily, too – healthy fats like olive and coconut oils, avocado, nuts and nut butters increase beta-carotene's bioavailability. These orange avengers are great with hemp seeds and walnuts, or tossed with oil-based dressings that provide essential fats and help regulate blood-sugar levels. To enrich a sweet potato stew, stir in almond butter; blend in almonds, macadamias or cashews to sensationalize a sweet spud soup.

carrots

With a cartload of beta-carotene and carotenoids, the common carrot fends off infection on two fronts: strengthening skin and aiding mucus membranes in the respiratory and digestive tracts to battle bacteria looking to sneak into the bloodstream. Carrots' vitamin C, leading an army of antioxidants allied with fibre, rages against free radicals to cleanse the liver and colon; vitamin K, calcium, magnesium and phosphorus help to oxygenate the blood, lower cholesterol and make the heart, bones and nervous system happy. The clincher: the beta-carotene here is heat stable, and light cooking in stir-fries and soups, or steaming and puréeing for desserts and baked goods, makes it more bioavailable. Raw carrot, retaining its live enzymes and key nutrients, rocks in a salad. Juiced or whole, carrots add sweetness, flavour and colour to smoothies and desserts. As with sweet potatoes, pairing with healthy fats make the carotenoids go crazy.

superspices: cardamom and cinnamon

Loaded with minerals, cardamom injects exquisite flavour while working undercover as an antibiotic agent to ease sore throats, clear congestion in the lungs, kidney and stomach and stimulate metabolism and digestion. It also activates antioxidant glutathione, and its vitamins A and C deter cell degeneration. Mesmerizing in a myriad of blends, cardamom *does* like to be the star, so start with a pinch; ¼ teaspoon usually hits the sweet spot.

Cinnamon, a powerful antibacterial, antimicrobial, antiviral, antifungal and anti-inflammatory machine, pushes back pathogens, warms the body, increases circulation and stimulates the lymph. With calcium, manganese and fibre, this sassy spice strengthens bones and connective tissue and optimizes nerve function. Cinnamon has an ability to mimic insulin, helping move sugars from the blood into the cells and promoting immune health by preventing blood-sugar spikes.

superfoods: camu and goji

With beta-carotene, calcium, potassium and protein, camu amps up the antiviral, antibacterial and antifungal agenda. This berry, among the richest sources of vitamin C known, is tart, so boost orange, mango and peach smoothies with just ½ teaspoon of the freeze-dried powder to get your daily dose.

The howl of goji, the 'wolfberry', strikes terror into threatening intruders and helps to oxygenate cells, tissues and blood to reduce stress and inflammation and increase energy and vitality. With a slew of vitamins, minerals, fats, fibre and protein, goji promotes heart, eye, skin and digestive health, and improves memory and mood. Up to a tablespoon of the freeze-dried powder slips into smoothies and raw desserts unnoticed, putting this powerful predator on the prowl.

more hero foods

- açaí
- algae (chlorella, spirulina)
- berries
- black pepper (combined with turmeric)
- broccoli
- coconut
- cultured vegetables
- fermented foods (such as kefir, kombucha, rejuvelac, yogurt)
- ginger
- lemon and lime
- oregano
- mango
- papaya
- pineapple
- pomegranate
- red pepper
- tea (black, green, white)
- turmeric
- wheatgrass
- winter squash (such as butternut, pumpkin)

This cold-and-flu fighter tastes like a divine dessert. The bromelain in pineapple suppresses coughs and loosens mucus, mint clears respiratory congestion, ginger encourages sweating to flush out toxins, vitamin C in limes and pineapple acts as a natural antibiotic to fight infection, and powerful anti-inflammatories in pak choi and all the other ingredients combat congestion. For more medicinal mojo, add all three boosters. For a healthy immunity treat, freeze the mix in ice-lolly moulds.

pine-mint maximmunity

SERVES 2

480 ml (17 fl oz) unsweetened almond milk or macadamia milk (strained if homemade)

⅛ tsp finely grated lime zest, plus extra to taste

1 tbsp fresh lime juice, plus extra to taste

½ tsp probiotic powder (see page 154, optional)

40 g (1½ oz) baby pak choi, chopped

9 g (¼ oz) mint leaves, plus extra to taste

1 tsp finely chopped fresh ginger, plus extra to taste

480 g (17 oz) frozen pineapple

¼ small avocado, stoned and peeled

10 drops alcohol-free liquid stevia, or 2 chopped pitted dates, soaked (see page 171), plus extra to taste

optional boosters

25 g (1 oz) frozen raw broccoli florets

1 tbsp coconut oil (in liquid form)

½ tsp chlorella

Throw the milk, lime zest, lime juice, probiotic powder, pak choi, mint, ginger, half of the pineapple and the boosters into your blender, and blast on high for 30–60 seconds until the ingredients are pulverized. Add the remaining pineapple, avocado and sweetener and blast again for 10–20 seconds until creamy. (You could put everything in together, but you may have trouble blending with a conventional machine.) Tweak the lime zest, lime juice, mint and ginger to taste.

NUTRITIONAL FACTS (PER SERVING)

calories 283 kcal | fat 14 g | saturated fat 0.4 g | sodium 52.8 mg | carbs 40 g | fibre 8 g | sugars 25.2 g | protein 6.8 g | calcium 152.6 mg | iron 2.2 mg

From left: Carrot Cake
Crush (page 34), Pine-mint
Maximmunity (opposite)

From left: Sweet Potato & Cashew Dip
(opposite), Can't Beet This Dip (page 42),
Raw Red Hummus (page 142)

There's an addictive sweet potato, lentil and cashew dip sold in Australia. During an infamous road trip from Melbourne to Sydney, my partner, Scott, became dangerously dependent on it. He polished off four tubs of the stuff, and ever since has been begging me through gritted teeth and with shaking hands for a re-creation. Satisfied with this healthier version, he's spared the agony of culinary withdrawal. (To be honest, I wanted to nail this just as much for me.) 'You'll need a high-speed machine to make this, or you may bust your blender!' Good advice, Scott. 'If you roast the sweet potato beforehand, you can get your fix in 15 minutes. And you want the flesh to be nicely roasted – not charred.' Thanks again. Now, my tips: add the turmeric and Panaseeda oils to up the immunity ammunition. And: never let anyone eat four tubs of anything in the course of a 10-hour drive.

sweet potato & cashew dip

MAKES 720 G (1 LB 9 OZ)

1 large orange-flesh sweet potato

5 tbsp extra virgin olive oil

150 g (5½ oz) yellow onion, diced

2 tsp finely chopped garlic (about 2 cloves)

1 tsp natural salt (see page 139), plus extra to taste

4 tbsp fresh lemon juice

1 tsp apple cider vinegar

140 g (5 oz) raw unsalted cashews, soaked (see page 171)

1 tsp coconut sugar

1 tsp mild yellow curry powder, plus extra to taste

1½ tsp ground coriander

1 tsp ground cumin

¾ tsp sweet paprika

optional boosters

⅛ tsp ground turmeric

2 drops Panaseeda black cumin oil (see page 211)

2 drops Panaseeda coriander oil (see page 211)

Preheat the oven to 200°C/400°F/Gas mark 6.

Either wrap the sweet potato in foil or lightly brush it with olive oil. Bake for about 1 hour until soft. Allow to cool, remove the skin and mash the flesh. Set aside 250 g (9 oz) of the mashed flesh.

In a frying pan, heat 1 tablespoon of the olive oil over a medium heat and sauté the onion and garlic with a pinch of the salt for about 5 minutes until soft and translucent. Allow to cool slightly. Pour the remaining 4 tablespoons of olive oil into a high-speed blender with the lemon juice and vinegar. Add the onion mixture, the mashed sweet potato and the remaining ingredients, including boosters, and the rest of the salt. Blast on high for about 1 minute until smooth and creamy. You may need to periodically stop the machine and scrape down the sides of the container. The dip will keep in the fridge for about 5 days.

NUTRITIONAL FACTS (PER SERVING, BASED ON 8 SERVINGS)

calories 205 kcal | fat 16.3 g | saturated fat 2.6 g | sodium 306.6 mg | carbs 13.1 g | fibre 1.9 g | sugars 3.4 g | protein 4 g | calcium 25.8 mg | iron 1.7 mg

This brilliant beauty converts raw-beetroot resistors into raw-beetroot rowdies. A divine dressing of orange, lemon, chives, ginger, garlic, vinegar and chilli flakes (add the camu for a bigger immune boost) envelops the earthiness of the beetroot and the sweetness of the carrots in intoxicating flavours that open and expand across the palate. Spiralizing the beetroot and carrots delivers gorgeous presentation (see photo on page 20), or shred the beetroot, carrots and cabbage fast in a food processor fitted with the coarse-shredding disc. Toss, dress, chill and taste how this brilliant bouquet blooms.

righteous roots

SERVES 6 AS A STARTER, 4 AS A MAIN; DRESSING MAKES 480 ML (17 FL OZ)

dressing

1 tsp finely grated orange zest

180 ml (6 fl oz) fresh orange juice

80 ml (2¾ fl oz) extra virgin olive oil

4 tbsp fresh lemon juice

12 g (½ oz) finely chopped chives

1½ tbsp finely chopped fresh ginger, plus extra to taste

1½ tbsp pure maple syrup

1½ tsp Dijon mustard

1 tsp finely chopped garlic (about 1 clove)

1 tsp natural salt (see page 139)

½ tsp apple cider vinegar

¼ tsp chilli flakes, plus extra to taste

salad

540 g (1 lb 3 oz) raw beetroot (about 4 medium beetroot), peeled and grated or spiralized

440 g (15½ oz) raw carrots (about 4 medium carrots), grated or spiralized

180 g (6 oz) green apple (about 2 medium apples), peeled and grated or spiralized

160 g (5¾ oz) raw almonds, sliced

11 g (¼ oz) finely chopped mint leaves

Natural salt to taste (see page 139)

optional boosters

50 g (1¾ oz) green cabbage, shredded

75 g (2¾ oz) English cucumber, peeled and diced

1 tsp camu powder (see page 23)

Throw all of the dressing ingredients into your blender along with the camu powder booster and blast on high for 30–60 seconds until well combined. Tweak the ginger and chilli to taste.

To make the salad, toss together the beetroot, carrots, apples, almonds and mint in a large bowl. Add the cabbage and cucumber boosters. Pour the dressing onto the salad and toss to coat evenly. Enjoy immediately, or chill for about 1 hour to allow the flavours to develop, then serve.

NUTRITIONAL FACTS (PER SERVING, BASED ON 6 SERVINGS)

calories 379 kcal | fat 25.9 g | saturated fat 2.8 g | sodium 525.7 mg | carbs 33.8 g | fibre 9.1 g | sugars 19.8 g | protein 8.4 g | calcium 130.5 mg | iron 2.3 mg

Inspired by a mega mango pudding my family and I worship at our local dim sum joint, this healthier (and, we think, tastier) immune-boosting incantation substitutes condensed milk, cane sugar and gelatine with coconut, maple syrup and agar powder. That bit of non-traditional casting lets the mango headline the show *and* work its medicinal magic. To up the antioxidant ante, add the goji booster. Packed with enzymes and fibre to aid with assimilation and elimination, this tummy tamer dials up digestive detox. A boost with coconut extract enhances your tropical trip, and cardamom adds exquisite flavour as well as natural antibiotic agents. Immunity angel? Dessert demon? Both, on one plate!

tropi-panna cotta

SERVES 6

1 (398 ml/14 fl oz) can full-fat coconut milk (shake, then pour)

480 g (17 oz) fresh mango, roughly chopped, plus 120 g (4½ oz) fresh mango pieces

4 tbsp pure maple syrup

1 tbsp coconut oil (in liquid form)

1 tsp agar powder (see page 211)

17 g (½ oz) toasted coconut chips (or flakes)

optional boosters

1 tbsp goji powder (see page 23)

½ tsp natural coconut extract/flavour

½ tsp ground cardamom

Throw the coconut milk, roughly chopped mango, maple syrup, coconut oil, along with the goji powder, coconut extract and cardamom boosters, into your blender, and blast on high for 30–60 seconds until smooth and creamy.

Pour the mixture into a saucepan and whisk in the agar powder.

Over a medium heat, bring the mixture to a gentle simmer, stirring constantly, and heat for about 5 minutes until the agar is completely dissolved and the mixture has thickened.

Lightly grease a 6-hole standard muffin tin and distribute the mixture evenly among the holes. Chill in the fridge for at least 2 hours to set.

To serve, gently slide a butter knife around the edge of each panna cotta. Place a chopping board over the top of the muffin tin, and, holding the two together, gently turn upside down. Tap the base of each muffin hole to dislodge each panna cotta.

Serve on small plates topped with the fresh mango pieces and toasted coconut chips.

NUTRITIONAL FACTS (PER SERVING)

calories 261 kcal | fat 18.1 g | saturated fat 15.8 g | sodium 12.3 mg | carbs 27.1 g | fibre 1.6 g | sugars 21.7 g | protein 2.3 g | calcium 37.5 mg | iron 2.5 mg

Grain-free, paleo-friendly, probiotic-rich, immune-boosting and incredibly cleansing, this bowl bursts with a zesty tang and vibrant, fresh flavour that will shoot straight down your spine like a citrus shower. If you think you can't eat beetroot and beetroot greens raw, the simple marinade of lemon juice, salt and paprika (that I stole from my friend Geoffrey, who stole it from a farmers' market vendor) may change your mind. The marinated beetroot and greens, served as a sexy summer salad, make a divine dish on their own. But go for the whole production number (see photo on page 101). The salty, sweet, spicy and tangy cast of this dish will tap dance on the taste buds and have everyone round the table whistling and cheering for an encore.

grain-free abundance

SERVES 8

cauliflower rice

2 medium heads cauliflower, cut into florets

4 tbsp extra virgin olive oil or coconut oil (in liquid form)

1 tsp natural salt (see page 139)

marinated beetroot

4 small or 3 large golden beetroot, peeled and very thinly sliced with a mandoline (about 280 g/10 oz)

180 ml (6 fl oz) fresh lemon juice

1 tbsp natural salt (see page 139)

1 tbsp sweet paprika

roasted vegetables

3 courgettes, sliced diagonally

3 tbsp extra virgin olive oil

¾ tsp natural salt (see page 139)

Chilli flakes

396 g (14 oz) trimmed green beans

3 carrots, diagonally sliced

1 bunch beetroot greens, roughly chopped (about 120 g/4½ oz)

220 g (7¾ oz) Love Your Gut (page 164) or other sauerkraut

260 g (9 oz) Ripper Roasted Red Pepper Purée (page 100)

optional boosters

7 g (¼ oz) finely chopped flat-leaf parsley leaves

70 g (2½ oz) blanched flaked almonds

1 tsp finely chopped lemon zest

Preheat the oven to 190°C/375°F/Gas mark 5. Line a large baking sheet with a silicone liner or baking paper.

To make the cauliflower rice, put the cauliflower florets in a food processor and pulse about five times until it has the texture of couscous. You may have to process in two batches. In a large bowl, stir the oil and salt into the cauliflower until well combined. Transfer the 'rice' to the prepared baking sheet and bake for about 15 minutes. Remove from the oven, stir with a spatula or wooden spoon and return to the oven for a further 15–20 minutes until the cauliflower begins to brown. Stir in the parsley booster and set aside until ready to serve.

Increase the oven temperature to 200°C/400°F/Gas mark 6. Line two large baking sheets with silicone liners or baking paper.

To marinate the beetroot, in a bowl, toss the beetroot slices with the lemon juice, salt and paprika. Cover and allow the beetroot to release their juices and marinate for about 1 hour.

To roast the vegetables, put the courgette slices in a bowl, toss with 1 tablespoon of the olive oil, ¼ teaspoon of the salt and a pinch of chilli flakes. Transfer them to one of the prepared baking sheets and arrange them in a single layer. In the same bowl, toss the beans and carrots with the remaining 2 tablespoons olive oil, the remaining ½ teaspoon salt and a pinch of chilli flakes. Transfer the beans and carrots to the second prepared baking sheet and arrange them in a single layer. Roast the courgettes for about 25 minutes until al dente; roast the beans and carrots for about 20 minutes until al dente.

Throw the beetroot greens into a large bowl and drain the beetroot marinade onto the beetroot greens. Toss to evenly coat.

To assemble the bowls, divide the cauliflower rice equally among eight bowls. Arrange equal portions of the beans, courgettes and carrots around the circumference of each bowl on top of the 'rice'. With tongs, place an equal amount of beetroot greens in the centre of each bowl and top with beetroot slices. Place 60 g (2¼ oz) of the fermented vegetables on the side of each bowl and top with 1 tablespoon of the almond booster and a pinch of the grated lemon zest booster. Spoon the roasted red pepper purée into a squeeze bottle and add a generous couple of squeezes over each bowl. Alternatively, use a 1 tablespoon measure to drizzle on the purée. Serve immediately and pass any remaining red pepper purée around the table.

NUTRITIONAL FACTS (PER SERVING)

calories 324 kcal | fat 20.6 g | saturated fat 2.5 g | sodium 2235.6 mg | carbs 33.5 g | fibre 11.4 g | sugars 17.5 g | protein 8.6 g | calcium 141.7 mg | iron 3.5 mg

tom kha

SERVES 8 AS A STARTER, 6 AS A MAIN; PASTE MAKES 293 G (10 OZ)

paste

1 tsp coconut oil (in liquid form)

135 g (4 1/2 oz) shallot, diced

4 tbsp fresh lime juice

88 g (3 oz) finely chopped fresh lemongrass

10 g (1/4 oz) dried shiitake mushroom powder (see Note, below)

21 g (3/4 oz) finely chopped coriander root (or stems)

25 g (1 oz) galangal, peeled and sliced

2 tbsp finely chopped garlic (about 6 cloves)

1 tbsp finely grated lime zest

1 tbsp chopped fresh kaffir lime leaves

1 1/2 tsp natural salt (see page 139)

soup

960 ml (1 3/4 pints) full-fat canned coconut milk (shake, then pour)

960 ml (1 3/4 pints) vegetable stock

2 1/2 tsp Bragg Liquid Aminos, gluten-free soy sauce or tamari

3/4 tsp fresh lime juice, plus extra to taste

1 1/2 tsp natural salt (see page 139), plus extra to taste

1 1/2 tsp coconut sugar

1/2 kabocha squash, unpeeled and deseeded, cut into 5 cm (2 in) cubes (420 g/15 oz)

80 g (3 oz) shiitake mushrooms, sliced

7 g (1/4 oz) coriander leaves

17 g (1/2 oz) diagonally sliced salad onion (green parts only)

Lime wedges, to serve

optional boosters

130 g (4 1/2 oz) courgette, diced

90 g (3 1/4 oz) rice stick noodles

1/4 tsp black sesame seeds, to garnish

To make the paste, in a small frying pan, heat the coconut oil over a medium heat. Add the shallot and sauté for about 10 minutes until the shallot is translucent and just starting to brown. Allow to cool slightly, then transfer to your blender. Add the rest of the paste ingredients and blast on high for about 1 minute until smooth. You may have to stop the machine and scrape down the sides of the container.

To make the soup, in a large pot over a medium heat, mix together 480 ml (17 fl oz) of the coconut milk with 236 g (8 oz) of the paste and stir for about 5 minutes until the oil comes to the surface and the coconut oil just starts to separate. Stir together until the paste is completely dissolved.

Add the remaining 480 ml (17 fl oz) of coconut milk, the stock, liquid aminos, lime juice, salt and sugar until well combined. Add the kabocha squash and the courgette booster and simmer over a medium heat for about 5 minutes until the vegetables are just tender. Add the mushrooms and the rice noodle booster and simmer for about 2 minutes until the mushrooms and noodles are just tender. Tweak lime juice and salt to taste.

Ladle the soup into bowls and serve topped with the coriander, salad onion and a sprinkle of the black sesame seeds, if liked. Offer the lime wedges on the side.

Note: To make mushroom powder, grind dried mushrooms in a spice grinder or coffee grinder until they are finely ground. On average, 2 g (1/16 oz) dried mushrooms will make about 1 tablespoon of powder.

Chef Eda Denjakul makes the best *tom kha* I've ever tasted. With fellow chef
Michelle Smith, we veganized Eda's family recipe, letting mushroom powder do
duty for fish stock. Verdict? Mind-blowing. Immunity martial artists like coconut,
garlic, shiitake and lemongrass ward off microbes while they kick-box in even
more flavour. OK, the paste takes some work – but this soup is oh-so worth it! I make
double and triple batches of the paste and keep it on hand, in the freezer, so this
sublime soup's a snap.

NUTRITIONAL FACTS (PER SERVING, BASED ON 8 SERVINGS)

calories 308 kcal | fat 26.4 g | saturated fat 23.1 g | sodium 931.7 mg | carbs 19.9 g | fibre 2.5 g | sugars 3.7 g |
protein 4.7 g | calcium 61.8 mg | iron 5.4 mg

This little gem that Karen Kipp (The Juice Goddess) and I whip up at all our juice-cleanse retreats never fails to wow the participants. An exotic elixir (see photo, page 25), it brings together the vitamin C in carrot, lemon and orange (camu sends that into the stratosphere) with the immune-boosting, anti-inflammatory power of coconut oil, ginger and cinnamon. The turmeric and black pepper boosters add more medicinal magic and a tasty twist. Here's a cold-crushing detox concoction that tastes like a treat and really does live up to its name!

carrot cake crush

SERVES 2

480 ml (17 fl oz) filtered water

270 g (9½ oz) carrots, roughly chopped

1½ medium oranges, peeled and segmented

½ medium green apple, cored and roughly chopped

Pinch of finely grated lemon zest, plus extra to taste

½ small lemon, peeled and deseeded

1 tbsp coconut oil (in liquid form), plus extra to taste

1½ tsp finely chopped fresh ginger, plus extra to taste

¾ tsp natural vanilla extract, plus extra to taste

½ tsp ground cinnamon, plus extra to taste

5 drops alcohol-free liquid stevia, plus extra to taste

Pinch of natural salt (see page 139)

optional boosters

1 tsp camu powder (see page 23)

¼ tsp ground turmeric

Pinch of freshly ground black pepper

Throw everything except the boosters into your blender and blast on high until the ingredients are completely pulverized. Strain through a filtration bag, nut milk bag or sheer piece of clean nylon hosiery. Tweak the coconut oil, ginger, vanilla, cinnamon and stevia to taste. Rinse the blender container. Pour the juice back into the blender, add the boosters and blast on high for 10–20 seconds until well combined.

NUTRITIONAL FACTS (PER SERVING)

calories 182 kcal | fat 7.3 g | saturated fat 6 g | sodium 244.3 mg | carbs 29.1 g | fibre 7.3 g | sugars 17.6 g | protein 2.3 g | calcium 109.2 mg | iron 0.7 mg

If you like a little cream on the top, this is a healthy immune-boosting option. The coconut oil thickens the mixture while it's in the fridge and adds antiviral, antifungal and antibacterial power. Yeah, tell yourself that as you spoon it on everything in sight. If you don't have coconut meat, raw unsalted cashews work great, too. I serve this with the Blueberry & Lemon Cashew Cream Crêpes (page 204) and Classic Cheesecake (page 67), boosted with lemon and cinnamon. But this cream works nicely with just about any aromatic, so try those you like.

coconut cream

MAKES 330 G (11¾ OZ)

240 ml (8½ fl oz) full-fat canned coconut milk (shake, then pour)

180 g (6 oz) young coconut meat

2 tbsp coconut oil (in liquid form)

1 tbsp pure maple syrup, plus extra to taste

1 tsp natural vanilla extract, plus extra to taste

Pinch of natural salt (see page 139)

optional boosters

½ tsp finely grated lemon zest, plus extra to taste

½ tsp fresh lemon juice, plus extra to taste

⅛ tsp ground cinnamon, plus extra to taste

Pour all of the ingredients, including the boosters, into your blender and blast on high for 30–60 seconds until smooth and creamy. Tweak the vanilla, lemon and cinnamon to taste. Use immediately, or chill in the fridge.

NUTRITIONAL FACTS (PER SERVING, BASED ON 8 SERVINGS)

calories 123 kcal | fat 11.2 g | saturated fat 8.6 g | sodium 44 mg | carbs 4.6 g | fibre 0.7 g | sugars 2.3 g | protein 1.1 g | calcium 8.5 mg | iron 1.2 mg

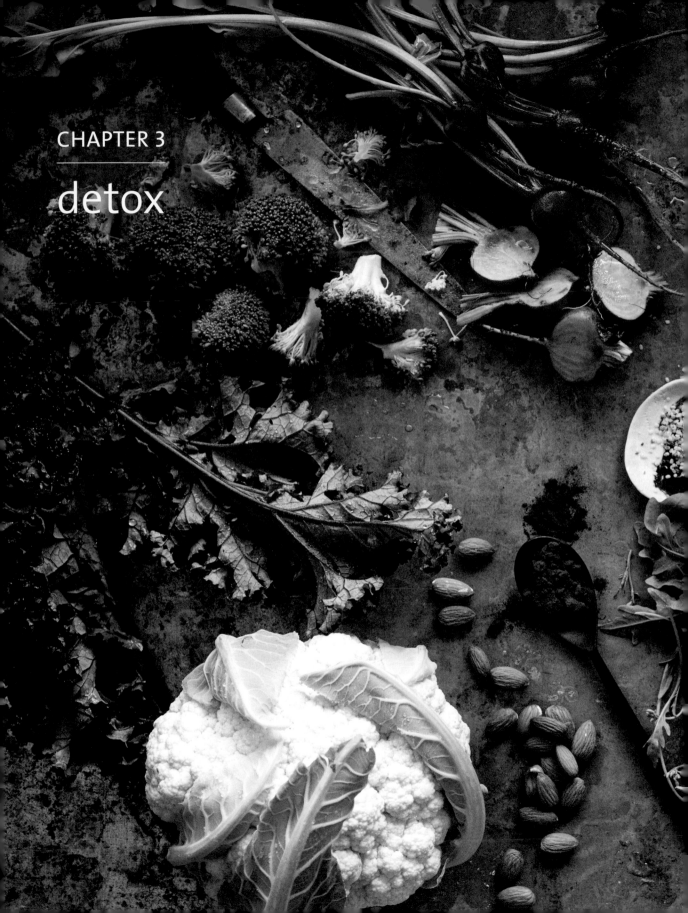

CHAPTER 3

detox

detox

Our bodies have built-in cleansing mechanisms, but the barrage of toxins coming at us from environmental pollutants, processed foods, drugs, stress, sedentary living and illness easily overwhelm them. Since we've amped up the toxins we take in, we need to dial up detox support in our diets, too. Detox takes place in two phases: our bodies tag and bag the rubbish, then take it out. Fewer nutrients support phase two, so we need to consume them routinely to keep the major protective players — liver, skin, intestines, kidneys, lymphatic system and blood — at peak performance.

broccoli

A green, mean detox machine, broccoli (especially the florets) is rich in toxin-tackling glucosinolates, ranking highest in one kind, glucoraphanin, which the body converts to the detox phytonutrient sulforaphane. (Broccoli sprouts deliver even more.) The conversion relies on myrosinase, an enzyme found in broccoli, mustard, radish and horseradish. Antioxidants (glutathione plus vitamins C and E), alkalizing minerals (magnesium, zinc), flavonoids, carotenoids and omega-3s combat oxidation and inflammation, vitamin K, folate and iron oxygenate the blood, vitamin C aids iron absorption, and fibre battles bad bacteria for better digestion. Raw broccoli provides live enzymes and more bioavailable glucoraphanin; to maximize those benefits, serve it in salads with mustard-laced dressings. Frozen raw florets fortify smoothies without altering flavour. Broccoli cooked for less than 5 minutes binds carcinogenic bile acids even better than raw. Don't discard the leaves — they're high in calcium and antioxidants like vitamins A and C. Use them like chard, for raw wraps, and sautéed in stir-fries, soups and stews.

beetroot

Detox depends on mineral-rich blood, and beetroot, with iron, copper, magnesium and potassium, vitamin C, fibre and dietary nitrates, are brilliant blood builders. Full of folate, beetroot's a cell regenerator, too. Anti-inflammatory betaine fights infections, crushes cancer cells and buddies up with glutathione to ice infiltrators. Clearing congestion from the colon, leveraging the lymph and lifting toxins from the liver, beetroot will clean you out! Rock on with the roots, but don't let the leaves languish — they pack more nutrients. Raw, beetroot roots and greens blast full phytonutrition into smoothies and salads; for cooked cleanse karma in soups and dips, steam or simmer, or rustically roast those roots.

rocket

This lightning-bolt leaf launches health into high orbit and vaporizes toxic torpedoes! Vitamins A, B, C and K, and minerals like iron, copper, manganese and phosphorous, fizzle free radicals. A happy hydrator, rocket cools and calms, but is detox dynamite in the liver, detonating heavy metals and agrotoxins, while enzymes advance the antibacterial and antiviral agenda. Anti-inflammatory power fires up cellular, enzymatic and metabolic functions, making rocket a fat foe, too. Rocket is a great garnish for soups, stews and pizzas, and brings a peppery note to salads and smoothies.

artichokes

Along with divine flavour, artichokes deliver diuretic and digestive detonators, to keep the liver, gallbladder and kidneys squeaky clean. Their abundant fibre helps eliminate toxins, too! Antioxidant caffeoylquinic acids and cynarin stimulate bile production to digest fats efficiently. Along with luteolin, they regulate blood pressure and cholesterol and ward off digestive disturbances. Vitamin C makes this delicious thistle an anti-inflammatory immunity activist, boosting collagen to heal wounds and fighting free radicals formed during macronutrient metabolism. 'Chokes provide vitamin K and aid iron absorption to help build blood. Steam or roast, then dip leaves and hearts in aioli; throw hearts into soups, salads and dips. My go-to is defrosted frozen; canned need a rinse and drain; avoid marinated for these recipes. With artichokes on their own or in dishes, drizzle truffle oil and lemon — you'll ban the butter!

coriander

Heavy metals get viruses and bacteria disco dancing in our organs, tissues, cells and blood, and invite in diverse disorders from cancer to depression. To add insult to injury, they enlarge fat cells into cellulite. Once they get past the velvet rope, they're in no hurry to leave – until chelators in coriander step up as the club's bouncers and strong-arm mercury, aluminium and lead to the exits. They boot out other toxins, too, and alkalizing minerals lend a hand against acid wastes. A phenomenal phalanx of phytonutrients, healing antioxidants and essential fatty acids stop oxidation, inflammation and stress at the door. Herb and spice in one, coriander's leaves and seeds are strikingly different flavour enhancers. The leaves' clean citrus quality sings along with sweet and savoury tunes in smoothies, soups, salsas, spreads, sauces, dressings, stews and stir-fries. (If coriander tastes soapy to you, use parsley.) Coriander seed adds a sharp sweet note to curries, dips, soups and stir-fries.

parsley

As mighty a detox dynamo as coriander, parsley exiles heavy metals while its diuretic properties banish baddies from the bladder and kidneys. Its arsenal of cleansing compounds includes myristicin, a volatile oil that activates antioxidant glutathione to crush environmental carcinogens; luteolin, a flavonoid antioxidant; and alkalizing minerals and anti-inflammatory vitamins. A heaped tablespoon of chopped parsley provides the RDA of vitamin K. A handful of the leaves transforms a smoothie into a magic metabolism-boosting tonic, a digestive aid and an ace against airborne allergens. To add vibrant colour and flavour, toss parsley into raw or cooked veggies, dips, sauces and dressings. These recipes are best with flat-leaf parsley, which is more fragrant than the curly kind and less bitter.

algae: spirulina and chlorella

Chlorella, a true algae, contains more chlorophyll than any leafy green, and spirulina, a blue-green algae, offers lots, too, with phycocyanin, a pigment that protects cells from oxidative damage. These water-born agents purify, oxygenate and alkalize the blood, aid tissue growth and repair, cleanse the liver and skin and clear toxins from the bowels. Their chelators flush heavy metals and offset the effects of radiation and chemotherapy. Prebiotic as well, these algae feed friendly bacteria for digestive detox. Their vitamins A, B and K, along with iron and some forty other minerals, calm inflammation and boost immunity. 'Cracked wall' powders are the most digestible. Given the pungent aquarium aroma, start with ⅛ teaspoon. Banana, mango, pineapple, lemon and mint mellow the murk.

more hero foods

- almonds
- asparagus
- avocado
- berries
- cabbage
- cauliflower
- cayenne
- celery
- coconut and coconut oil
- cucumber
- cultured vegetables
- garlic
- ginger
- leafy greens (such as pak choi, chard, spring greens, dandelion, kale, spinach)
- lemon and lime
- radish (mooli, red, white)
- sea vegetables
- sprouts (such as alfalfa, broccoli, pea)
- turmeric
- wheatgrass

This blend whips beetroot, oranges and ginger into a detox delight. Depending on the character of your oranges, add stevia to taste. But, be warned: beetroot moves the bowels, especially if you add the aloe, prune and apple cider vinegar boosters.

smooth moves

SERVES 2

120 ml (4 fl oz) filtered water

⅛ tsp finely grated orange zest, plus extra to taste

4 medium oranges, peeled and quartered

2 tbsp fresh lemon juice, plus extra to taste

150 g (5½ oz) raw beetroot (grated for conventional blenders), peeled and cubed

2 tsp finely chopped fresh ginger, plus extra to taste

Pinch of natural salt (see page 139)

Alcohol-free liquid stevia (optional)

125 g (4½ oz) ice cubes, plus extra to taste

optional boosters

2 tbsp pure aloe vera juice

1 pitted prune, chopped

¼ tsp apple cider vinegar

Throw everything except the ice, but including the boosters, into your blender and blast on high for 30–60 seconds until pulverized. Add the ice and blast again for 10–20 seconds until chilled. Drink immediately for the most balanced flavour. Strain through a filtration bag, nut milk bag, sheer piece of clean nylon hosiery or fine-mesh sieve for a smoother consistency.

NUTRITIONAL FACTS (PER SERVING)

calories 210 kcal | fat 0.6 g | saturated fat 0.1 g | sodium 211.4 mg | carbs 51.8 g | fibre 11 g | sugars 39.9 g | protein 4.8 g | calcium 166 mg | iron 1 mg

How can you add green powders to smoothies without gagging? Pair with mango, lift with lemon and beat with basil. (Dial up the detox with the cauliflower, seed oil and cayenne boosters.) These cleansing and immunity rock stars turn lemons into tasty lemonade.

it's so easy being green

SERVES 2

480 ml (17 fl oz) raw coconut water or filtered water

1 tsp finely grated lemon zest, plus extra to taste

4 tbsp fresh lemon juice, plus extra to taste

25 g (1 oz) curly green kale leaves, torn (1 or 2 large leaves with stalk removed, ripped into small pieces)

25 g (1 oz) basil leaves, plus extra to taste

1 tsp wheatgrass powder (see page 171)

1 tsp chlorella (see page 39)

½ tsp probiotic powder (see page 154, optional)

480 g (17 oz) frozen mango chunks

optional boosters

30 g (1 oz) frozen raw cauliflower florets

1 tbsp flaxseed oil or chia seed oil

Pinch of cayenne pepper

Throw all of the ingredients into your blender, including the boosters, and blast on high for 30–60 seconds until smooth and creamy. Tweak the lemon zest, lemon juice and basil to taste.

NUTRITIONAL FACTS (PER SERVING)

calories 211 kcal | fat 1.8 g | saturated fat 0.7 g | sodium 260 mg | carbs 48.7 g | fibre 7.3 g | sugars 40.1 g | protein 5.6 g | calcium 126.2 mg | iron 4.8 mg

On my website, this dip (see photo, page 26) gets raves from one-time beetroot sceptics. My friend Judy made a beetroot dip for her eight-year-old students, and had them hopping into it like it was hamburgers! I spiced things up with more garlic, chilli and salt; boosted the detox potential with ginger, plus powerful Panaseeda immunity oils; and hit the jackpot. You *will* need a high-speed blender or a food processor for this one. Still, don't miss it. In all its variations, this is unbeetable!

can't beet this dip

MAKES ABOUT 370 G (13 OZ)

600 g (1 lb 5 oz) raw beetroot, peeled and cubed

4 tbsp extra virgin olive oil

½ tsp natural salt (see page 139), plus extra to taste

¾ tsp cumin seeds

¾ tsp coriander seeds

2 tsp finely chopped garlic (about 2 cloves), plus extra to taste

2 tsp deseeded and finely chopped green chilli, plus extra to taste

2 tsp fresh lemon juice, plus extra to taste

9 g (¼ oz) finely chopped coriander leaves

optional boosters

¾ tsp finely chopped fresh ginger

2 drops Panaseeda black cumin oil (see page 211)

2 drops Panaseeda coriander oil (see page 211)

Preheat the oven to 200°C/400°F/Gas mark 6. Line a baking sheet with a silicone liner or baking paper. Toss the beetroot with 2 tablespoons of the olive oil and ¼ teaspoon of the salt. Arrange the beetroot on the baking sheet in a single layer and roast for about 1 hour, tossing periodically, until the beetroot is tender. (You don't want any burnt bits.) You should have 320 g (11½ oz).

Heat the cumin and coriander seeds in a small heavy frying pan over a medium-high heat for about 2 minutes, stirring constantly, until they release their fragrance and change colour slightly. Be careful not to burn them or they will develop bitterness. Grind the seeds in a spice grinder or crush with a pestle and mortar.

Throw the beetroot into a high-speed blender or food processor and add the remaining 2 tablespoons of olive oil, the toasted and ground seeds, the garlic, chilli, lemon juice, the remaining ¼ teaspoon of salt and any boosters. Blast until well combined. Tweak the garlic, chilli, lemon juice and salt to taste. Transfer the dip to a bowl and stir in the coriander.

NUTRITIONAL FACTS (PER SERVING, BASED ON 8 SERVINGS)

calories 94 kcal | fat 7 g | saturated fat 1 g | sodium 205.1 mg | carbs 7.7 g | fibre 2.3 g | sugars 5.1 g | protein 1.3 g | calcium 17.3 mg | iron 0.8 mg

Bursting with fabulous fresh flavour and vibrant shades of green in contrast with hues of ivory and white, this salad is an elegant dish you can get on the table in 30 minutes. And, it won't push out the paunch. The rocket, basil, coriander, lime, cucumber, tomatoes and chilli all contribute to the aromatic complexity while cleansing the body, and the dish's high water content aids digestion.

aromatic rocket

SERVES 8 AS A STARTER, 6 AS A MAIN; DRESSING MAKES 300 ML (10 FL OZ)

dressing

120 ml (4 fl oz) extra virgin olive oil

¼ tsp finely grated lime zest, plus extra to taste

4 tbsp fresh lime juice, plus extra to taste

40 g (1½ oz) coriander leaves

50 g (1¾ oz) basil leaves

1 tbsp finely chopped shallot

2 tsp finely chopped garlic (about 2 cloves)

1 tbsp coconut nectar or other liquid sweetener

½ tsp deseeded and finely chopped green chilli, plus extra to taste

½ tsp natural salt (see page 139)

⅛ tsp freshly ground black pepper

salad

132 g (4½ oz) rocket

140 g (5 oz) canned hearts of palm, drained and cubed

150 g (5½ oz) English cucumber (unpeeled), cubed

225 g (8oz) water chestnuts, cubed

115 g (4 oz) green tomatoes, diced

70 g (2½ oz) blanched flaked almonds

Natural salt (see page 139)

Freshly ground black pepper

optional boosters

180 g (6 oz) cooked cannellini beans

1 avocado, stoned, peeled and cubed

1 tsp finely grated lime zest

To make the dressing, throw all of the dressing ingredients into your blender and blast on high for 30–60 seconds until smooth. Tweak the lime zest, lime juice and chilli to taste.

In a large bowl, gently toss 180 ml (6 fl oz) of the dressing with the rocket, hearts of palm, cucumber, water chestnuts, tomatoes, almonds and the cannellini bean booster. Season to taste with salt and pepper. Serve topped with the avocado and lime zest boosters. Enjoy immediately, and pass the remaining dressing around the table.

NUTRITIONAL FACTS (PER SERVING, BASED ON 8 SERVINGS)

calories 215 kcal | fat 18.4 g | saturated fat 2.3 g | sodium 309 mg | carbs 11.2 g | fibre 4.1 g | sugars 4.4 g | protein 4.4 g | calcium 120 mg | iron 2.5 mg

You'll swear this soup totes a ton of carbs and gobs of cheese and cream. But the rich, cheesy sauce is a healthy blend of cauliflower, lemon juice, nutritional yeast and miso paste that thickens and flavours the broccoli stock without deterring the detox or packing on calories. Add the thyme, cayenne and truffle oil to elevate the experience to ethereal. Even the most devout dairy diehard won't know this is vegan. Happy, healthy comfort food.

cheezy broccoli

SERVES 6 AS A STARTER, 4 AS A MAIN; CHEEZE SAUCE MAKES 355 G (12 OZ)

soup base

1.4 litres (2½ pints) vegetable stock

600 g (1 lb 5 oz) broccoli florets, roughly chopped

¼ tsp natural salt (see page 139), plus extra to taste

Freshly ground black pepper

cheeze sauce

1 tbsp extra virgin olive oil

150 g (5½ oz) yellow onion, diced

2 tsp finely chopped garlic (about 2 cloves)

4 tbsp vegetable stock

195 g (7 oz) steamed cauliflower florets

6 tbsp nutritional yeast flakes

2 tbsp white miso paste

1½ tbsp fresh lemon juice

1 tsp natural salt (see page 139)

Finely chopped flat-leaf parsley, to garnish

optional boosters

1 tsp finely chopped fresh thyme, plus extra to taste

Pinch of cayenne pepper, plus extra to taste

Truffle oil

To make the soup base, combine the stock and broccoli in a large saucepan. The stock may not completely cover the broccoli but the broccoli will release liquid as it simmers. Over a high heat, bring the mixture to the boil. Reduce the heat to medium and simmer for 3–5 minutes just until the broccoli is al dente and still vibrant green. Be careful not to overcook. Allow to cool slightly.

To make the cheeze sauce, in a small frying pan, heat the olive oil over a medium-high heat and sauté the onion and garlic for about 5 minutes until soft and translucent. Transfer to your blender and add the stock, cauliflower, nutritional yeast, miso, lemon juice and salt. Blast on high for 30–60 seconds until smooth and creamy. Transfer to a bowl.

In batches, pour the soup base into the blender (no need to wash after blending the sauce) along with the thyme and cayenne boosters and process on medium-high speed for 10–15 seconds until well combined and mostly puréed; there should still be speckles of broccoli. Add more thyme and cayenne to taste. (For conventional blenders, remove the small centre lid cap and cover the opening with a tea towel so steam can escape while you blend.) Return the soup to the saucepan and warm it over a low heat. Stir in the cheeze sauce and combine well. Season to taste with the salt and pepper. Ladle the soup into bowls, garnish with a few drops of the truffle oil booster and the parsley and serve.

NUTRITIONAL FACTS (PER SERVING, BASED ON 6 SERVINGS)

calories 132 kcal | fat 3.6 g | saturated fat 0.5 g | sodium 775.6 mg | carbs 17.9 g | fibre 8.1 g | sugars 4.9 g | protein 12.5 g | calcium 71.9 mg | iron 1.9 mg

Detoxing does not mean your dinners have to diminish in decadence. This beautiful buffet, featuring hearty roasted vegetables and steamed artichokes accompanied by an awesome aioli drizzle-and-dip, is crazy-good and a great example of how you can cleanse with class.

artichokes & roasted veg with rosemary pine nut aioli

SERVES 4; AIOLI MAKES 315 G (12 OZ)

aioli

120 ml (4 fl oz) unsweetened almond milk (strained if homemade)

3 tbsp fresh lemon juice, plus extra to taste

2 tbsp extra virgin olive oil

1½ tsp apple cider vinegar, plus extra to taste

140 g (5 oz) raw pine nuts, soaked (see page 171)

1 tsp finely chopped garlic (about 1 clove)

2 tsp finely chopped fresh rosemary

½ tsp natural salt (see page 139), plus extra to taste

vegetables

20 Brussels sprouts, trimmed and halved

3 tbsp plus 1 tsp extra virgin olive oil

Natural salt (see page 139)

2 fennel bulbs, stalks removed, halved lengthways

4 artichokes

240 g (8½ oz) green beans, trimmed

1 bunch asparagus, trimmed

optional boosters

1⅛ tsp fresh lemon juice, plus extra to taste

Garlic powder

Chilli flakes

To make the aioli, throw all of the aioli ingredients into your blender and blast on high for about 1 minute until smooth and creamy. Tweak the lemon juice, vinegar and salt to taste. Transfer to a container and chill in the fridge. It will thicken. Or make just prior to serving for a thinner consistency.

Preheat the oven to 180°C/350°F/Gas mark 4. Line two large rectangular baking dishes with baking paper.

Toss the Brussels sprouts with 2 tablespoons of the olive oil, ¼ teaspoon of salt, ¼ teaspoon of the lemon juice booster, ⅛ teaspoon of the garlic powder booster and ⅛ teaspoon of the chilli flake booster. Brush each fennel piece with ½ teaspoon of the olive oil and sprinkle with a pinch of salt, ⅛ teaspoon of the lemon juice booster, a pinch of the garlic powder booster and a pinch of the chilli flake booster. Place the Brussels sprouts and fennel (cut sides down) in one of the baking dishes and roast for about 1 hour until cooked through. Set the vegetables aside.

Trim the stalks off the artichokes and place them cut side down in a wide saucepan. Add 960 ml (1¾ pints) of filtered water and bring to the boil over a high heat. Reduce the heat to medium to maintain a high simmer, cover and steam the artichokes for about 40 minutes until tender and cooked through. Check the pan periodically and add more water as needed.

While the artichokes are cooking, toss the green beans with 1 teaspoon of the olive oil, and ⅛ teaspoon of salt, ⅛ teaspoon of the lemon juice booster, ⅛ teaspoon of the garlic powder booster and ⅛ teaspoon of the chilli flake booster. Place in the second baking dish. Toss the asparagus with the remaining 1 teaspoon of olive oil, ⅛ teaspoon of salt, the remaining ¼ teaspoon of the lemon juice booster, ⅛ teaspoon of the garlic powder booster and a ⅛ teaspoon of the chilli flake booster. When the Brussels sprouts and fennel have been in the oven for 45 minutes, place the baking dish with the beans and asparagus in the oven. Roast for 10–15 minutes until al dente.

To serve, place an artichoke on each of four plates, and then divide the Brussels sprouts, fennel, beans and asparagus among the plates. Divide two-thirds of the aioli among four ramekins amd pour the remaining aioli into a squeeze bottle. Squeeze some aioli over the vegetables, and then place a ramekin of aioli on each plate. Or place all of the vegetables and the aioli on a large platter and serve family style.

NUTRITIONAL FACTS (PER SERVING, BASED ON 4 SERVINGS)

calories 582 kcal | fat 44.3 g | saturated fat 4.5 g | sodium 943.6 mg | carbs 43.1 g | fibre 18.7 g | sugars 12.6 g | protein 16.6 g | calcium 211.7 mg | iron 7.9 mg

This sugar-free dessert tastes like a gourmet treat. Bromelain, an enzyme in pineapple, clears respiratory congestion, loosens mucus, breaks down proteins, clears toxins from the blood, calms inflammation and tames excess gastric juices. Rosemary, a brilliant digestive and cleansing aid, stimulates circulation and acts as a mild diuretic to promote kidney health and reduce bloating. Along with its awesome accent flavour, this herb delivers powerful antioxidant, antibacterial and anticarcinogenic action. The lemon juice doubles down on detox. This grand granita will clean you out!

rosemary-lemon granita

SERVES 6–8

960 g (2 lb 1 oz) fresh pineapple (1 large pineapple), roughly chopped

½ tsp finely grated lemon zest, plus extra to taste

4 tbsp fresh lemon juice, plus extra to taste

1 tsp finely chopped fresh rosemary

5 drops alcohol-free liquid stevia, plus extra to taste

Pinch of natural salt (see page 139)

optional boosters

165 g (5¾ oz) English cucumber, peeled and chopped

60 g (2¼ oz) frozen raw cauliflower florets

1 tsp camu powder (see page 23)

Throw all of the ingredients, including any boosters, into your blender and blast on high for 30–60 seconds until smooth. Tweak the lemon zest, lemon juice and stevia to taste.

Transfer the mixture to an 18 x 28 cm (7 x 11 in) or 20 cm (8 in) square tin. Chill in the fridge for about 1 hour until really cold. Transfer the tin to the freezer and freeze for 15 minutes. Scrape the mixture with a fork, then return the tin to the freezer. Continue freezing, stirring and scraping every 15 minutes until the granita is completely frozen. This will take about 1 hour. Scrape the mixture one last time and keep covered in the freezer.

When you're ready to serve, scoop the granita into chilled bowls or stemmed glasses.

NUTRITIONAL FACTS (PER SERVING, BASED ON 6 SERVINGS)

calories 82 kcal | fat 0.2 g | saturated fat 0 g | sodium 50.2 mg | carbs 22 g | fibre 2.3 g | sugars 16 g | protein 0.9 g | calcium 22.7 mg | iron 0.5 mg

So I can make this basil bombshell any time we're in the mood for it, I always keep the ingredients on hand. It's simple and really cleansing. (Add the wheatgrass and chilli flakes for more detox dynamite.) I use it in so many different ways – drizzled over steamed or roasted vegetables, as a dipping sauce for grilled kebabs, slathered on sandwiches and wraps or stirred into grains. Add the capers for an added layer of flavour. One to two teaspoons (or more) of this sauce brings a touch of magic to chunky vegetable soups, and it's incredible as the star ingredient in the Gentle Lentils soup (page 59). Blending in one-quarter of an avocado makes an awesome green goddess dressing.

basil-is-the-bomb sauce

MAKES 240 ML (8½ FL OZ)

120 ml (4 fl oz) extra virgin olive oil

50 g (1¾ oz) basil leaves

20 g (¾ oz) finely chopped salad onion (white and green parts)

1½ tbsp fresh lemon juice

2 tsp finely chopped garlic (about 2 cloves)

¼ tsp apple cider vinegar

¼ tsp natural salt (see page 139), plus extra to taste

optional boosters

2 tsp capers, drained

1 tsp wheatgrass powder (see page 171)

⅛ tsp chilli flakes, plus extra to taste

Throw everything into your blender, including any boosters, and blast on high for 30–60 seconds until smooth and emulsified. Tweak the salt and chilli flakes to taste. This is best served immediately, but will keep, sealed and chilled, for about 5 days.

NUTRITIONAL FACTS (PER SERVING, BASED ON 4 SERVINGS)

calories 246 kcal | fat 27.1 g | saturated fat 3.7 g | sodium 147.5 mg | carbs 1.5 g | fibre 0.4 g | sugars 0.3 g | protein 0.6 g | calcium 29 mg | iron 0.7 mg

CHAPTER 4

protein

protein

Our bodies' proteins do a variety of jobs: *builders* construct cells, muscles, connective tissue, bones, tendons and skin; *transporters* carry nutrients; *messengers* send signals among players; *immuno-* and *hormonal* do what their names suggest; and *enzyme* proteins support metabolism. All are made up of amino acids; of the twenty in the body's proteins, nine are essential to our diets, since we can't manufacture them. 'Complete proteins' contain – in varying amounts – all nine essential amino acids. Our protein needs vary, too. Excess protein won't build more muscle or strength, and, like excess anything, can irritate and overwhelm the body.

hemp

The complete protein in hemp seed has a structure that makes for high digestibility, and its unique amino acid, edestin, is similar to the globulin in our blood, making hemp's amino acid profile the closest among plants to our own. Readily absorbed, hemp's protein gives muscle tone, improves circulation and aids tissue repair. A good source of omega-3s and -6s, hemp also combats inflammation, fires up fat metabolism and boosts brain function and mood. Hemp also contains the elusive GLA – aka 'GLAmour' – fatty acid, helping manage PMS, menopause and other hormonal shifts and strengthening hair, skin and nails. High in fibre, both soluble and insoluble, hemp packs no other carbohydrates, so it's a carb-lite crusader. Unlike many seeds, hemp requires no soaking or grinding. Toss whole seeds into smoothies, salads and soups. With a tad under 4 g protein per tablespoon, hemp's great to fortify dips, dressings, sauces and baked goods, and as a nut replacer in pesto. Boost smoothies with cold-pressed hemp oil; start with 1 teaspoon and work up slowly, or the flavour gets grassy. Hemp-protein powder and home-made hemp milk are also fine ways to get your fix.

quinoa

Boasting both complete protein and the highest protein content of any grain, quinoa is rich in the amino acids lysine, methionine and cysteine, building blocks of muscle and essential to tissue growth and repair. A low-GI food that's full of fibre and high in folate, magnesium, zinc, phosphorus, manganese and copper, this gluten-free glory is nutrient-dense, fills the belly and regulates blood sugar – it's ideal workout fuel. Antioxidant flavonoids, vitamin E, heart-healthy fats and omega-3s not compromised by cooking make quinoa an anti-inflammatory ally, too. Cook white, red, black or tri-colour mix quinoa, then toss with herbs and veggies, make gluten-free tabouli or go for the burgers on page 62.

tofu and tempeh

Soya is controversial. Here's my take: yes, this protein-rich bean's phytoestrogens can, in high amounts or consumed with other oestrogenic foods, mess up hormone balance. If you have or have had a hormone-linked condition, avoiding soya is prudent. For most of us, whole soya in moderation is fine and provides good protein. Much soya is genetically engineered, and soya flours, milks and protein isolates are processed with solvent extraction; commercial soya 'meats' involve yet more chemicals. Such products are nutritionally unbalanced, high in phytates that impair digestion and are no friends to our health. Organic tofu and tempeh (both minimally processed) are in the clear. Tofu and tempeh, with 15–20 g protein per 126 g (4½ oz), respectively, rank among the best vegetarian sources of protein. They're also great sources of calcium, alkaline buffers (see page 138) and omega-3s, boosting immunity along with bone and heart health.

Tempeh and fermented tofu boast high digestibility, concentrated phytonutrients, bioactive peptide proteins, antioxidants, anti-inflammatories and beneficial probiotic agents. Tofu – curdled and pressed soya milk – is brilliant baked, stir-fried and grilled; firm and extra-firm are best. Use silken tofu in dressings, sauces and desserts. Fermented tofu, with a consistency like cream cheese, is a zesty spread and awesome for enriching dressings and sauces (see page 158). Tempeh, always fermented, is more firm in texture and pronounced in flavour than regular tofu. Plain or mixed with grains, tempeh (some kinds aren't gluten-free) is phenomenal fried and sliced or crumbled in salads (see Kale! Caesar, page 13), stir-fries and other savoury dishes. It's a sensational substitute for meat in chilli.

pumpkin seeds

These sweet seeds are high-fibre, low-glycaemic protein packers that help us feel full, provide lasting energy and come loaded with antioxidant phytonutrients, vitamins A, C, E and K, and omega-3s. Their mega-measure of magnesium supports heart, bones and teeth, while loads of zinc boost immunity, aid skin and eye health and regulate blood sugar levels. Zinc and phytosterols are pals to the prostate, with phytosterols also reducing LDL cholesterol. The seeds and their oil offer antiviral, antifungal and antimicrobial ammunition, too. To aid sleep, pumpkin seeds provide lots of tryptophan. They add crunch and flavour to salads, stews and desserts. Tip: blended with almonds, pumpkin seed oil conjures up a peanut-butter flavour (page 56).

cashews

These buttery bandits are high in protein, low glycaemic, lower in fat than most nuts and high in monounsaturated mojo. Packing antioxidants, fibre and minerals, cashews fire on free radicals, contribute to collagen and elastin for healthy bones and connective tissue, up iron utilization for bomb-proof blood and are terrific for our teeth. Mounds of magnesium make these nuts nifty for the nervous system, too. The cow of the vegan world, yielding rich butter and cream, this nut cranks up culinary creativity, adds crunch to salads and savouries and gives velvety texture to smoothies, soups, sauces, dressings, sweet creams and desserts. Since cashews are acid- and fungus-forming, munch in moderation.

legumes

This family of foods includes beans (chickpea, cannellini, soya/edamame, pinto, adzuki, black, kidney, butter and others), lentils and peas (green, mange tout and snap) – all great sources of protein. Low in fat, high in complex carbs, fibre and slow-digested proteins, legumes are satiating energy foods. Like bananas, they have resistant starch (see page 6), that fills us up and boosts metabolism. Their fibre content, with their protein, helps regulate blood sugar and digestion. Nutritional profiles vary, but legumes are typically rich in B vitamins and minerals. The downside: as both starch and protein, they're difficult to digest (see Well Combined, page 170), and feed fermentation in the gut and candida growth. I eat legumes in moderation, in salads, veggie burgers, soups and Mexican classics like nachos, tacos, burritos and enchiladas.

more hero foods

- almonds
- amaranth
- artichokes
- broccoli
- buckwheat
- chia seeds
- coconut
- kale
- millet
- nutritional yeast flakes
- pistachios
- sesame seeds and tahini
- sorghum
- spinach
- spring greens
- sprouts (such as broccoli, mung bean, pea)
- sunflower seeds
- walnuts
- watermelon seeds
- yogurt (almond, coconut, soya)

From left: Peach 'Yogurt' (opposite),
Happy Horchata (page 68)

This epic combo tastes like dairy yogurt flavoured with blended fruits. You'll get the best results with canned or jarred peaches in natural juice. Fresh and frozen lack the strength of flavour this blend needs. The chia bumps up the protein and omega fatty acids, and the camu comes in with vitamin C to boost immunity. Don't miss the cardamom for Indian-inspired elation.

peach 'yogurt'

SERVES 2

180 ml (6 fl oz) filtered water

½ tsp finely grated lemon zest, plus extra to taste

4 tbsp fresh lemon juice, plus extra to taste

½ tsp probiotic powder (see page 154, optional)

400 g (14 oz) canned or jarred peaches in natural fruit juice, drained

140 g (5 oz) raw unsalted cashews, soaked (see page 171)

1 tsp natural vanilla extract

½ medium banana (fresh or frozen)

30 g (1 oz) frozen raw cauliflower florets

125 g (4½ oz) ice cubes, plus extra to taste

optional boosters

1 tbsp chia seeds (black or white)

1 tsp camu powder (see page 23)

¼ tsp ground cardamom, plus extra to taste

Throw the water, lemon zest, lemon juice, probiotic powder, peaches, cashews and vanilla, plus the boosters, into your blender and blast on high for about 60 seconds until smooth and creamy. Add the banana, cauliflower and ice and blast again for 10–20 seconds until smooth and chilled. Tweak the lemon zest, lemon juice, cardamom and ice to taste. Drink immediately.

NUTRITIONAL FACTS (PER SERVING)

calories 517 kcal | fat 31 g | saturated fat 5.5 g | sodium 25.1 mg | carbs 54 g | fibre 6.2 g | sugars 29.6 g | protein 14.7 g | calcium 56.2 mg | iron 5.4 mg

This almond-butter-based take on satay is divine, and if you add the pumpkin seed oil your sauce will taste pretty close to the traditional peanut version. Don't miss the herb boosters for gorgeous presentation and added flavour.

satay skewers

MAKES 8 SKEWERS; SAUCE MAKES 345 G (12 OZ)

marinade

2 tbsp gluten-free soy sauce or tamari

2 tbsp toasted sesame oil

1 tbsp finely chopped garlic (about 3 cloves)

1 tsp natural salt (see page 139)

1/2 tsp freshly ground black pepper

1/2 tsp finely chopped fresh ginger

1/4 tsp chilli flakes

vegetables and tofu

1 red pepper, deseeded and cut into 3 cm (1¼ in) chunks

1 yellow pepper, deseeded and cut into 3 cm (1¼ in) chunks

1 small red onion, cut into 8 chunks

2 courgettes, cut into 1 cm (½ in) rounds

8 button mushrooms, halved

16 cherry tomatoes

1 (397 g/14 oz) packet extra-firm tofu, cut into 16 equal pieces

sauce

1/2 tsp extra virgin olive oil

35 g (1¼ oz) shallot, finely chopped

120 ml (4 fl oz) full-fat canned coconut milk (shake, then pour)

130 g (4½ oz) roasted almond butter

2 tbsp pumpkin seed oil, plus extra to taste (see intro above, optional)

2 tbsp gluten-free soy sauce or tamari

1½ tbsp fresh lime juice

2 tsp finely chopped garlic (about 2 cloves)

2 tsp finely chopped fresh ginger

2 tsp coconut nectar, plus extra to taste

1 tsp red curry paste, plus extra to taste

1/4 tsp chilli flakes, plus extra to taste

1/8 tsp natural salt (see page 139), plus extra to taste

optional boosters

1 tsp finely chopped flat-leaf parsley

1 tsp finely chopped coriander

1 tsp finely chopped basil

If using bamboo skewers, soak eight in water for 30 minutes so the skewers won't burn.

To make the marinade, whisk all of the ingredients together in a large mixing bowl.

Add all of the vegetables (not the tofu) and toss to coat evenly. Transfer the vegetables to another bowl and use the marinade left in the bowl to coat the tofu by gently rolling the pieces in the marinade or by applying the marinade with a pastry brush so the pieces don't break up.

Preheat the oven to 220°C/425°F/Gas mark 7. Line one large baking sheet or two smaller baking sheets with silicone liners or baking paper.

Assemble the skewers by threading the vegetables and tofu onto each of eight skewers in the following order: 1 tomato, 1 mushroom half, 1 courgette round, 1 red pepper piece, 1 yellow pepper piece, 1 tofu cube, 1 red pepper piece, 1 yellow pepper piece, 1 onion chunk, 1 courgette round, 1 tofu cube, 1 mushroom half, 1 tomato. Place the skewers lengthways on the prepared baking sheets. Reserve any remaining marinade.

Roast the skewers for 15–20 minutes until the vegetables are lightly browned. Remove from the oven, gently turn the skewers over and roast for a further 15 minutes until the vegetables are tender. (Alternatively, grill the skewers over a high heat for about 10 minutes on each side.)

While the skewers are cooking, make the sauce. Throw all of the sauce ingredients into your blender and blast on high for 30–60 seconds until smooth and creamy. You may have to scrape down the sides of the container. Tweak the pumpkin seed oil, coconut nectar, curry paste, chilli flakes and salt to taste.

Brush the cooked skewers with the reserved marinade and sprinkle with the herb boosters. Serve immediately and pass the sauce around the table.

NUTRITIONAL FACTS (PER SERVING, BASED ON 8 SERVINGS)

calories 324 kcal | fat 24.1 g | saturated fat 4.9 g | sodium 786.5 mg | carbs 18.2 g | fibre 5.6 g | sugars 6.5 g | protein 14.8 g | calcium 429.1 mg | iron 3.4 mg

When my friend Denise goes lentil, I go mental. Add my Basil-is-the-bomb Sauce (page 49) to her protein-powered soup, and ka-pow! You've got a knockout. The sauce is essential and rockets this rustic vegetable and legume soup into the stratosphere. The lemon juice is key, brightening and lifting the flavours, and I never say no to a dollop of So Good! Soured Cream (page 183). Top with slices of avocado and greens for some raw nutrition.

gentle lentils

SERVES 8 AS A STARTER, 6 AS A MAIN

2 tbsp grapeseed oil or extra virgin olive oil

2 tsp finely chopped garlic (about 2 cloves)

150 g (5½ oz) yellow onion, diced

132 g (4½ oz) celery, diced

160 g (5¾ oz) carrots, diced

1 tsp natural salt (see page 139), plus extra to taste

370 g (13 oz) dry green lentils

1 tbsp finely chopped fresh thyme, plus extra to taste

½ tsp ground black pepper

2 litres (3½ pints) vegetable stock

Fresh lemon juice

240 ml (8½ fl oz) Basil-is-the-bomb Sauce (page 49) with the chilli flakes booster

optional boosters

1 avocado, stoned, peeled and sliced

So Good! Soured Cream (page 183)

40 g (1½ oz) pea sprouts

Heat the oil in a large saucepan over a medium-low heat and sauté the garlic, onion, celery, carrot and ½ teaspoon of the salt for about 5 minutes until the vegetables soften slightly. Stir in the lentils, thyme, pepper and stock. Increase the heat to medium-high, bring the mixture to a lively simmer (not a full boil) and cook for about 5 minutes. Reduce the heat to medium-low, cover, add the remaining ½ teaspoon salt and simmer for about 20 minutes until the lentils and vegetables are tender but not mushy. Add salt to taste.

Ladle the soup into bowls and add about ¼ teaspoon lemon juice to each serving. Drizzle 1 tablespoon of the Basil-is-the-bomb sauce over the top of each bowl and serve with a few of the avocado slices, a dollop of soured cream and some of the pea sprouts. Pass the remaining Basil-is-the-bomb Sauce and more lemon juice around the table.

NUTRITIONAL FACTS (PER SERVING, BASED ON 8 SERVINGS)

calories 339 kcal | fat 17.7 g | saturated fat 2.3 g | sodium 431.1 mg | carbs 35.3 g | fibre 6.5 g | sugars 3.3 g | protein 12.4 g | calcium 60.7 mg | iron 3.6 mg

Raw florets not a fave? I'm betting the delectable dressing on this salad will change your mind. This recipe, among the most popular on The Blender Girl website, is one people go nuts over! The mayo-style dressing is thick, to achieve the 'stick to your ribs' effect raw dishes often lack. In this salad, creamy, crunchy and chewy textures complement bright, tangy, sweet and spicy flavours. Finely dicing the vegetables is critical, to make sure all the ingredients are uniformly dressed and that you get all the flavours with every bite. The base recipe is spectacular and loaded with high-quality protein. Boosting with the watermelon seeds and edamame adds even more. The sultanas bring in a delightful sweetness. With any or all of the boosters, or without, this salad will make you crazy for crucifers.

raw broccoli brilliance

SERVES 6 AS A STARTER, 4 AS A MAIN; THE DRESSING MAKES 450 G (1 LB)

dressing

80 ml (2¾ fl oz) filtered water

80 ml (2¾ fl oz) extra virgin olive oil

80 ml (2¾ fl oz) fresh lemon juice

140 g (5 oz) raw unsalted cashews, soaked (see page 171)

30 g (1 oz) cauliflower florets, chopped

2½ tbsp apple cider vinegar

2 tbsp coconut sugar

1½ tsp prepared yellow mustard

1 tsp natural salt (see page 139)

¼ tsp chilli flakes

salad

450 g (1 lb) broccoli florets, finely chopped

260 g (9 oz) celery, finely diced

80 g (3 oz) salad onion (white and green parts), finely chopped

160 g (5¾ oz) raw almonds, sliced

60 g (2¼ oz) shelled hemp seeds

70 g (2½ oz) raw sunflower seeds

70 g (2½ oz) raw pumpkin seeds

Natural salt (see page 139)

Freshly ground black pepper

optional boosters

320 g (11½ oz) shelled raw edamame

70 g (2½ oz) raw sprouted watermelon seeds

80 g (3 oz) sultanas

To make the dressing, throw all of the ingredients into your blender and blast on high for about 1 minute until smooth and creamy. Chill in the fridge.

To assemble the salad, in a large bowl, toss the broccoli, celery, salad onion, almonds, hemp seeds, sunflower seeds and pumpkin seeds, along with the edamame, watermelon seeds and sultana boosters. Add the dressing and toss. Season to taste with salt and pepper.

NUTRITIONAL FACTS (PER SERVING, BASED ON 6 SERVINGS)

calories 582 kcal | fat 48.1 g | saturated fat 6.1 g | sodium 466 mg | carbs 28.2 g | fibre 7.2 g | sugars 8.6 g | protein 19.1 g | calcium 162.9 mg | iron 5.3 mg

These are epic! And I don't mind sayin'. Everybody I serve these veggie burgers to pronounces them the best ever. It took me a long time to get the mix juuust right. Diehard kitchen accomplice Denise and I clocked so many hours trialling these that we actually shed tears of joy and did a delirious dance when I finally nailed them. They've got the mighty meaty look of a traditional burger, a brilliant barbecue flavour, and a moist but firm texture that stands up to cooking and doesn't fall apart – all with the high-quality proteins of beans and quinoa. (While I'm singing my own praises, the wedges are pretty spesh, too!) Now, remember: good things come to those who wait. Making these prize puppies is a two-hour commitment. Invest the time to reach for the sublime. I promise you won't be sorry.

bbq mushroom & bean burgers with wedges

SERVES 8

burgers

120 ml (4 fl oz) extra virgin olive oil

150 g (5½ oz) yellow onion, diced

1 tbsp finely chopped garlic (about 3 cloves)

2 tbsp vegetable stock

1 tbsp fresh lemon juice

180 g (6 oz) cooked cannellini beans

1 tsp natural salt (see page 139)

420 g (15 oz) chestnut mushrooms, diced

3 tbsp Bragg Liquid Aminos, gluten-free soy sauce or tamari

3 tbsp red miso paste

160 g (5¾ oz) cooked brown lentils

1 tbsp Dijon mustard

270 g (9½ oz) cooked quinoa

160 g (5¾ oz) fresh gluten-free breadcrumbs (do not use commercial breadcrumbs; see Note, page 64)

6 tbsp chickpea flour

3 tbsp balsamic vinegar

1 tbsp nutritional yeast flakes

37 g (1½ oz) finely chopped flat-leaf parsley leaves

1 tsp smoked paprika

⅛ tsp cayenne pepper

wedges

8 red-skinned potatoes (or other all-purpose potatoes), unpeeled and scrubbed

3 tbsp extra virgin olive oil

1 tsp natural salt (see page 139), plus extra to taste

⅛ tsp freshly ground black pepper, plus extra to taste

to serve

8 gluten-free vegan hamburger buns or flatbreads

Extra virgin olive oil, to brush the buns

8 lettuce leaves

1 medium tomato, sliced into 8 rounds

½ medium red onion, sliced into 8 rounds

1 large gherkin, sliced into 8 thin rounds

Prepared yellow mustard

Ketchup

Barbecue sauce

Mayo

optional boosters

1 tsp onion powder

1 tsp garlic powder

¾ tsp smoked paprika

To make the burgers, in a large frying pan over a medium heat, heat 1 tablespoon of the oil and sauté the onion and garlic for about 5 minutes until soft and translucent. Allow to cool slightly.

Add the vegetable stock, lemon juice, cannellini beans, ¼ teaspoon of the salt and the onion mixture to your blender and blast on high for about 20 seconds until combined. You may need to stop the machine and scrape down the sides of the container. Set aside.

In a large frying pan over a medium heat, heat 3 tablespoons of the olive oil and sauté the mushrooms with 1 tablespoon of the liquid aminos for 3–5 minutes until just cooked and reduced. Reduce the heat to low, add the miso paste and stir for about 2 minutes until well combined. Drain the mushroom mixture in a fine-mesh sieve to remove any liquid.

In a large bowl, stir together the cannellini bean mixture, the mushroom mixture and the mustard, then add the quinoa, breadcrumbs and chickpea flour. Mix until well combined. Add the remaining 2 tablespoons of liquid aminos, the balsamic vinegar, nutritional yeast, parsley, smoked paprika, cayenne and the remaining ¾ teaspoon of salt. Stir well, cutting the mixture with a spatula or spoon until thoroughly combined.

Line a baking sheet with kitchen paper (to absorb excess moisture). Using your hands, scoop up 120 g (4½ oz) of the mixture, form it into a 7.5 cm (3 in) round patty, and place on the prepared baking sheet. Repeat with the remaining mixture to form eight patties. Cover and chill in the fridge for 1–2 hours until firm. While the burgers are chilling, prepare the wedges.

Preheat the oven to 200°C/400°F/Gas mark 6.

Halve the potatoes lengthways, then cut each half lengthways into quarters to create eight long wedges from each potato.

Line a large baking sheet (or two smaller baking sheets) with kitchen paper. Lay the potato wedges in a single layer on top and cover with a second layer of kitchen paper. Pat the potatoes dry to remove all surface moisture. (This will help the oil and boosters coat the wedges better and will enable even crisping and baking.)

In a large bowl, combine the olive oil, salt, pepper and the onion powder, garlic powder and smoked paprika boosters. Using your hands, toss the potatoes in this seasoning mixture until evenly coated.

Line the same baking sheet(s) with baking paper. Using your hands (or tongs), transfer the potatoes one by one to the baking sheet(s), arranging them in a single layer with one cut side down. (If you empty the bowl onto the baking sheet you will get excess oil.)

Roast for about 30 minutes until the potatoes start to brown, then flip all of the wedges and roast for a further 20–30 minutes until lightly browned and crispy on the outside and tender on the inside. Tweak the salt and pepper to taste.

continued

While the potatoes are roasting, fry the burgers. In a very large frying pan (or two frying pans) over a medium-high heat, heat the remaining olive oil (½ tablespoon for each burger in the pan) until hot but not smoking. Add the burgers and fry for about 2 minutes until golden brown, but not burnt. Use two spatulas to carefully flip the burgers and fry for a further 2 minutes until golden brown.

Line a baking sheet with baking paper or a non-stick silicone sheet. With two spatulas, transfer the burgers to the baking sheet. Place in the oven for about 15 minutes until warmed through. Transfer immediately to a cool plate to avoid burning on the base.

While the burger patties are warming, toast the burger buns. Line a baking sheet with baking paper and place each half of the bun on the sheet, inside side up. Brush with olive oil, and bake until toasted to your liking.

Serve family style, with the toppings in bowls on the table. Place two halves of the burger bun on a plate, place a burger on top of one half. Serve with wedges, and allow people to assemble their burgers the way they like.

Note: Shop-bought gluten-free or wheat breadcrumbs are too heavy and overwhelming in these burgers. Make your own gluten-free breadcrumbs by pulsing 4 slices of gluten-free bread in a food processor for 10–20 seconds until the bread has the consistency of bread-crumbs. This makes about 160 g (5½ oz) breadcrumbs.

NUTRITIONAL FACTS (PER SERVING)

calories 811 kcal | fat 23.6 g | saturated fat 3.6 g | sodium 1708.3 mg | carbs 128.6 g | fibre 16.7 g | sugars 12.4 g | protein 25.1 g | calcium 223.8 mg | iron 8.8 mg

Blend, freeze, slice and eat voraciously. That's how easy this cake is! Once you have your cashews soaked (essential for a righteously creamy consistency), this decadent dessert takes less than 15 minutes to put together. It looks and tastes just like dairy-drenched cheesecake, but my family and friends tell me they crave this more than the conventional kind. Add the lemon and poppy seeds for an awesome twist and a drizzle of strawberry sauce to up the indulgence.

classic cheesecake

MAKES 10 SLICES

crust

160 g (5½ oz) raw whole almonds

170 g (6 oz) pitted dates, chopped, plus extra as needed

filling

180 ml (6 fl oz) coconut oil (in liquid form)

120 ml (4 fl oz) full-fat canned coconut milk (shake, then pour)

120 ml (4 fl oz) fresh lemon juice

120 ml (4 fl oz) pure maple syrup

420 g (15 oz) raw unsalted cashews, soaked (see page 171)

1 tsp natural vanilla extract

Pinch of natural salt (see page 139)

Coconut Cream (page 35), to serve (optional)

optional boosters

1 tbsp finely grated lemon zest, plus extra to taste and decorate

1 tbsp poppy seeds

Sweet Strawberry Sauce (page 119), to serve

To make the crust, grease a 23 or 25 cm (9 or 10 in) springform tin with coconut oil. Process the almonds and dates in a food processor until the mixture is well combined and clumps together. Form the mixture into a ball; if it doesn't hold together, you may need to add a bit more chopped date and process again. Press the mixture into the base of the prepared tin and set aside.

To make the filling, throw all of the ingredients into your blender in the order listed, including the lemon zest booster, and blend for about 1 minute until rich and creamy. To achieve the smoothest filling, stop the machine periodically and scrape down the sides of the container. Add the poppy seed booster once the filling is completely blended, then blast for just a few seconds to combine. Pour the filling into the crust. Cover the tin with foil and freeze the cheesecake for 6–8 hours until solidified.

To serve, transfer the tin from the freezer to the fridge and defrost for about 30 minutes. Gently release and remove the sides of the springform tin, then cut the cheesecake into 10 even slices with a very sharp knife. Keeping the slices together on the springform tin base, return the cheesecake to the fridge to continue defrosting for a further 30 minutes before serving. Serve the slices plain or drizzle each one with 2 tablespoons of the Sweet Strawberry Sauce booster and top with a dollop of the Coconut Cream. Pass the remaining strawberry sauce and coconut cream around the table.

Note: Because of the coconut oil, this filling will melt if left out at room temperature.

NUTRITIONAL FACTS (PER SERVING, BASED ON 10 SERVINGS)

calories 594 kcal | fat 45.2 g | saturated fat 20.2 g | sodium 38 mg | carbs 44.8 g | fibre 5 g | sugars 28 g | protein 11.8 g | calcium 91.8 mg | iron 4 mg

A healthier take on Mexican rice milk, this blend discards the soaking liquid for better digestion (see page 171) and the chia seeds (and watermelon seed booster) punch up the protein. Awesome chilled or over ice, this combo (see photo, page 54) is creamy, sweet and oh so tasty – especially with the nutmeg and cloves.

happy horchata

SERVES 2

190 g (6¾ oz) uncooked medium- or long-grain brown rice

Natural salt (see page 139)

½ tsp apple cider vinegar or lemon juice

140 g (5 oz) blanched flaked almonds

960 ml (1¾ pints) filtered water, plus extra for soaking

4 tbsp full-fat canned coconut milk (shake, then pour)

3 tbsp pure maple syrup, plus extra to taste

2 tbsp white chia seeds

1 tbsp natural vanilla extract, plus extra to taste

1 tbsp ground cinnamon, plus extra to taste and to garnish

Ice cubes, to serve

optional boosters

2 tbsp raw sprouted watermelon seeds

¼ tbsp ground nutmeg, plus extra to taste

Pinch of ground cloves, plus extra to taste

In a bowl, cover the rice with 480 ml (17 fl oz) of filtered water and add ¼ teaspoon of salt and ¼ teaspoon of the apple cider vinegar. In a separate bowl, cover the almonds with 480 ml (17 fl oz) of filtered water and add ¼ teaspoon of salt and the remaining ¼ teaspoon apple cider vinegar. Leave the rice and almonds to soak for at least 8 hours, or for up to 12 hours. Drain the rice and almonds and rinse thoroughly; discard the soaking liquids.

Transfer the drained rice and almonds to your blender with the 960 ml (1¾ pints) of filtered water and blast on high for about 60 seconds until the rice and almonds are completely pulverized.

Strain the mixture with a nut milk bag or filtration bag, and rinse the blender container and lid. Pour the strained rice/almond milk back into the blender. Add the coconut milk, maple syrup, chia seeds, vanilla, cinnamon, a pinch of salt and any boosters and blast for about 10 seconds until smooth and creamy. Tweak the maple syrup, vanilla, cinnamon, the nutmeg booster and the clove booster to taste.

Chill in the fridge for a couple of hours, then serve over ice. Sprinkle each glass with cinnamon.

NUTRITIONAL FACTS (PER SERVING)

calories 981 kcal | fat 48.5 g | saturated fat 9.3 g | sodium 764 mg | carbs 114.8 g | fibre 15.3 g | sugars 23 g | protein 24.4 g | calcium 378.3 mg | iron 6.1 mg

This versatile cheeze sauce is great for Nosh-on-'em Nachos (see photo, page 11), spectacular over pasta and wonderful for jazzing up vegetables. I've kept it quick and easy, so you can throw it together (once you've soaked the cashews) in 5 minutes. If you've got an extra 10 minutes, you can add sautéed onion and garlic in place of the garlic and onion powders, as I've done for the sauce in the Cauliflower Mac 'n' Cheeze (page 196). A bit of a fresh herb, such as thyme or parsley, goes brilliantly in this, too. Add the cayenne for kick and the tahini for added creaminess, more protein and another layer of flavour. For a taste reminiscent of smoked Gouda, add the smoked paprika. This sauce thickens in the fridge, so when reheating, you may want to add a splash of water or vegetable stock.

it's-better-with-cheeze sauce

MAKES 375 G (13 OZ)

120 ml (4 fl oz) vegetable stock, plus extra as needed

140 g (5 oz) raw unsalted cashews, soaked (see page 171)

3 tbsp nutritional yeast flakes

2 tbsp fresh lemon juice, plus extra to taste

1 tbsp white miso paste

½ tsp onion powder, plus extra to taste

½ tsp garlic powder, plus extra to taste

½ tsp natural salt (see page 139), plus extra to taste

⅛ tsp ground turmeric

optional boosters

1 tbsp hulled tahini

¼ tsp smoked paprika, plus extra to taste

Pinch of cayenne pepper, plus extra to taste

Throw everything except the boosters into your blender and blast on high for about 1 minute until smooth and creamy. Tweak the lemon juice, onion powder, garlic powder and salt to taste, and add any boosters. Blend again. You may want to add about 1 tablespoon more vegetable stock for a thinner consistency.

NUTRITIONAL FACTS (PER SERVING, BASED ON 10 SERVINGS)

calories 96 kcal | fat 6.4 g | saturated fat 1.1 g | sodium 186.5 mg | carbs 6.6 g | fibre 1.8 g | sugars 1.3 g | protein 5.2 g | calcium 7.5 mg | iron 1.2 mg

CHAPTER 5

weight loss

weight loss

In managing energy use, our bodies carry out millions of chemical processes. All taken together, they're termed 'metabolism'. Along with what we eat, factors like age, gender, muscle mass, body size, genes, hormones, environment, drugs and physical activity influence these processes, so no one's metabolism is the same as anyone else's. Base metabolic rate (BMR) measures energy use at rest; above-base metabolic rates vary with activity and stress. When we take in more energy than our metabolic rates are putting to use, our bodies store the surplus – as fat. A healthy diet, in conjunction with regular exercise, is our best metabolism regulator. While it's true that we are what we eat, we are most literally what we digest and absorb. Weight management calls for a healthy digestive system both to deliver nutrients where they're needed and to get rid of waste efficiently. Since nutrient-dense, low glycaemic, high-fibre foods provide quality calories, contain compounds that optimize energy uptake and utilization, and (along with water) fill us up, they're our mightiest allies in the weight-loss war.

green tea

Amped up by antioxidants, the anti-inflammatory epigallocatechin gallate (EGCG) makes green tea an ultimate fat fighter. Teamed with caffeine and the amino acid L-theanine, this hero muscles up for metabolic mojo. Packed with vitamins and minerals, and catechin flavonoids to cleanse the liver and kidneys, green tea has astronomical antioxidant benefits, too. Matcha powder packs the most power, with 100 times the EGCG of regular brewed green tea. While caffeine is a diuretic, green tea's a happy hydrator, boosting immunity and energy. Steep green tea leaves briefly to avoid bitterness.

chia seeds

Tiny titans, these fibre-filled seeds absorb ten times their weight in water, so they fill us up, and bulkify food for digestive cleansing and weight loss. With more than 90 per cent of its carbs taking the form of fibre, chia slows conversion of starches for sustained release of energy. With amino acids for muscle building and repair, chia is ace for athletes, and boosts stamina and endurance. A rich source of omega-3s, chia supports immune responses and enhances brain and nerve function, and its alkaline minerals are a boon to the blood. Sprinkle chia seeds, black or white, on yogurt, cereals, soups, stews and salads; blend into smoothies; stir into energy drinks; or whisk into milk or juice to make puddings. For a fantastic replacement for one large egg in baked goods, whisk 1 tablespoon chia seeds into 3 tablespoons water and leave to thicken.

chillies

Spice things up and shed the pounds! The capsaicin found in peppers acts as an appetite suppressant, heating the body to boost metabolism, burn fat and dial up detox. Rich in carotenoid antioxidants, chillies combat oxidative stress to boost immunity, too. In these recipes, I've used fresh Serrano, jalapeño and Anaheim chillies, along with dried chilli flakes and cayenne pepper (see page 155). Their heat varies, so start small and add to taste. Chillies add kick and medicinal magic to sweet and savoury dishes, and they're fantastic in smoothies, lifting the pungency of leafy greens and the earthiness of beetroot. They're sensational with chocolate, too.

raspberries

Rally round raspberries and reap the rewards. Anthocyanin pigments and flavonoid rheosmin (aka raspberry ketone) fire up metabolism and block fat absorption, while fellow flavonoid tiliroside moderates starch digestion to regulate blood sugar. These gems are jam-packed with alkalizing, antioxidant and anti-inflammatory agents, high in vitamins, minerals and fibre, and low in fat, sugar and calories. So gorge on raspberries by the gobfull; toss onto cereals, pancakes and desserts; and blend into smoothies, drinks, sauces and dressings.

grapefruit

Low in fat and sugar, high in water and pectin fibre, grapefruit burns fat, promotes the flow of gastric juices and bulks up food in the colon to accelerate elimination. This sassy citrus is a weight loss-friendly food, helping to lower insulin (reducing fat storage), while the phytonutrient limonoid supports antioxidant glutathione production to help the liver expel fats and sugars. One medium red grapefruit serves up the RDA of vitamin C along with bioflavonoids that beat the bloat. Delivering carotenoids for vitamin A, potassium and folic acid, grapefruit is an infection and inflammation fighter that regulates cholesterol and blood pressure. (It reacts adversely with most blood pressure meds, though.) While the white kind contains slightly fewer calories, pink and ruby are your best bet – they've got more free-radical-fighting flavonoids, anthocyanins and lycopenes. Like other citrus, grapefruit is chemically acidic, but alkaline forming when digested. Use it as a tummy-tamer in juices, smoothies and salads.

apples

An apple a day keeps the doctor away and your skinny jeans in play! Apple's pectin interacts with key antioxidants to lower blood-fat levels; the phytonutrient quercetin inhibits digestive enzymes so carbs break down less readily into sugar. Galacturonic acid (in pectin) lowers the body's demand for insulin, cleverly keeping apples' glycaemic index low. By stimulating bile production, pectin also helps the liver offload toxins and sweeps the colon. Valuable nutrients, quercetin included, are concentrated in the skin, so skip peeling. For low sugar content, I go with Granny Smith, but any variety works. My sweetener of choice for alkaline smoothies and drinks, apple gives fruit and vegetable salads awesome flavour; it's righteous raw or stewed on cereals and in desserts, and unsweetened apple sauce is a brilliant egg replacer in vegan baking.

pears

Yep, these buttery babes are high in fructose, but the sweetest and most water soluble of the simple sugars helps a pear satisfy a craving with less sugar overall. Since fructose is an excellent transport vehicle for B vitamins and antioxidants, that juicy pear's an immunity promotor, too! Fat free and full of fibre, pears fill us up and digest easily. The pectin acts as a diuretic and laxative, binding bile acids and scouring the gut and colon of wastes, for effective elimination. All varieties offer concentrated carotenoids and flavonoids, but go for red-skinned ones. Their peels contain flavonols that lower insulin levels to boost fat metabolism. Most of a pear's phytonutrients and fibre are in the skin, so put away the peeler. Pears bring a sublime sweetness to smoothies, juices and desserts.

more hero foods

- açaí
- almonds
- apple cider vinegar
- artichoke
- avocado
- berries (blackberries, blueberries, strawberries)
- broccoli
- Brussels sprouts
- cabbage
- cauliflower
- cinnamon
- coconut
- courgette
- cucumber
- ginger
- hemp seeds
- leafy greens (such as pak choi, chard, spring greens, kale, spinach, watercress)
- legumes
- sesame seeds
- watermelon

Weight-loss and metabolism-boosting superheroes – green tea, grapefruit, raspberries and mint – blend up a low-calorie treat that's crisp and refreshing. Add the pepper for flavour fever, and the broccoli and avocado for nutrient power and satiating energy.

tone it down with berries & tea

SERVES 2

1 green teabag

240 ml (8½ fl oz) boiling water

½ tsp probiotic powder (see page 154, optional)

180 g (6 oz) peeled and deseeded grapefruit pieces

1 green apple, cored and chopped (do not peel)

20 g (¾ oz) mint leaves

1 tbsp chia seeds (black or white)

5 drops alcohol-free liquid stevia, plus extra to taste

320 g (11¼ oz) frozen raspberries

optional boosters

25 g (1 oz) frozen raw broccoli florets

35 g (1¼ oz) red pepper, deseeded and chopped

¼ avocado, stoned and peeled

Steep the teabag in the boiling water for about 1 minute. Allow to cool, then chill in the fridge. Pour the chilled tea into your blender and add the probiotic powder, grapefruit, apple, mint, chia, stevia and the pepper and avocado boosters and blast on high for 30–60 seconds until well combined. Add the raspberries and the frozen broccoli booster, and blast again for 20–30 seconds until smooth. Tweak the stevia to taste. Enjoy immediately.

NUTRITIONAL FACTS (PER SERVING)

calories 187 kcal | fat 2.7 g | saturated fat 0.2 g | sodium 6.7 mg | carbs 40.7 g | fibre 15.8 g | sugars 21.7 g | protein 4.1 g | calcium 99.3 mg | iron 2.6 mg

In an immunity elixir that's *not* for the faint-hearted, ginger and cayenne fire up metabolism and digestion. Add the green boosters for a shot of cleansing chlorophyll and bulk up your bliss with some chia. Or keep the mix unstrained, and blast with ice for instant gratification.

lose it! lemonade

SERVES 2

480 ml (16 fl oz) filtered water

120 ml (4 fl oz) fresh lemon juice

1 small thin-skinned lemon, quartered and deseeded

2 green apples, cored and quartered (do not peel)

1 tsp finely chopped fresh ginger, plus extra to taste

Pinch of cayenne pepper, plus extra to taste

Pinch of natural salt (see page 139)

15 drops alcohol-free liquid stevia, plus extra to taste

1 tbsp chia seeds (black or white, optional)

Ice cubes, to serve (optional)

optional boosters

44 g (1½ oz) baby spinach

1 tsp wheatgrass powder (see page 171)

¼ tsp chlorella powder (see page 39)

Throw everything except the chia but including the spinach, wheatgrass and chlorella boosters into your blender and blast on high for about 60 seconds until well combined. Tweak the ginger, cayenne and stevia to taste. Strain the mixture using a filtration bag, nut milk bag or fine-mesh sieve. Enjoy immediately over ice or whisk in the chia seeds and chill in the fridge for a couple of hours.

NUTRITIONAL FACTS (PER SERVING)

calories 115 kcal | fat 0.6 g | saturated fat 0.1 g | sodium 157.9 mg | carbs 33.4 g | fibre 5.2 g | sugars 21 g | protein 1 g | calcium 27.6 mg | iron 0.4 mg

I've been serving up this little gem since the last millennium, and it never goes out of style. On the table in under 20 minutes, it's one of my go-to last-minute lifesavers when I've got no energy, little time (but a bit of thyme) and virtually nothing in the way of fresh food on hand. It's low in fat but high in flavour (add the boosters in any combination for even more). Punch up the nutrition and satiating quality by throwing in some leafy greens, celery, carrots and courgette. Or go hearty if you like, with a scoop of whole grains or pasta. This soup is as versatile as it is sensational.

cheeky chickpea & rosemary soup

SERVES 6 AS A STARTER, 4 AS A MAIN

1.2 litres (2¼ pints) vegetable stock

44 g (1½ oz) sun-dried tomatoes packed in oil, drained, dried and roughly chopped

2 tbsp finely chopped garlic (about 6 cloves)

1 tsp grapeseed oil or extra virgin olive oil

75 g (2¾ oz) yellow onion, diced

1 tsp natural salt (see page 139)

1 (411 g/14.5 oz) can diced tomatoes with their juice

1 tbsp finely chopped fresh rosemary

540 g (1 lb 3 oz) cooked chickpeas or 2 (425 g/15 oz) cans, rinsed and drained

20 g (¾ oz) finely chopped salad onion (green parts only)

Freshly ground black pepper

optional boosters

⅛ tsp chilli flakes, plus extra to taste

½ tsp finely chopped fresh thyme, plus extra to taste

45 g (1½ oz) chard, shredded

Add 240 ml (8½ fl oz) of the vegetable stock to your blender along with the sun-dried tomatoes, 1 tablespoon of the garlic and the chilli flakes booster and blast on high for 30–60 seconds until smooth. Set aside.

In a large pot, heat the oil over a medium heat and sauté the onion and the remaining garlic with ¼ teaspoon of salt for about 5 minutes until soft and translucent. Add the tomatoes, rosemary and thyme booster and sauté for a few minutes until fragrant. Add the blended mixture, remaining stock and ½ teaspoon of the salt. Increase the heat to high and bring to the boil. Reduce the heat to medium-low and add the chickpeas. Simmer, partially covered, for 10 minutes. Stir in the chard booster and let the greens wilt as the soup cools slightly. Add the salad onion just before serving. Season with the remaining salt and with pepper to taste.

NUTRITIONAL FACTS (PER SERVING, BASED ON 6 SERVINGS)

calories 194 kcal | fat 4.5 g | saturated fat 0.5 g | sodium 736 mg | carbs 31.6 g | fibre 9.1 g | sugars 6.9 g | protein 9.3 g | calcium 90.8 mg | iron 3.4 mg

This rockin' roasted vegetable salad *feels* decadent, but it's light and easily digested. Add the pine nut and lemon zest boosters for an extra burst of flavour, and spice up the dressing with chilli flakes. Tarragon likes to headline any show, and here's her time to shine!

roasted veggies with lemon tarragon trickle

SERVES 6 AS A STARTER, 4 AS A MAIN; DRESSING MAKES 210 G (7 OZ)

dressing

1 head of garlic

120 ml (4 fl oz) plus 1 tsp extra virgin olive oil

Natural salt (see page 139)

¼ tsp finely grated lemon zest

4 tbsp fresh lemon juice

1 tbsp Dijon mustard, plus extra to taste

2 tsp finely chopped shallot

2 tsp coconut nectar or pure maple syrup

⅛ tsp freshly ground black pepper

1 tbsp roughly chopped fresh tarragon

vegetables

1 head cauliflower, cut into florets with the stems attached

2 yellow peppers, deseeded and cut into long strips

2 courgettes, cut lengthways into eighths

½ red onion, cut into eighths

3 tbsp plus 1 tsp extra virgin olive oil

Natural salt (see page 139)

Freshly ground black pepper

2 bunches broccolini

1 romaine lettuce heart, roughly chopped (175 g/6 oz)

2 tbsp flat-leaf parsley, plus extra to taste

2 tbsp finely chopped chives, plus extra to taste

Lemon juice, to taste

optional boosters

Pinch of chilli flakes, plus extra to taste

35 g (1¼ oz) dry-toasted pine nuts

⅛ tsp finely grated lemon zest

Preheat the oven to 190°C/375°F/Gas mark 5. Line two large baking sheets with baking paper.

Cut off the top of the head of garlic, brush with the 1 teaspoon of oil and sprinkle with a pinch of salt. Wrap the head in baking paper, then in foil (to allow the garlic to steam and not burn, and to reduce aluminium transfer) and roast for 40–60 minutes until tender. Allow the garlic to cool, then squeeze the pulp out of the skins. This should make about 2 tablespoons of roasted garlic. Set aside.

To prepare the vegetables, toss the cauliflower, peppers, courgettes and red onion with 2 tablespoons of the oil, ½ teaspoon of salt and ½ teaspoon of pepper. Arrange the vegetables on one of the prepared baking sheets in a single layer and roast for 30–40 minutes until lightly browned.

Toss the broccolini with 1 tablespoon of the oil, ¼ teaspoon of salt and ¼ teaspoon of pepper. Arrange the broccolini in a single layer on the second prepared baking sheet and roast for about 15 minutes, until al dente.

While the veggies are roasting, finish making the dressing. Throw the remaining 120 ml (4 fl oz) of olive oil, ½ teaspoon of salt, the roasted garlic pulp, the lemon zest, lemon juice, mustard, shallot, coconut nectar, black pepper and the red chilli flake booster into your blender and blast on high for about 30 seconds until emulsified and creamy. Tweak the chilli flakes to taste. Add the tarragon and pulse a few times just to break it down and evenly disperse it. You don't want to overprocess the tarragon.

In a large bowl, combine the roasted veggies, the romaine lettuce, parsley, chives, lemon juice to taste and the pine nut booster and toss with 120 ml (4 fl oz) of the dressing. Add more dressing to taste and season with salt and pepper. Serve topped with lemon zest booster. Pass extra dressing around the table.

NUTRITIONAL FACTS (PER SERVING, BASED ON 6 SERVINGS)

calories 330 kcal | fat 27.3 g | saturated fat 3.9 g | sodium 324.5 mg |
carbs 20.9 g | fibre 5.4 g | sugars 7.2 g | protein 5.5 g |
calcium 90.1 mg | iron 2.1 mg

These dehydrated veggie crisps, a healthy alternative to fried potato crisps, have an incredible flavour that makes for a magnificent munch. They're low in calories, loaded with live enzymes and nutrients and inexpensive to make. To get just the right crunch, cut your courgettes in thin, even slices. You'll get the best results with a mandoline, but you can use a very sharp knife. Add the spice boosters for mindblowing flavour. I make double and triple batches because these little treats vanish as soon as they're ready to eat.

cheezy courgette crisps

MAKES ABOUT 52 G (1¾ OZ)

4 tbsp filtered water

1½ tbsp fresh lemon juice

1 tbsp extra virgin olive oil

2 tbsp raw sunflower seeds, soaked (see page 171)

2 tbsp nutritional yeast flakes

1 tbsp garlic powder

1 tbsp onion powder

½ tsp natural salt (see page 139)

2 medium courgettes

optional boosters

¼ tsp smoked paprika

⅛ tsp ground turmeric

⅛ tsp cayenne pepper

Throw the water, lemon juice, olive oil, sunflower seeds, yeast, garlic powder, onion powder, salt and any boosters into your blender and blast on high for 30–60 seconds until smooth and creamy. You may have to stop the machine and scrape down the sides of the container.

With a mandoline, slice the courgettes to a thickness of 1.5mm (¹⁄₁₆ in), or if using a sharp knife, slice them as thinly as possible. In a large bowl, massage the paste into the courgette slices with your hands until evenly coated.

Lay the courgette crisps on mesh dehydrator trays lined with non-stick sheets. Set the temperature to 46°C (115°F) and dry for about 12 hours or until dry. Gently remove the crisps from the non-stick sheets and lay them on the mesh trays. Dry for another 6 hours or until crispy. Store in an airtight container in a cool, dry place. The courgette crisps will keep for a few weeks, but they never last that long.

NUTRITIONAL FACTS (PER SERVING, BASED ON 4 SERVINGS)

calories 109 kcal | fat 6.2 g | saturated fat 0.8 g | sodium 304.5 mg | carbs 9.9 g | fibre 3.9 g | sugars 3.4 g | protein 6.7 g | calcium 29.7 mg | iron 1.2 mg

If I had a grain of sand for every request I get for a healthy, dairy-free coffee creamer, I'd live on my own private beach. I beta-tested this with a big cohort of my coffee-drinking friends. They went so bonkers I was tempted to brew up a pot and guzzle it myself. A thinner version of the cashew cream in *The Blender Girl* cookbook got good reactions from the javaholics, but this mixture of alkaline almond and coconut milk took the blue ribbon. The base recipe will rock your mug with richness *sans* sugar. That's why I tag it to the weight-loss category. Bump up the flavour with the vanilla booster. If slimming is not your objective, go mad with the maple syrup or go off the charts with the Kahlua. Whether you flavour this blend or stay with the basics, you'll never buy creamer again.

dream creamer

MAKES 480 ML (17 FL OZ)

160 g (5¾ oz) raw whole almonds, soaked (see page 171)

360 ml (12 fl oz) filtered water

4 tbsp full-fat canned coconut milk (shake, then pour)

optional boosters

1 tbsp natural vanilla extract

3 tbsp pure maple syrup

6 tbsp Kahlua, plus extra to taste

Throw the almonds and the filtered water into your blender and blast on high for about 60 seconds until pulverized. Strain the almond mixture with a nut milk bag, filtration bag or sheer piece of clean nylon hosiery. Rinse the blender, pour the strained milk back into the blender and add the coconut milk. Process on high for just a few seconds until well combined. Use the creamer unsweetened, or add the vanilla, maple syrup and/or Kahlua boosters for an incredible flavoured creamer. This will keep in the fridge for about 3 days (because of the soaked almonds). To store longer, do not soak the almonds, and the creamer will keep for about 5 days.

NUTRITIONAL FACTS (PER SERVING, BASED ON 6 SERVINGS)

calories 172 kcal | fat 15.3 g | saturated fat 2.8 g | sodium 3.9 mg | carbs 6 g | fibre 3.3 g | sugars 1.2 g | protein 5.8 g | calcium 75.2 mg | iron 1.3 mg

Thai-food maestro Eda Benjakul taught me the secret to an exceptional curry: a home-made paste. Brilliant bursts of flavour will make you scoff at the commercial stuff. Since the paste means a trip to the Asian supermarket and then a chop-a-thon, I've made the quantity generous. Freeze the extra portions of paste separately, so you can whip up two more batches of curry when the whim strikes. Which – trust me – it will.

greedy green curry

SERVES 4; CURRY PASTE MAKES 322 G (11½ OZ)

curry paste

1 tsp coconut oil (in liquid form)

70 g (2½ oz) shallot, finely chopped

2 tbsp fresh lime juice

2 tbsp filtered water

25 g (1 oz) Thai basil leaves, cut into ribbons

42 g (1½ oz) coriander roots (or stems), finely chopped

3 tbsp thinly sliced fresh lemongrass

6 tbsp chopped green chillies (including seeds)

2 tbsp dried shiitake powder (see Note, opposite)

2 tbsp dried porcini powder (see Note, opposite)

1½ tbsp chopped fresh kaffir lime leaves

1½ tbsp sliced galangal

1 tbsp finely chopped garlic (about 3 cloves)

1 tsp natural salt (see page 139)

curry

1 tbsp coconut oil (in liquid form)

960 ml (1¾ pints) full-fat canned coconut milk (shake, then pour)

240 ml (8½ fl oz) vegetable stock

½ tsp Bragg Liquid Aminos, gluten-free soy sauce or tamari

¼ tsp natural salt (see page 139), plus extra to taste

184 g (6½ oz) Chinese or Indian aubergine, cut into 4 cm (1½ in) pieces

115 g (4 oz) red pepper, deseeded and cubed

198 g (7 oz) firm tofu, cut into cubes

2 tbsp Thai basil leaves, cut into ribbons

2 tbsp finely chopped coriander

1 tsp finely chopped kaffir lime leaves

540 g (1 lb 3 oz) cooked quinoa or brown rice

optional boosters

37 g (1¼ oz) raw or roasted cashews, crushed

25 g (1 oz) beansprouts

½ tsp finely grated lime zest

To make the curry paste, in a frying pan over a medium-high heat, heat the coconut oil and sauté the shallot for about 5 minutes until lightly browned. Allow to cool slightly, then transfer to your blender with the rest of the paste ingredients. Blast on high for about 1 minute until smooth. You may have to stop the machine and scrape down the sides of the container.

To make the curry, in a large pot over a medium heat, heat the coconut oil and sauté 107 g (3½ oz) of the curry paste for 1–2 minutes until fragrant. Stir in 480 ml (17 fl oz) of the coconut milk and simmer for about 5 minutes until the oil comes to the top. Stir together until the paste is completely dissolved. Add the remaining coconut milk, the vegetable stock, liquid aminos

and salt and increase the heat to medium-high to bring the mixture to a simmer; do not allow the mixture to boil. Reduce the heat to low and simmer, uncovered, for about 30 minutes until the oils start to come to the top again, the coconut begins to skim and separate and the mixture reduces. Add the aubergine and simmer for 5 minutes until softened. Add the red pepper and simmer for 3–5 minutes until just softened. Gently stir in the tofu just to warm it. Into four bowls, scoop 135 g (4¾ oz) of quinoa and top with curry, then top with the Thai basil, coriander and kaffir lime, as well as with the cashew, beansprouts and lime zest boosters.

Note: To make the shiitake powder and the porcini powder, grind dried mushrooms in a spice grinder or coffee grinder until very fine. The powder will keep in a sealed container in the storecupboard for months.

NUTRITIONAL FACTS (PER SERVING)

calories 860 kcal | fat 61.2 g | saturated fat 47.8 g | sodium 834.4 mg | carbs 67 g | fibre 11.1 g | sugars 6.7 g | protein 23.7 g | calcium 462.5 mg | iron 13.3 mg

If you're watching your waistline, poached pears make a perfect treat. And this red-wine-and-raspberry rendition rocks! Add all three boosters for a brilliantly balanced burst of flavour – the vanilla, zest and spices all marry to create magic. True, the sauce has a lot of natural sugar in it, but you're giving just a tiny drizzle to each serving. Choose pears that are ripe but firm, so they don't break up while poaching, and core them with care, from the bottom, for the most elegant visual effect.

NUTRITIONAL FACTS (PER SERVING)

calories 179 kcal | fat 0.4 g | saturated fat 0 g | sodium 9.8 mg | carbs 27.2 g | fibre 3.1 g | sugars 19.4 g | protein 0.7 g | calcium 42.9 mg | iron 0.9 mg

pears poached to perfection

SERVES 8

1 (750 ml) bottle merlot

720 ml (1¼ pints) filtered apple juice

80 ml (2¾ fl oz) pure maple syrup

1 vanilla pod, sliced down the middle

1 cinnamon stick

3 cm (1¼ in) piece fresh ginger, sliced

1 tbsp finely grated lemon zest

8 firm Bartlett, Bosc or Conference pears with the stems intact

320 g (11¼ oz) fresh raspberries

Ice cream or Coconut Cream (page 35), to serve

optional boosters

2 star anise pods

¼ tsp whole cloves

1 tbsp mint leaves, cut into ribbons

Pour the wine, apple juice and maple syrup into a pot large enough to hold 8 pears, and add the vanilla pod, cinnamon stick, ginger slices, lemon zest and the star anise and clove boosters. Bring the mixture to the boil, then reduce the heat to medium-low, keeping the mixture at a simmer. With a sharp knife, cut a slice off the bottom of each pear so that it stands up. With a ¼ teaspoon measuring spoon, core the pears from the bottom and peel them, leaving the stems intact. With a large spoon, gently add the pears to the wine mixture. Lay a piece of baking paper (with a hole cut in the centre to allow steam to escape) on the top of the pears to keep them submerged so that they don't discolour. Keep the liquid just below a simmer and cook for 15–20 minutes, turning the pears every few minutes to ensure they cook and coat evenly. The pears are done when a paring knife easily pierces the flesh. Remove from the heat, remove the pears from the liquid with a slotted spoon and place them on a plate to cool.

Throw the raspberries into your blender and blast on high for about 30 seconds until fully puréed. Strain the mixture through a fine-mesh sieve to remove the seeds. Discard the seeds, wash the sieve, then strain the wine mixture. Transfer the strained liquid to a small pot and stir in the raspberry purée until well combined. Simmer the mixture for about 90 minutes until reduced to about 420 ml (14¾ fl oz); the reduced liquid should be thick enough to lightly coat a spoon. Allow the syrup to cool and thicken further.

To serve, stand each pear up on a small plate and pour 2 tablespoons of the syrup over the top, allowing the syrup to drip down and pool under the fruit. Decorate with the mint leaf booster and serve with a scoop of ice cream or Coconut Cream.

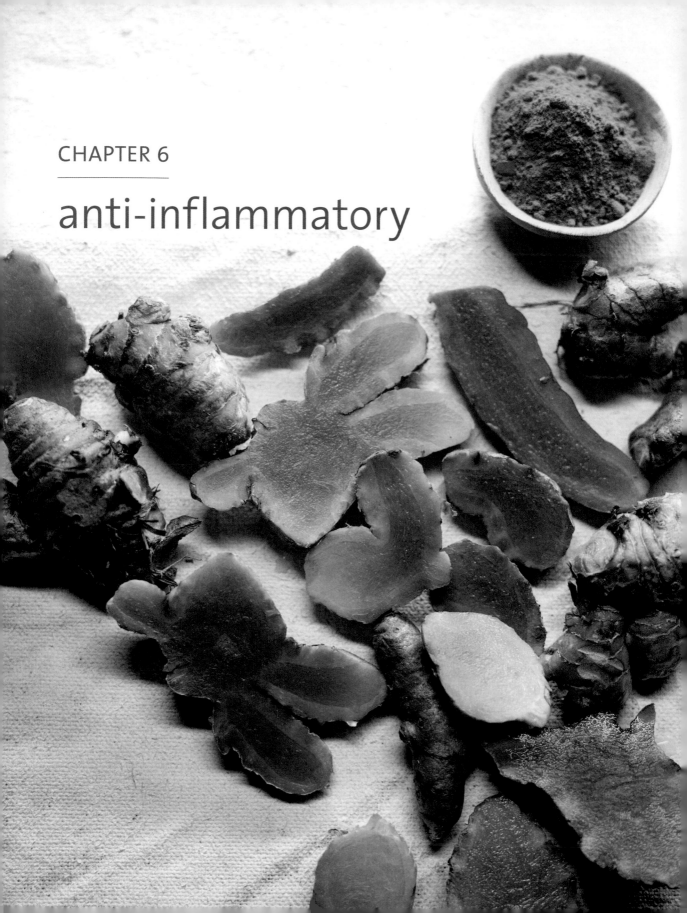

CHAPTER 6

anti-inflammatory

anti-inflammatory

Toxins barrage us in our food, water, air and elsewhere in our environments. Along with drugs, poor health, chronic disease, dietary deficiencies, lack of exercise, stress and other hazards of modern life, toxins throw our oxygen metabolism out of whack, prompting excessive, unhealthy inflammatory responses that promote disease. Strategic foods recalibrate our systems for healthy inflammatory responses critical to our built-in immune function.

ginger

Gingerol, biochemical cousin of capsaicin (in peppers), gives ginger power to calm inflammation and relieve pain and swelling. This aromatic root stimulates the lymphatic system and sweats out toxins, particularly in the lungs, sinus passages and colon. Ginger settles the stomach; alleviates nausea, gas and bloating; repairs the intestines; and its antibiotic properties fight infection. You'll get the fullest flavour and nutrition with fresh; to maximize them, don't peel – just scrub. For accuracy, grate or finely chop, then measure. Giving a citrusy zing and comforting warmth to drinks, soups, stir-fries, salad dressings, desserts and baked goods, fresh ginger's a secret weapon for lifting bitter or earthy flavours in green smoothies. Ground dried ginger works well for baking mixed with spices like cinnamon, nutmeg, cardamom and cloves.

turmeric

This relative of ginger is a medicinal master. Curcumin, which gives turmeric a vibrant orange hue, promotes healthy inflammatory responses and relieves joint pain and swelling, making turmeric an arthritis ace. It also clears congestion, fires up fat metabolism, reduces gas and bloating and inhibits abnormal cell growth. Since fresh turmeric isn't always available, I've worked up these recipes around dried. A pinch of the powder adds a stimulant to a smoothie, drink, dessert, soup, dressing or dip without altering flavour. In most recipes, ⅛–¼ teaspoon (¼–½ teaspoon fresh, finely chopped) adds a mild spicy note; amp up for more warmth

and turmeric tenacity. Since curcumin absorbs better paired with piperine in chillies and black pepper, add one of those and you're golden.

brussels sprouts

Loaded with antioxidant disease-fighting glucosinolates (see broccoli, page 38), vitamins C and K and providing omega-3s in the bargain, Brussels sprouts help regulate inflammatory responses. The cutest of crucifers is a chemoprotective crusader as well, armed with a specific compound that prevents environmental, toxin-triggered changes to our DNA. With a host of alkaline minerals and fibre, this brilliant brassica regulates blood sugar and cholesterol, combats oxidative damage and aids digestion. Shred raw or roasted b-sprouts and serve with a mustard dressing for delectable detox dining.

pak choi

This Asian avenger provides more than seventy phenolic antioxidants, unique sulfur compounds (glucosinolates), gobs of beta-carotene (for vitamin A) and vitamin C, alkaline minerals, folate, B₆, omega-3s and fibre. It also tops in vitamin K. All that makes these sexy stalks anti-inflammatory superstars, bolstering resistance to infection, staving off oxidative damage, fostering healthy muscle and nerve function, building bones and blood and boosting metabolism. Baby pak choi, more tender and mild, is easily masked by other flavours in a green smoothie. Young or mature, this beauty works her magic into salads, soups and stir-fries.

walnuts

This anti-inflammatory scavenger (best eaten raw) wages war on disease. Highest of all nuts in omega-3s, bursting with antioxidant phytonutrients, and rich in monounsaturated fats, walnuts contain L-arginine, which converts to nitric oxide, relaxing blood vessels and unclogging arteries. This heart-healthy hero fizzles free radicals, and regulates blood pressure and cholesterol to keep the blood flowing freely! As their alkaline minerals neutralize acids, walnuts are sensational skin savers, too, repairing collagen and protecting cell integrity. One of the few food sources of melatonin, they calm the nervous system and aid sleep. With omega-3s, vitamin E and folate, melatonin delivers neuroprotective properties, making walnuts brilliant brain food. For optimal digestion, soak 'em (see page 171) and then dehydrate. Toss into smoothies and desserts, mix with dates for raw crusts, or combine with sun-dried tomato and spices for an awesome raw minced meat substitute to go in tacos, salads and wraps.

spring greens

Full of fibre, alkalizing chlorophyll, antioxidant glucosinolates, vitamin K and omega-3s, spring greens amp up the anti-inflammatory agenda, binding bile acids, banishing bacteria and increasing enzyme activity for detox and digestion – while helping to oxygenate blood and enhance circulation. Shred the greens and splash with lemon juice; this activates enzymes and cranks up the sulforaphane (see broccoli, page 38). Spring greens are feisty; removing stems and chopping the leaves helps bring down bitterness. For raw wraps and cooked enchiladas, the leaves are a brilliant swap for tortillas.

flax

The triumvirate of essential fatty acids, lignans and mucilage fibre makes flaxseed a wellness wonder. Loaded with omega-3s, flax combats inflammation and boosts cellular cleansing and immune responses. The omega-3 alpha-linolenic acid is heat stable, making flax a great addition to baked goods. Lignans are phytoestrogens that balance hormones, preventing breast and prostate cancers, reducing menopausal symptoms, easing PMS and increasing fertility. Mucilage, a water-soluble fibre, drives detox. Grinding increases bioavailability and absorption of some of the nutrients, so toss ground flax into smoothies, cereals and desserts. The mucilage gels, so eat your raw flax-fortified foods fast, or for an 'eggsalent' egg replacer in baked treats, whisk 1 tablespoon ground flax into 3 tablespoons water and let thicken. The mild flavour of flax oil makes it my go-to booster for smoothies, raw soups and desserts; 1 tablespoon goes unnoticed in any blend.

pomegranate powder

Antioxidant punicalagins in pomegranate (juice and peel) fight free radicals. Packed with those and other phytonutrients, vitamins C and K, folate, alkalizing minerals and fibre, this superfruit is an antiviral agent, too, and boosts immunity. Since the freeze-dried powder (see page 211) is convenient, retains most of the fresh fruit's power and has a milder flavour than the juice, I use 1 tablespoon to boost smoothies, drinks and raw desserts.

more hero foods

- alliums (such as chives, garlic, onions)
- almonds
- apples
- apple cider vinegar
- asparagus
- avocado
- berries (blackberries, blueberries, raspberries, strawberries)
- cauliflower
- celery
- cherries (tart)
- chillies and cayenne
- cinnamon
- coconut
- cucumber
- fermented foods (such as kefir, rejuvelac, vegetables)
- leafy greens (such as beetroot, chard, kale, spinach)
- lemon and lime
- quinoa
- shiitake mushrooms
- tomatoes

Beetroot, beetroot greens and grapefruit are powerful cleansing and anti-inflammatory foods, but they're not always crowd pleasers. Dress them up with the tartness of pomegranate, the sweetness of strawberries and pineapple and an exotic twist of rosemary – all of them fellow anti-inflammatory stars – and you'll have a detox dynamo disguised as a cocktail. For more medicinal magic, add all three boosters. If your fruit's tart, a few drops of stevia will sweeten the deal. Omit the rosemary and you'll have a pink pint of pleasure that kids'll love, too.

pink punch

SERVES 2

360 ml (12 fl oz) unsweetened pomegranate juice

½ tsp probiotic powder (see page 154, optional)

160 g (5¾ oz) red grapefruit, peeled (pith removed), deseeded and chopped

15 g (½ oz) beetroot greens

80 g (3 oz) raw beetroot, peeled and diced (or grated for conventional blenders)

1 tsp finely chopped fresh rosemary, plus extra to taste

½ small avocado, stoned and peeled

160 g (5¾ oz) frozen strawberries

160 g (5¾ oz) frozen pineapple

Alcohol-free liquid stevia, to taste

optional boosters

1 tbsp flaxseed oil or chia seed oil

1 tbsp pomegranate powder (see page 89)

1 tbsp chia seeds (black or white)

Throw the juice, probiotic powder, grapefruit, beetroot greens, beetroot, rosemary and the boosters into your blender and blast on high for 30–60 seconds until the ingredients are pulverized. Add the avocado, strawberries and pineapple and blast for a further 30 seconds until smooth and creamy. Add rosemary and sweetener to taste. Enjoy immediately for the most balanced flavour.

NUTRITIONAL FACTS (PER SERVING)

calories 274 kcal | fat 6.3 g | saturated fat 1 g | sodium 69.2 mg | carbs 56.5 g | fibre 7.9 g | sugars 43.5 g | protein 3.4 g | calcium 82.7 mg | iron 1.6 mg

From left:
Magic Mylk (page 103),
Pink Punch (opposite)

Big thanks to my friend Jody, for the photo and suggestion that inspired this dish. Eating at a café in Sydney, she snapped a shot of an avocado *del sur* and sent it with the caption, 'Your chimichurri would be so good on this!' The alkalizing, anti-inflammatory ace that resulted is a showstopper. The lime juice, herbs and chilli of the chimichurri meld with the buttery notes of the avocado and the tang of the tomato for a beautiful bite of bliss.

avocado avenger

SERVES 4–8; CHIMICHURRI MAKES 300 ML (10 FL OZ)

chimichurri

180 ml (6 fl oz) extra virgin olive oil

1½ tbsp finely grated lime zest

2 tbsp fresh lime juice

2 tbsp fresh lemon juice

1½ tbsp finely chopped garlic (about 4 cloves)

1 tsp natural salt (see page 139)

¼ tsp chilli flakes, plus extra to taste

30 g (1 oz) mint leaves, plus extra to garnish

30 g (1 oz) coriander leaves, plus extra to garnish

24 g (1 oz) finely chopped chives, plus extra to garnish

4 avocados, halved, stoned and peeled

35 g (1¼ oz) English cucumber, peeled and finely diced

35 g (1¼ oz) tomatoes, deseeded and finely diced

optional boosters

55 g (2 oz) shaved courgette ribbons (½ small courgette)

70 g (2½ oz) watermelon, deseeded and finely diced, plus extra to taste

35 g (1¼ oz) raw sprouted watermelon seeds

To make the chimichurri, throw the olive oil, lime zest, lime juice, lemon juice, garlic, salt and chilli flakes into your blender and blast on high for 10–20 seconds until the sauce is emulsified and the zest, garlic and chilli flakes have been completely pulverized. Add the mint, coriander and chives, and pulse on high for a few seconds, then on low for a few seconds just to break down the herbs, but keeping the dressing very loose and not completely blended.

On a large platter, lay out the courgette ribbon booster. Then place the avocado halves cut sides up on top of the courgette, like boats. Drizzle 1 tablespoon of the chimichurri into each stone hole. Next, place 1 teaspoon diced cucumber and 1 teaspoon diced tomato into each stone hole or on top of each avocado. Place 1 teaspoon of the watermelon booster on top. With a squeeze bottle or a spoon, drizzle more chimichurri sauce onto the avocados. Top with a sprinkle of mint, coriander, chives and the watermelon seed booster. Sprinkle with the remaining tomato and cucumber and with the remaining (or more) watermelon booster if liked. Enjoy immediately.

NUTRITIONAL FACTS (PER SERVING, BASED ON 8 SERVINGS)

calories 350 kcal | fat 35 g | saturated fat 5 g | sodium 301.5 mg | carbs 13.9 g | fibre 7.4 g | sugars 1.2 g | protein 2.5 g | calcium 30.3 mg | iron 1 mg

sesame soba

SERVES 4–8; DRESSING MAKES 180 ML (6 FL OZ)

salad

1 (269 g/9½ oz) packet buckwheat soba noodles

2 tsp toasted sesame oil

110 g (4 oz) baby pak choi, shredded

250 g (9 oz) asparagus, thinly sliced diagonally

110 g (4 oz) Brussels sprouts, shredded

1½ tbsp gluten-free soy sauce or tamari

120 g (4½ oz) English cucumber, halved lengthways and thinly sliced (do not peel)

30 g (1 oz) salad onion, thinly sliced diagonally (white and green parts)

13 g (½ oz) finely chopped coriander

2 tsp black sesame seeds, plus extra to taste

Fresh lime juice, to serve

dressing

3 tbsp toasted sesame oil

3 tbsp rice vinegar

3 tbsp gluten-free soy sauce or tamari

1½ tbsp finely chopped fresh ginger, plus extra to taste

1 tsp finely chopped garlic (about 1 clove)

1 tsp mirin

optional boosters

⅛ tsp chilli flakes, plus extra to taste

160 g (5¾ oz) shelled raw edamame

2 g (1/16 oz) nori sheets, julienned, plus extra to taste

Cook the soba noodles according to the instructions on the packet. Do not overcook or your noodles will be gluey. Drain, rinse and soak for a few minutes in cold water, then drain again to remove as much of the starch as possible.

To make the dressing, throw all of the dressing ingredients, including the chilli flake booster, into your blender and blast on high for 30–60 seconds until the ginger, garlic and chilli flakes are completely pulverized. Tweak the ginger and chilli flakes to taste. Set aside.

In a large wok or frying pan over a medium-high heat, warm the sesame oil and sauté the pak choi, asparagus and Brussels sprouts with the tamari for 1–2 minutes, just until the vegetables are soft and wilted. Allow to cool.

In a large bowl, toss the cooked vegetables with the soba noodles and dressing, and add the cucumber, salad onion, coriander, black sesame seeds and the edamame booster. Serve the salad family style topped with a splash of lime juice and the nori booster.

NUTRITIONAL FACTS (PER SERVING, BASED ON 8 SERVINGS)

calories 200 kcal | fat 7 g | saturated fat 1 g | sodium 839.3 mg | carbs 30.1 g | fibre 1.8 g | sugars 1.7 g | protein 7.6 g | calcium 52.6 mg | iron 2.3 mg

When you're craving a noodle or two and concerned about inflammation, one hundred per cent buckwheat soba is the one to stick to. To avoid a gluey gulp, cook the noodles just 'til soft, chill quickly in cold water and drain. Soba with sesame is a classic, and baby pak choi, Brussels sprouts, asparagus, cucumber and coriander make this salad a great way to enjoy your noodles while balancing out the carbo-blast. Bring in the sesame oil, vinegar, tamari, ginger and garlic all to taste, and boost with lime juice to lift and brighten the flavours. The edamame add colour and texture along with protein, and the nori (which I throw in with reckless abandon) is an alkaline aid.

The wow factor here is that a simple soup can taste so good. Give orange-flesh sweet potatoes a gentle roast to caramelize them without scorching. Roasting the veggies a day in advance makes this a 15-minute meal. Stir through some spinach for an injection of chlorophyll. A splash of lime juice brightens the flavours, a drizzle of macadamia oil highlights the nutty element and a sprinkle of crushed macadamias and coriander enlivens the presentation. Sweet spuds calm inflammation in brain and nerve tissues; coupled with ginger and turmeric, they help ease joint pain and swelling, so you've got a 'souper' arthritis aid.

NUTRITIONAL FACTS (PER SERVING, BASED ON 8 SERVINGS)

calories 219 kcal | fat 11.9 g | saturated fat 1.6 g | sodium 173 mg | carbs 27.2 g | fibre 4.8 g | sugars 6.5 g | protein 2.9 g | calcium 57.6 mg | iron 1.2 mg

sweet potato &
macadamia magic

SERVES 8 AS A STARTER, 6 AS A MAIN

2 medium red onions, peeled and quartered

1 kg (2 lb 2 oz) orange-flesh sweet potatoes, peeled and cut into chunks

3 tbsp extra virgin olive oil

¼ tsp natural salt (see page 139), plus extra to taste

1.9 litres (3 pints) vegetable stock

2 tsp finely chopped fresh ginger

½ tsp ground turmeric

Pinch of cayenne pepper, plus extra to taste

70 g (2½ oz) raw unsalted macadamias

Fresh lime juice, to serve

Finely chopped coriander, to serve

optional boosters

80 g (3 oz) baby spinach (or other leafy greens)

Macadamia oil, to serve

Finely chopped raw unsalted macadamias, to serve

Preheat the oven to 180°C/350°F/Gas mark 4. Line a large baking sheet with a silicone liner or baking paper.

Toss the onions and sweet potatoes with the oil and salt and spread them out on the prepared baking sheet. Roast for about 1 hour until the vegetables are tender but not burnt. You don't want any black bits.

Transfer the roasted vegetables to a large saucepan and add the vegetable stock, ginger, turmeric and cayenne. Bring the mixture to the boil, then lower the heat to medium-high and simmer, partially covered, for about 15 minutes to allow the flavours to infuse.

Remove the pan from the heat and stir in the macadamias. Allow the mixture to stand for 10 minutes to soften the nuts and cool the soup slightly. Working in batches, pour the soup into your blender and purée on high for 1–2 minutes until smooth and creamy. (For conventional blenders, remove the small centre lid cap and cover the opening with a tea towel so steam can escape while you blend.) Return the soup to the saucepan, and warm it over a low heat, and tweak the salt and cayenne to taste. Stir in the spinach booster until the leaves are just wilted.

To serve, ladle the soup into bowls and splash each serving with lime juice. Garnish with a drizzle of the macadamia oil booster, and sprinkle with the coriander and the chopped macadamia booster.

In this epic offering, seasoned canned jackfruit masquerades as shredded chicken. When my pal Geoffrey and I whipped some up, the omnivores were astounded. Try the healthy tweak and use spring greens instead of tortillas. I like to stack the deck – with pumpkin seeds, coriander, salad onions, guac, pico and jalapeño chillies. Like any enchiladas, these are a couple of hours work. Preparing the sauce, *crema* and filling the day before makes assembly a snap. One bite and you'll be jumping for jackfruit.

jazzy jackfruit enchiladas

SERVES 6; SAUCE MAKES 720 ML (1¼ PINTS),
SUNFLOWER CREMA MAKES 632 G (1 LB 6 OZ)

sauce

663 g (1 lb 7 oz) Roma tomatoes, rinsed

1 medium white onion, cut into 16 wedges

8 garlic cloves (do not peel)

2 tbsp extra virgin olive oil

1¾ tsp natural salt, plus extra to taste (see page 139)

1 Poblano chilli (or long green chilli)

1 tbsp fresh lime juice

25 g (1 oz) coriander leaves and a bit of stems

sunflower crema

180 ml (6 fl oz) filtered water

2 tbsp extra virgin olive oil

2 tbsp fresh lime juice

155 g (5½ oz) raw sunflower seeds, soaked (see page 171)

2 tbsp nutritional yeast flakes

2 tsp white miso paste

1½ tsp apple cider vinegar

¾ tsp natural salt (see page 139)

½ tsp garlic powder

½ tsp onion powder

⅛ tsp smoked paprika

Pinch of cayenne pepper (optional)

filling

1 tbsp extra virgin olive oil

95 g (3¼ oz) yellow onion (½ large onion), sliced

1 tsp finely chopped garlic (about 1 clove)

1 tsp natural salt (see page 139)

½ tsp ground cumin

1 (280 g/10 oz) can young green jackfruit in brine, drained, rinsed and roughly sliced

Pinch of chilli flakes

180 ml (6 fl oz) filtered water

1 tsp finely chopped fresh oregano

⅛ tsp smoked paprika

⅛ tsp Bragg Liquid Aminos, gluten-free soy sauce or tamari

to assemble

12 corn tortillas or ribbed spring greens

4 tbsp extra virgin olive oil

1 avocado, stoned, peeled and thinly sliced

2 tbsp raw pumpkin seeds

2 tbsp finely chopped coriander

2 tbsp finely chopped salad onion (white and green parts)

Herbed Roasted Rice (page 18), to serve (optional)

optional boosters

240 g (8½ oz) guacamole (see page 10)

200 g (7 oz) pico de gallo (see page 10)

1 jalapeño chilli, deseeded and thinly sliced

To make the sauce, preheat the oven to 200°C/400°F/Gas mark 6. Lay the tomatoes, onion wedges and whole garlic cloves in a rimmed baking dish and toss with the olive oil and 1 teaspoon of the salt. Roast for about 40 minutes until the tomatoes are cooked and have released their juices. Remove from the oven and allow to cool slightly.

While the tomatoes are cooking, roast the Poblano chilli by moving it over an open flame until blistered on all sides. Place in a plastic bag and seal the bag. Allow the chilli to cool, then remove the skin and seeds.

Squeeze the garlic pulp out of the skins and into your blender. Pour the rest of the contents of the baking dish, including the juices, into the blender. Add the lime juice, coriander, half of the Poblano chilli and the remaining ¾ teaspoon of salt. Blast on high for 30–60 seconds until well combined. Tweak the Poblano chilli and salt to taste. Set aside.

To make the sunflower *crema*, throw all the *crema* ingredients into your blender and blast on high for about 60 seconds until smooth and creamy. Set aside.

To make the filling, in a shallow saucepan over a medium heat, warm the olive oil and sauté the onion, garlic, ½ teaspoon of the salt and the cumin for 5–10 minutes until the onion is soft and translucent. Add the jackfruit, ¼ teaspoon of the salt and the chilli flakes; increase the heat to high. Sauté for 5 minutes until the jackfruit is starting to soften and brown. Stir in 174 g (6 oz) of the sauce, the water, oregano, smoked paprika and liquid aminos and stir to combine. Reduce the heat to low, cover and allow to steam, stirring occasionally, for 15–20 minutes until the liquid has reduced and the jackfruit has broken down further. Mash the jackfruit with a fork to shred the 'meat' until it resembles shredded chicken. Add the remaining ¼ teaspoon of salt.

Preheat the oven to 180°C/350°F/Gas mark 4. Line a plate with kitchen paper. Lightly grease a 23 x 33 cm (9 x 13 in) baking dish with olive oil. If using tortillas, in a small frying pan over a high heat, warm 1 teaspoon of the olive oil. Place a tortilla in the pan and heat for about 10 seconds until rippling. Flip the tortilla and fry for a further 10 seconds until soft, pliable and just starting to crisp. Set aside on the prepared plate. Repeat with remaining olive oil and tortillas.

To assemble, fill each tortilla or spring green with 1½ tablespoons of the filling and roll. Place in the baking dish seam side down. Repeat with the remaining tortillas (or spring greens) and filling, spacing the enchiladas about 1 cm (½ in) apart. Ladle the remaining sauce and drizzle 180 g (6 oz) of the *crema* (or more) over the enchiladas. Bake for 10–15 minutes until the enchiladas are heated through and just starting to brown and bubble. Remove from the oven and top with the avocado slices, pumpkin seeds, coriander and salad onion, and with the guacamole, pico de gallo and sliced jalapeño chilli boosters. Serve with the Herbed Roasted Rice.

NUTRITIONAL FACTS (PER SERVING)

calories 642 kcal | fat 43.4 g | saturated fat 5.7 g | sodium 1478.2 mg | carbs 58.1 g | fibre 13.8 g | sugars 8.3 g | protein 15 g | calcium 126.4 mg | iron 4 mg

For most people, red peppers promote a healthy inflammatory response because of their high levels of vitamin C, phytonutrients, carotenoids and capsaicin (a natural pain reliever). But for those sensitive to nightshades, peppers can exacerbate excessive inflammation. I use peppers as anti-inflammatory agents, and this super-easy staple is fantastic with pasta, grains or veggies. To keep it simple and accessible, I've created it around jarred roasted peppers. If you've got time, freshly roasted are even better. As in the Terrific Tomato Sauce (page 189), sun-dried tomatoes bring a lot to the flavour table, and if your peppers are a little bitter, more sun-dried tomatoes will balance the blend. With kids in mind, I've kept the base recipe mild, but I never make it without chilli flakes and paprika. Boosted, it's magical as part of the Grain-free Abundance bowl photographed here (see recipe on page 30). If enjoying the purée raw, add the probiotic powder booster to aid digestion.

ripper roasted red pepper purée

MAKES 360 G (12 OZ)

4 tbsp extra virgin olive oil

2 tbsp filtered water

1 tbsp fresh lemon juice, plus extra to taste

1 (340 g/12 oz) jar roasted red peppers or 1 large roasted pepper

22 g (¾ oz) sun-dried tomatoes packed in oil, drained, dried and roughly chopped

1 tbsp finely chopped garlic (about 3 cloves)

1½ tsp finely chopped shallot

27 g (1 oz) roughly chopped raw walnuts

¼ tsp natural salt (see page 139), plus extra to taste

⅛ tsp Bragg Liquid Aminos, gluten-free soy sauce or tamari

optional boosters

½ tsp sweet paprika, plus extra to taste

½ tsp probiotic powder (if eating the purée raw, see page 154)

Pinch of chilli flakes, plus extra to taste

Throw everything into your blender, including the boosters, and blast on high for 30–60 seconds until smooth and creamy. Tweak the lemon juice, salt, paprika and chilli flakes to taste.

NUTRITIONAL FACTS (PER SERVING, BASED ON 8 SERVINGS)

calories 104 kcal | fat 9.2 g | saturated fat 1.2 g | sodium 86.4 mg | carbs 5 g | fibre 1.5 g | sugars 3 g | protein 1.4 g | calcium 11.8 mg | iron 0.6 mg

From left: Ripper Roasted
Red Pepper Purée (opposite),
Grain-free Abundance (page 30)

Joy of the Jingslingers has a secret weapon for magical sugar-free desserts: a perfect blend of birch xylitol and stevia. Thanks to that combo, this dessert diva belts out bold anti-inflammatory notes (of cacao, coconut, walnut and tart cherry) *sans* sugar and that bitter stevia aftertaste. Chaga mushroom chimes in with caramel-y antioxidant ammo, with back-up from the Blue Majik spirulina extract. This act won't keep you up all night, either. The magnesium in cacao and melatonin in the walnuts and cherries help you sleep. Tart cherries are anti-inflammatory; sweet ones not so much. When they're not available fresh, defrost some frozen ones, or go with raspberries. Whatever fruit she's crowned with, this punched-up puddin's a showstopper.

life-changing chocolate pudding

SERVES 4

120 ml (4 fl oz) full-fat canned coconut milk (shake, then pour)

360 g (12 oz) raw young coconut meat

36 g (1¼ oz) cacao powder or unsweetened cocoa powder

 3 tbsp powdered birch xylitol (see page 155), plus extra to taste

1 tsp natural vanilla extract

1 tsp ground cinnamon, plus extra to taste

½ tsp alcohol-free chocolate-flavoured (or plain) liquid stevia, plus extra to taste

⅛ tsp natural salt (see page 139)

155 g (5½ oz) pitted tart cherries

60 g (2¼ oz) raw walnuts, crushed

optional boosters

1 tbsp coconut oil (in liquid form)

1 tsp E3Live Blue Majik (see page 211) or spirulina

1 tsp chaga mushroom powder (see page 211)

Throw the coconut milk, coconut meat, cacao powder, xylitol, vanilla, cinnamon, stevia, salt and any boosters into your blender and blast on high for 30–60 seconds until smooth and creamy. You may need to stop the machine and scrape down the sides of the container. Tweak the sweeteners and cinnamon to taste.

Spoon the mixture into four dessert bowls or cocktail glasses and chill in the fridge for a couple of hours to firm up.

Serve topped with the cherries and walnuts.

NUTRITIONAL FACTS (PER SERVING)

calories 309 kcal | fat 22.9 g | saturated fat 7.3 g | sodium 93.6 mg | carbs 22.2 g | fibre 8 g | sugars 6.7 g | protein 6.9 g | calcium 46.3 mg | iron 3.8 mg

This immunity angel and anti-inflammatory avenger is a supercharged medicinal version of Sleep Spell, in *The Blender Girl* cookbook. I make a batch of this sugar-free milk (see photo, page 91) every week, rarely get sick and sleep like a baby. To keep the drink alkaline and fully empower the almond, ginger, cinnamon and turmeric warriors, this one's sweetened with stevia. If you're looking for a more decadent experience, add dates or maple syrup. I enjoy this elixir cold. But boost with the coconut, cardamom and clove, warm it up slightly, and this mylk's even more magical!

magic mylk

SERVES 2–3; MAKES ABOUT 720 ML (1¼ PINTS)

160 g (5¾ oz) raw whole almonds, soaked (see page 171)

720 ml (1¼ pints) filtered water

1½ tbsp finely chopped fresh ginger, plus extra to taste

2½ tsp ground turmeric, plus extra to taste

2½ tsp ground cinnamon, plus extra to taste

1 tsp natural vanilla extract

15 drops alcohol-free vanilla-flavoured (or plain) liquid stevia, plus extra to taste

Pinch of freshly ground black pepper

optional boosters

1 tbsp coconut oil (in liquid form)

¼ tsp ground cardamom, plus extra to taste

Pinch of ground cloves

Throw all of the ingredients, including the boosters, into your blender and blast on high for about 1 minute until the almonds are completely pulverized. Tweak the ginger, turmeric, cinnamon, stevia (or other sweetener) and cardamom to taste. Strain the mixture through a filtration bag, nut milk bag, fine-mesh sieve or sheer piece of clean nylon hosiery. You may have to strain twice to get a really smooth consistency, if liked. Gently warm on the hob (or if using a high-speed blender, continue blending until warm) or serve chilled.

NUTRITIONAL FACTS (PER SERVING, BASED ON 2 SERVINGS)

calories 495 kcal | fat 40.1 g | saturated fat 3.1 g | sodium 17 mg | carbs 23.1 g | fibre 12.5 g | sugars 4.2 g | protein 17.4 g | calcium 264.5 mg | iron 4.8 mg

fabulous fats

fabulous fats

Quality fats are not just good for us, they are essential for optimal health. The catchphrase 'low fat', coined by the commercial food industry to describe chemistry projects that substitute fats with sugar, is a trap. With fat, as with carbs, choose quality sources in appropriate quantities. Plant-based fats promote wellness, but we can get too much of a good thing. Since not much in the plant kingdom that contains fat is naturally 'low fat', here are some foods that are either low in fat or contain efficient fats that support health.

coconut

This spherical superstar comes off the tree fully loaded with high-efficiency saturated fats, chiefly medium-chain triglycerides that break down easily to release energy, rather than being stored as body fat. Coconut fats boost endocrine function – thyroid especially – and amp up metabolic rates to burn calories. These healthy fats also promote the effective utilization of blood glucose, enhancing the secretion of insulin to regulate blood sugar, reducing stress on the pancreas, liver, kidneys, gall bladder and adrenals, all while satisfying and sustaining us in ways that unfab fats just don't. High in protein, vitamins, minerals, antioxidants and anti-inflammatory agents, coconut supports strong bones and teeth, and helps regulate blood pressure and cholesterol for heart health. This dynamic drupe's down with detox as well, facilitating the absorption of alkalizing angels like calcium and magnesium. Chock-a-block with lauric, caprylic, capri and myristic acids, which annihilate the lipid membranes of viruses, bacteria, yeast and fungi, coconut is an immunity idol, too.

Crack one and reap the rewards. Young (green) coconuts double the fun: the soft meat makes a creamy base for desserts, smoothies, sauces and dehydrated wraps. Fresh, raw, unpasteurized coconut water is a natural isotonic energy drink, loaded with enzymes and hydrating potassium electrolytes that boost the function of the liver, thyroid, kidneys and gall bladder for cleansing karma.

Low in calories and carbs, the water is almost completely fat-free, and makes a brilliant energizing addition to smoothies, drinks, cocktails, elixirs and raw soups and desserts. Creamed coconut (the dehydrated meat, ground to a smooth paste) is a convenient way to infuse tropical magic into smoothies and curries. It's coconut oil that really rocks the house. Temperature-stable, so it forms no free radicals when heated, this is the healthiest oil to cook with, especially at high temperatures. Because it solidifies when kept cool, it's sublime for setting raw desserts (see page 67) and brilliant as a base for chocolates (see page 134).

sesame seeds

Rich in heart-healthy monounsaturated fats in the form of oleic acid and loaded with magnesium, sesame seeds have the highest phytosterol content among common nuts and seeds and contain the unique lignans sesamin and sesamolin. All these components work together to regulate blood pressure and cholesterol. Loaded with copper, key to anti-inflammatory activities, sesame reduces pain and swelling, combats free radicals and boosts collagen and elastin regeneration; with iron to build blood, it's got your immunity covered, too. As one of the most concentrated plant-based sources of calcium and loaded with zinc, these tiny super-seeds are proof that the best things for bone health really do come in small packets. Both whole sesame seeds and tahini deliver easily absorbable protein, in combo with low-GI carbs for long-lasting energy. With a nutty flavour, sesame seeds make a great substitute for cashews, and they're fantastic sprinkled on anything that takes your fancy.

blueberries

Full of fibre, low in sugar and with a high-efficiency combo of healthy fats, blueberries metabolize like a low-GI fruit, regulating blood sugar and sweeping out toxins to aid digestion and detox. Bursting with antioxidant anthocyanin pigments, these brilliant balls shoot a ballistic blast at free radicals, burn fats to give us an edge in the weight war and boost brain function for greater mental clarity, memory and cognitive function. Get your resveratrol (the polyphenol in grape skins that has put red wine back on so many do lists) with blueberries, too; it enhances cardiac action and – along with other antioxidants and B vitamins – ups energy and endurance. Blueberries also boast the natural antibiotics celebrated in cranberries, to help ban bacterial growth from the urinary tract. Carotenoid flavonoids and a string of vitamins and minerals make blueberries an immunity idol for healthy eyes, skin and hair. Their natural gelatinous quality binds a smoothie, so enjoy a blended treat fast to steer clear of sludge (or freeze it for ice lollies – see Blue Card Pops, page 117). The natural built-in thickener adds body to a sweet sauce, too. Let these blue babies, cooked or in the raw, punch up your pancakes, puddings and parfaits. Or keep things simple, go for instant gratification, and bop a fistful right into your mouth.

cranberries

Fruits typically have a low fat content (and those are efficient fats), and these smart little tarts are low in sugar, too. It's the unique array of antioxidant phytonutrients, though, that make cranberries a health-promoting star. Heavy on the flavonoids and the same anthocyanin antioxidants as blueberries, cranberries also provide proanthocyanidins, whose antibiotic and antiviral properties block harmful bacteria and viruses in the stomach, bladder and uterus. Many of the phytonutrients in cranberries offer anti-inflammatory benefits, particularly for the digestive and cardiovascular systems, and since cranberries help regulate cholesterol, they're heart-healthy heroes as well. Loaded up with vitamins C, E and K; manganese; copper; and pantothenic acid, these super cell-structure savers also guard DNA against oxidative damage. Get cosy with cranberries in smoothies, sauces and desserts for low-sugar sensations.

maqui

This Patagonian warrior storms into battle armed with quality fats, a few simple sugars, an arsenal of vitamins, minerals, fibre, potent polyphenols, anti-inflammatory agents and those powerful anthocyanins that power up blueberries. It fights free radicals with more antioxidants than any other food to keep our immune systems soldiering on. Maqui bolsters metabolism and regulates blood sugar and digestion, too. Flavour-wise, it flies below the radar to let other ingredients lead the charge. A battalion of foods, especially smoothies and raw desserts, enlists a hint of mild maqui that goes all but unnoticed. Since the vibrant purple colour is hard to miss, blend with pretty blue and red picks like berries and beetroot. Just 2 teaspoons of the freeze-dried powder (see page 211) has you covered. This superhero likes things raw and ready, and is allergic to oxygen, so add it and enjoy it fast!

more hero foods

- almonds
- apples
- asparagus
- avocado
- broccoli
- Brussels sprouts
- cabbage
- cauliflower
- celery
- chia seeds
- flaxseeds
- grapefruit
- hemp seeds
- leafy greens (such as rocket, kale, lettuce, spinach)
- lemon and lime
- olives and olive oil
- pumpkin seeds
- sea vegetables
- sunflower seeds
- walnuts

A spectacular blend of savoury, sweet and spicy, this strawberry-tomato gazpacho smoothie sings with all the ingredients in perfect harmony and the balsamic vinegar hitting a tangy, sharp note. You'll get the best flavour with cherry tomatoes and ripe strawberries. Tweak the sweetener according to the character of your fruits and your own preference. The olive oil and pepper boosters heighten things on the savoury side, and the goji powder rounds out nutrition and boosts immunity.

red basil balsamic blast

SERVES 2

180 ml (6 fl oz) raw coconut water or filtered water

3 tbsp fresh lime juice

½ tsp probiotic powder (see page 154, optional)

175 g (6 oz) cherry tomatoes

25 g (1 oz) basil leaves, plus extra to taste

70 g (2½ oz) red pepper, deseeded and diced

37 g (1¼ oz) English cucumber (do not peel), diced

1 tsp diced red onion

1 tsp deseeded and finely chopped green chilli, plus extra to taste

½ tsp balsamic vinegar, plus extra to taste

¼ tsp natural salt (see page 139), plus extra to taste

1 tsp finely chopped garlic (about 1 clove)

320 g (11¼ oz) frozen strawberries

5 drops alcohol-free liquid stevia, plus extra to taste

optional boosters

1 tbsp goji powder (see page 23)

1 tsp extra virgin olive oil

Pinch of freshly ground black pepper, plus extra to taste

Throw everything into your blender, including the boosters, and blast on high for 30–60 seconds until smooth and creamy. Tweak the basil, chilli, vinegar, salt and stevia to taste.

NUTRITIONAL FACTS (PER SERVING)

calories 103 kcal | fat 0.7 g | saturated fat 0.2 g | sodium 395.6 mg | carbs 24.3 g | fibre 5.9 g | sugars 12.9 g | protein 3.2 g | calcium 90.8 mg | iron 2.2 mg

A deconstruction of my favourite smoothie from *The Blender Girl* cookbook, this more textured incantation benefits from a 12-hour chill that allows the flavours to develop. Every sublime spoonful will take your taste buds places where they'll forget you're cleansing.

pineapple cucumber gazpacho

SERVES 8 AS A STARTER, 6 AS A MAIN

1.9 kg (4 lb 6 oz) fresh pineapple (about 2 large pineapples), peeled and diced

1 tsp finely grated lime zest

2 tbsp fresh lime juice, plus extra to taste

2 tbsp deseeded and finely chopped jalapeño chilli

600 g (1 lb 5 oz) English cucumber, peeled and diced

14 g (½ oz) finely chopped coriander

20 g (¾ oz) finely chopped salad onion (white and green parts)

1 tbsp extra virgin olive oil

1½ tsp natural salt (see page 139), plus extra to taste

Freshly ground black pepper

optional boosters

1 tbsp finely chopped fresh ginger

⅛ tsp ground turmeric

65 g (2¼ oz) raw macadamias, finely chopped

Throw 1.2 kg (2 lb 12 oz) of the pineapple along with the lime zest, lime juice, jalapeño chilli and ginger and turmeric boosters into your blender and blast on high for 30–60 seconds until the ingredients are pulverized. Pour the mixture into a large mixing bowl and add the remaining pineapple, the cucumber, coriander, salad onion, olive oil and salt, and season to taste with pepper; stir to combine. Cover and chill in the fridge for at least 3 hours, but preferably 12 hours. Tweak the lime juice and salt to taste and serve chilled, topped with the macadamia booster.

NUTRITIONAL FACTS (PER SERVING, BASED ON 8 SERVINGS)

calories 152 kcal | fat 2.1 g | saturated fat 0.3 g | sodium 441.4 mg | carbs 35.9 g | fibre 4 g | sugars 25.8 g | protein 1.9 g | calcium 48.6 mg | iron 1 mg

Tofu is a great source of plant-based protein, but served raw it gets nobody excited – until you bring on a delicious sauce and some tasty toppings. This chic starter, featured in an entertaining menu I created for *Vegetarian Times*, had me overwhelmed with e-raves from people who swore they hate tofu. (Be sure to use firm silken tofu to ensure a creamy texture.) With a wonderful combination of savoury, sweet and spicy elements, and a beautifully minimalist presentation, this quick, easy dish takes you on a flavourful journey. Kick things up a notch by adding the boosters. Either way, you'll look like a gourmet chef.

chilled silken tofu with wasabi, lime & cucumbers

SERVES 8

cucumbers

4 tbsp fresh lime juice

2 tsp coconut nectar or other liquid sweetener

1 tsp rice vinegar

½ tsp natural salt (see page 139)

½ medium English cucumber, halved lengthways and thinly sliced or spiral sliced

dressing

4 tbsp gluten-free soy sauce or tamari

2 tbsp fresh lime juice

4 tsp rice vinegar

4 tsp coconut nectar or other liquid sweetener

1 tbsp wasabi paste

1 tsp finely chopped fresh ginger

tofu

2 (349 g/12 oz) packets firm silken tofu, well chilled, drained and each block cut into 4 equal-sized squares

1 tsp gomasio (ground sesame seeds and sea salt, see page 210) or white sesame seeds

optional boosters

4 tsp finely chopped salad onion (green parts only)

½ small red radish, very thinly sliced, then julienned

¼ sheet nori, julienned into short strips

To prepare the cucumbers, whisk the lime juice, sweetener, vinegar and salt in a bowl. Add the cucumber and stir to evenly coat. Set aside.

To make the dressing, throw all of the dressing ingredients into your blender and blast on high for about 30 seconds until well combined. Or, throw the ingredients into a glass jar, seal and shake vigorously to combine.

To assemble, place a tofu square into each of eight shallow bowls and cover each square with 1 tablespoon of the dressing. Gently drain the cucumbers so that they are still coated with marinade, mound 2 tablespoons of cucumber on top of each tofu square and sprinkle with a pinch of gomasio. Serve topped with ½ teaspoon of the salad onion booster and a sprinkle of the radish and nori boosters. Pass the remaining dressing around the table. Alternatively, serve dressed tofu squares family style on a large platter.

NUTRITIONAL FACTS (PER SERVING)

calories 88 kcal | fat 3.8 g | saturated fat 0.8 g | sodium 594.2 mg | carbs 7.8 g | fibre 1.4 g | sugars 4.7 g | protein 7.9 g | calcium 183.5 mg | iron 1.6 mg

If you're in a low-fat funk and longing for luscious, this creamy and crunchy white stunner is salad porn. The cut of the vegetables is the key to an elegant presentation and perfect balance of flavour. Julienne the celeriac, leek and apple and add tiny diced celery and fennel. Dousing the celeriac and apple with lime juice and dressing the salad fast is essential, to avoid oxidation. The 30-minute chill allows the flavours to marry and the dressing's zesty tang to permeate all the ingredients. The cucumber and avocado boost the crunch and cream. I always include the chilli, which complements the tart and sweet. However you opt to go, this one will make you serious about celeriac.

sexy celeriac slaw with lime & poppy seeds

SERVES 8 AS A STARTER, 6 AS A MAIN; DRESSING MAKES 360 ML (12 FL OZ)

dressing

180 ml (6 fl oz) fresh lime juice

4 tbsp extra virgin olive oil

70 g (2½ oz) raw unsalted cashews, soaked (see page 171)

3 tbsp pure maple syrup

1 tbsp finely chopped garlic (about 3 cloves)

1 tbsp finely chopped fresh ginger

1 tsp finely grated lime zest

¾ tsp natural salt (see page 139)

salad

360 g (12¾ oz) celeriac, peeled and julienned (I use a mandoline to slice it)

150 g (5½ oz) leek (white parts only), julienned

170 g (6 oz) green apple (do not peel), julienned

66 g (2¼ oz) celery, finely diced

44 g (1½ oz) fennel, finely diced

2 tbsp fresh lime juice

8 g (¼ oz) finely chopped mint leaves, plus extra to garnish

7 g (¼ oz) finely chopped coriander, plus extra to garnish

1½ tsp poppy seeds, plus extra to garnish

optional boosters

125 g (4½ oz) English cucumber, peeled, deseeded and julienned

2 tsp deseeded and finely chopped green chilli, plus extra to taste

1 avocado, halved, stoned, peeled and sliced

To make the dressing, throw all of the dressing ingredients into your blender and blast on high for about 60 seconds until smooth and creamy.

In a large salad bowl, gently massage (to avoid bruising) the celeriac, leek, apple, celery, fennel and the cucumber booster with the lime juice to reduce oxidation and brighten the flavours. Gently fold in the dressing, the mint, coriander, poppy seeds and the chilli booster. Chill, covered, in the fridge for about 30 minutes to allow the flavours to open and mingle. Garnish with more mint, coriander and poppy seeds and top with the sliced avocado booster, if liked. Serve family style or mounded on individual plates.

NUTRITIONAL FACTS (PER SERVING, BASED ON 8 SERVINGS)

calories 184 kcal | fat 11.1 g | saturated fat 1.7 g | sodium 280.4 mg | carbs 21.1 g | fibre 2.6 g | sugars 9.5 g | protein 3.1 g | calcium 65.4 mg | iron 1.6 mg

These baked beauties are scrumptious and are baked instead of deep-fried. Serve in wraps, buffet style, with assorted add-ins and toppings, or just go with gobs of the tahini sauce (which offers health-promoting fat). These are best enjoyed right after they're made, since they dry out if stored.

no-fry falafels

SERVES 4; MAKES 20 BALLS, 245 ML (8½ FL OZ) SAUCE

falafels

260 g (9 oz) cooked chickpeas or 1 (425 g/15 oz) can, rinsed and drained

25 g (1 oz) finely chopped flat-leaf parsley leaves

50 g (1¾ oz) red onion, diced

20 g (¾ oz) salad onion (white and green parts), finely chopped

1 tbsp finely chopped garlic (about 3 cloves)

1 tbsp fresh lemon juice, plus extra to taste

2 tbsp chickpea flour

1 tsp ground cumin

¾ tsp natural salt (see page 139), plus extra to taste

½ tsp ground coriander

¼ tsp apple cider vinegar

¼ tsp Bragg Liquid Aminos, gluten-free soy sauce or tamari

⅛ tsp freshly ground black pepper

Pinch of cayenne pepper, plus extra to taste

1 tbsp extra virgin olive oil

tahini sauce

80 ml (3 fl oz) filtered water

4 tbsp fresh lemon juice, plus extra to taste

120 g (4½ oz) hulled tahini

1 tsp finely chopped garlic (about 1 clove), plus extra to taste

¼ tsp natural salt (see page 139), plus extra to taste

Pinch of freshly ground black pepper, plus extra to taste

to serve

1–2 hearts romaine lettuce, with leaves pulled apart

180 g (6 oz) tomato, deseeded and diced

150 g (5½ oz) Persian or English cucumber, deseeded and diced

160 g (5¾ oz) gherkins, diced

37 g (1¼ oz) red onion, diced

8 g (¼ oz) finely chopped dill

8 g (¼ oz) finely chopped mint

optional boosters

2 tsp deseeded and finely chopped green chilli, plus extra to taste

⅛ tsp ground turmeric

2 tbsp finely chopped coriander

To make the falafels, throw all of the falafel ingredients, except the olive oil but including the chilli and turmeric boosters, into a food processor and pulse for about 30 seconds until well combined. Tweak the lemon juice, salt, cayenne and chilli to taste. Transfer the mixture to a bowl and bring it together with your hands.

Line a baking sheet with kitchen paper (to absorb excess moisture). Using a 1 tablespoon measuring spoon, scoop out portions of the falafel mix and roll them between your hands to form balls. Place on the prepared baking sheet and transfer to the fridge to firm up for about 30 minutes.

To make the tahini sauce, throw those ingredients, including the coriander booster, into your blender and blast on high for 20–30 seconds until smooth and creamy. You may need to stop the machine and scrape down the sides of the container, and you may need to add

1 tablespoon or more of filtered water to get the mixture to blend. Tweak the lemon juice, garlic, salt and pepper to taste. Transfer to a serving bowl.

Preheat the oven to 200°C/400°F/Gas mark 6. Line a baking sheet with baking paper.

Transfer the falafels to the prepared baking sheet in rows 1 cm (½ in) apart. Using your thumb, flatten each ball ever so slightly.

Pour the olive oil into a small bowl and, with a pastry brush, brush the tops of the falafel balls with a generous slather so that the oil runs down the sides and hits the baking sheet. Lift each ball and dip it in the olive oil that has run down so that the bottom is coated as well.

Bake the falafels for 10–15 minutes until the bottoms are slightly browned. Gently flip over each falafel and bake for a further 10–15 minutes until lightly browned. Remove from the oven and allow to cool slightly or completely.

Serve the falafels and tahini dressing buffet style with the romaine leaves, tomato, cucumber, gherkins, onion, dill and mint on the table. To assemble, take a romaine leaf and place 1 or 2 falafels (depending on the size of the leaf) on top. Add the tomato, cucumber, gherkins, onions, dill and mint, and a drizzle of tahini sauce.

NUTRITIONAL FACTS (PER SERVING)

calories 387 kcal | fat 22.3 g | saturated fat 3.1 g | sodium 1137.4 mg | carbs 39 g | fibre 12.3 g | sugars 8.6 g | protein 14.6 g | calcium 264.9 mg | iron 7.2 mg

Whole-fruit ice lollies are my go-to dessert – super-easy, endless in flavour combinations, and a fun way to eat fruit! Unlike commercial ice lollies made with juice – and loads of sugar – these blend up whole blueberries, for full-fibre value. The natural gelatinous quality of the berries helps bind and sweep out toxins, promoting digestive health. Blueberries boast the heftiest levels of antioxidants of any fresh fruit (and the açaí and maqui boosters will send those into the stratosphere). Add the flaxseed oil for anti-inflammatory omega-3 fatty acids. Cardamom elevates the blueberry blast, making this proud lolly a free radical-crushing crusader on a stick.

blue card pops

MAKES 10–12 ICE LOLLIES

120 ml (4 fl oz) fresh orange juice

640 g (1 lb 6 oz) fresh blueberries

2 tbsp pure maple syrup

2 tbsp fresh lemon juice

¼ tsp ground cardamom

Pinch of natural salt (see page 139)

optional boosters

1 tbsp flaxseed oil or chia seed oil

1 tbsp açaí powder (see page 122)

1 tsp maqui powder (see page 107)

Throw all of the ingredients, including any boosters, into your blender and blast on high for 30–60 seconds until smooth.

Pour the mixture into your ice lolly moulds, guiding it with a small spoon (the gelatinous quality of the blueberries makes the mixture thick) and freeze for about 8 hours or until fully frozen.

To serve, give the bottom half of the moulds a 2–3-second dip in warm water and ease the ice lollies free.

NUTRITIONAL FACTS (PER SERVING, BASED ON 10 SERVINGS)

calories 53 kcal | fat 0.2 g | saturated fat 0 g | sodium 30.4 mg | carbs 13.5 g | fibre 1.6 g | sugars 9.9 g | protein 0.6 g | calcium 9.7 mg | iron 0.2 mg

Rooibos is righteous. All the more so when it's blended with orange and cranberries. This fruity iced tea intoxicates your taste buds as they scramble to pin down the elements of that fabulous flavour. The pomegranate powder amps up the antioxidants, and the ginger and vanilla kick this up to wow.

rooibos refresher

SERVES 2

1 rooibos teabag (plain, not fruit-flavoured)

240 ml (8½ fl oz) boiling water

3 medium oranges, peeled and segmented

120 g (4½ oz) fresh or frozen and defrosted cranberries

125 g (4½ oz) ice cubes

Alcohol-free liquid stevia (or other sweetener, optional)

optional boosters

1 tbsp pomegranate powder (see page 89)

1½ tsp finely chopped fresh ginger, plus extra to taste

¼ tsp natural vanilla extract

Steep the teabag in the boiling water for about 5 minutes. Discard the teabag and chill the tea in the fridge until cold.

Pour the chilled tea into your blender with the oranges, cranberries, ice and the pomegranate, ginger and vanilla boosters and blast on high for 30–60 seconds until liquefied. Add stevia to taste and strain for a smoother consistency. Drink immediately.

NUTRITIONAL FACTS (PER SERVING)

calories 157 kcal | fat 0.4 g | saturated fat 0 g | sodium 8.5 mg | carbs 39.8 g | fibre 9.4 g | sugars 28.2 g | protein 2.8 g | calcium 120.6 mg | iron 0.4 mg

This quick, easy sauce is like a little black dress. It complements almost any dessert without upstaging it, fits into any menu and never goes out of style. Best of all, it takes less than 5 minutes to prepare. Enjoy it over ice cream, cakes or pies. Try it drizzled over the Classic Cheesecake (page 67). Depending on the quality of your berries and your preference, tweak the lemon juice to taste. With well-ripened fruit, I reduce the dates to 55 g (2 oz). But 85 g (3 oz) typically hits the sweet spot. For a sensational sauce, boost with the Grand Marnier, ginger and vanilla.

sweet strawberry sauce

MAKES 480 ML (17 FL OZ)

4 tbsp raw coconut water or filtered water

85 g (3 oz) pitted dates, soaked (see page 171)

300 g (10½ oz) hulled and halved fresh strawberries

1 tbsp fresh lemon juice, plus extra to taste

Pinch of natural salt (see page 139)

optional boosters

1 tsp Grand Marnier

1 tsp finely chopped fresh ginger, plus extra to taste

¼ tsp natural vanilla extract

Throw everything into your blender, including any of the boosters, and blast on high for 30–60 seconds until smooth. Tweak the dates, lemon juice and ginger to taste. This sauce will keep in the fridge for about 5 days.

NUTRITIONAL FACTS (PER SERVING, BASED ON 16 SERVINGS)

calories 20 kcal | fat 0.1 g | saturated fat 0 g | sodium 18.6 mg | carbs 5.5 g | fibre 0.7 g | sugars 4.5 g | protein 0.2 g | calcium 6.6 mg | iron 0.1 mg

CHAPTER 8

low carb

low carb

Tracking carbs gets boring, and it's far from the whole story. A better approach: go for quality whole foods, assessing the types of fibre, starches and sugars, *then* clock quantity. Nutrient-dense low-glycaemic foods regulate blood sugar and provide a better energy flow. Still, we can eat too much of them. Carbs are like the petrol in a car's tank – the highest octane may be powering your engine, but punch the pedal too hard, or keep it pressed to the floor, and you won't burn the fuel efficiently. Our bodies store unburned fuel as fat. For efficiency and sustained energy access, here are my picks at the pump.

cauliflower

This brilliant brassica delivers culinary versatility and miraculous medicinal power, in the company of high-quality carbs. Jam-packed with vitamins, minerals and antioxidant phytonutrients, including the mega-marvel glutathione, cauliflower helps our cells, tissues, organs and blood blossom, unwithered by free radicals, oxidation and inflammation. Bursting with the glucoraphanin found in broccoli (see page 38), cauliflower is a diva in the detox department. As for fabulous ways to enjoy it? Pulse raw chunks into cauli-couscous for use in salads (see page 176) or cook as cauliflower rice (see page 148). Steam, then purée, to add a creamy element to soups and sauces. Roasted, cauliflower rocks righteously with other veg. Frozen, it slips into smoothies without adding flavour funk.

kale

Go crazy with kale, not just 'cause it's low-carb, but to get your fill of its phenomenal phytonutrients, including forty-five flavonoids and those famed carotenoids. With chopping, blending or chewing, the leaves unleash those cancer-crushing compounds, along with antioxidant, antimicrobial and anti-inflammatory punch. With gobs of glutathione (the antioxidant that jump-starts the liver) and glucosinolates (see broccoli, page 38), kale drives detox, too. Loaded with fibre, protein and B vitamins to stabilize blood sugar for a sustained release of energy and to mend muscles, it's wonderful workout fuel. After a sugar orgy, I rely on the chlorophyll in kale to *adios* acidity. Cavolo nero is less bitter than the curly stuff. Get your fix raw in salads and smoothies, or cooked in soups, stews, stir-fries and bakes. Tip: massaging raw kale with lemon juice and olive oil takes off the bitter edge and activates enzymes.

cabbage

Long dissed as poor man's food, cabbage serves up an embarrassment of riches with no crap carbs. Fitted with those fantastic phytonutrients to calm inflammation and with antioxidants like vitamins A and E, this brassica will make your skin and eyes glow. Overflowing with glucosinolates and glutathione, this leafy legend has cleansing covered, too. Feathered with fibre, manganese, B vitamins and iodine, along with quality carbs, cabbage massages the muscles and soothes the nervous system while it fuels us. All varieties – white, Savoy, red – work in these recipes, but it's worth noting that red has more than six times the vitamin C of white and is loaded with antioxidant anthocyanins (see blueberries, page 106). Cabbage adds these nutrients and more to salads, soups, stews and stir-fries; fermented, it reigns in the probiotic palace (see page 164). To those who cringe when they consider crucifers: Thai Slaw (page 129) will have you crying out for cabbage.

açaí

The weight-loss industry's gone ape for açaí. So far, the evidence can't support extravagant fat-burning claims, but this palm fruit is low in sugar, with most of its carbs in the form of fibre, helping us feel full to punch down the poundage. Açaí is more like an olive than a berry, providing quality fats (like hemp's) with fibre. It's a super scavenger, too, raging against free radicals like a bull in a china shop. Bursting with anthocyanin pigments and vitamins C, E and K, this pretty purple pick surpasses even blueberries in antioxidant ammo. Purchase unsweetened frozen pulp or freeze-dried powder (see page 211). With a natural creaminess, and flavour that's like tart blackberry with a hint of chocolate, açaí is awesome in smoothies and raw desserts made with berries, beetroot, banana, nut or coconut milk or dates.

romaine

High in water and fibre and low in calories, romaine hydrates, energizes, detoxifies and assists heart health, all while boosting metabolism to aid weight loss. This nutritious lettuce is also rich in folate, potassium, vitamins A, C and K, and alkaline buffers, to build blood and counteract acidity. A sensational salad staple, it's also a superb swap for tortillas or flatbreads in low-carb tacos and wraps.

sprouts

My favourite sprouts are alfalfa, pea, sunflower and broccoli. Soak your goods in a Kilner jar with a flat metal lid and a ring top. Remove the lid from the ring and use it as a guide to cut a piece of muslin to cover the opening of the jar. Place the food you want to sprout in the jar, about one-third full, and fill the jar with warm water and a little natural salt. Close the jar with the breathable cover and ring and leave overnight. To drain, remove the ring and mesh, pour out the water, then fill the jar with fresh, warm water. Replace the flat metal lid and secure it with the ring. Shake the jar, drain and repeat. Refit the mesh, close the jar with the ring and lay the jar down at an angle. Leave the jar on its side to sit in natural light to drain. Repeat rinsing and draining every few hours, or at least twice a day. Most foods sprout in 1–4 days. When they are ready, rinse and drain thoroughly, then tilt the jar until the sprouts are dry. Store in the fridge.

red pepper

The capsaicin in low-carb, low-fat sweet peppers speeds metabolism without raising heart rate and blood pressure, while it regulates blood sugar and cholesterol. Vitamin B_6 comes in as a diuretic to flush wastes and banish bloating. Antioxidant phytonutrients and sulfur compounds that inhibit abnormal cell growth make this fabulous fruit an immunity idol. Winning the vitamin C sweeps, with 60 g (2¼ oz) delivering the recommended daily allowance, and providing good amounts of vitamin E, red pepper clears congestion and boosts collagen to aid the skin, bones and joints. Peppers are nightshades so may elevate inflammation in arthritis sufferers, but they can benefit heart health. Add raw to salads, wraps and smoothies or use raw or roasted for soup sensations.

more hero foods

- almonds
- asparagus
- avocado
- berries
- broccoli
- Brussels sprouts
- celery
- courgette
- cucumber
- fennel
- grapefruit
- hemp seeds
- leafy greens (such as rocket, pak choi, chard, spring greens, spinach)
- lemon and lime
- oils (coconut, olive, sesame)
- pumpkin seeds
- radishes (such as mooli, red and white)
- shiitake mushrooms
- walnuts
- watermelon

A full-fibre riff on the popular pickle juice in *The Detox Dynamo Cleanse,* this alkalizer pumps probiotic proliferation.

dill pickle party

SERVES 2

4 tbsp filtered water

3 tbsp fresh lemon juice, plus extra to taste

2 tbsp apple cider vinegar, plus extra to taste

1 tsp probiotic powder (see page 154)

1 English cucumber, roughly chopped (do not peel)

1 green apple, cored and chopped (do not peel)

100 g (3½ oz) green cabbage, shredded

2 tsp finely chopped dill, plus extra to taste

1 tsp finely chopped garlic (about 1 clove), plus extra to taste

1 tsp natural salt (see page 139), plus extra to taste

¼ tsp Dijon mustard, plus extra to taste

Pinch of cayenne pepper, plus extra to taste

½ small avocado, stoned and peeled

125 g (4½ oz) ice cubes

optional boosters

27 g (1 oz) baby spinach

35 g (1¼ oz) plain sauerkraut, drained

1 tsp inulin powder (see page 155)

Pour the water, lemon juice and vinegar into your blender. Then add the probiotic powder, cucumber, apple, cabbage, dill, garlic, salt, mustard, cayenne and any boosters. Blast on high for 30–60 seconds until the ingredients are pulverized. Add the avocado and ice and blast again for 20–30 seconds until smooth and creamy. Tweak the lemon juice, vinegar, dill, garlic, salt, mustard and cayenne to taste. Serve cold.

NUTRITIONAL FACTS (PER SERVING)

calories 148 kcal | fat 5.7 g | saturated fat 0.9 g | sodium 1190 mg | carbs 25.9 g | fibre 6.6 g | sugars 14.3 g | protein 2.7 g | calcium 62.9 mg | iron 1.1 mg

In this low-carb cocktail, avo wraps around rum like white on rice. Then Cointreau sets the blend on fire! My brother-in-law Leigh – aka the Silver Fox Bar Champion Extraordinaire – put me onto that little trick. Tweak the lime juice, zest and alcohol to taste. Be bold and add the green powder boosters (which you won't taste), and go craaaaaaaay-ay-ayzy with the cayenne! No, I haven't had too many of these . . . yet.

avocado daiquiri

SERVES 4

360 ml (12 fl oz) raw coconut water

1 tsp finely grated lime zest, plus extra to taste

80 ml (2¾ fl oz) fresh lime juice, plus extra to taste

80 ml (2¾ fl oz) light rum, plus extra to taste

½ medium avocado, stoned and peeled

½ medium banana, sliced (fresh or frozen)

1 tbsp Cointreau

1 tbsp coconut nectar or pure maple syrup

125 g (4½ oz) ice cubes, plus extra to taste

4 thin lime slices

optional boosters

1 tsp wheatgrass powder (see page 171)

¼ tsp spirulina or chlorella (see page 39)

Pinch of cayenne pepper

Throw everything, except the lime slices but including the boosters, into your blender and blast on high for 30–60 seconds until well combined. Tweak the lime zest, lime juice, rum and/or ice to taste. Pour into four martini glasses, garnish the rims with the lime slices and serve immediately.

NUTRITIONAL FACTS (PER SERVING)

calories 140 kcal | fat 3.9 g | saturated fat 0.7 g | sodium 99.4 mg | carbs 14.6 g | fibre 3.5 g | sugars 8.4 g | protein 1.4 g | calcium 30.6 mg | iron 0.5 mg

shiitake & asparagus lettuce cups with lime drench

MAKES 16 LETTUCE CUPS; SERVES 8 AS A STARTER, 4 AS A MEAL;
LIME DRENCH MAKES 160 ML (5½ FL OZ), FILLING MAKES 800 G (1 LB 12 OZ)

lime drench

4 tbsp fresh lime juice

3 tbsp brown rice vinegar

1 tbsp mirin

1 tbsp Bragg Liquid Aminos, gluten-free soy sauce or tamari

1 tsp finely chopped garlic (about 1 clove)

1 tsp finely chopped fresh ginger

1½ tsp coconut sugar or other sweetener

filling

2 tbsp extra virgin olive oil

1 tbsp finely chopped garlic (about 3 cloves)

1 small green chilli, deseeded and finely chopped

1 tbsp finely chopped fresh ginger

72 g (2½ oz) green onion (white and green parts), finely chopped

312 g (10½ oz) shiitake or chestnut mushrooms, finely diced

110 g (4 oz) courgette (½ medium courgette), finely diced

140 g (5 oz) asparagus (about 5 medium spears), finely diced

4 tbsp toasted sesame oil

3 tbsp Bragg Liquid Aminos, gluten-free soy sauce or tamari

14 g (½ oz) finely chopped coriander

16 large butter, looseleaf or romaine lettuce leaves (outer leaves of about 4 heads)

optional boosters

Pinch of chilli flakes

70 g (2½ oz) raw or dry-toasted pine nuts

2 tbsp gomasio (ground sesame seeds and sea salt, see page 210) or sesame seeds

To make the lime drench, throw all of the ingredients, including the red chilli flake booster, into your blender and blast on high for about 30 seconds until well combined. Transfer to a container and set aside.

To make the filling, in a large saucepan, heat the olive oil over a medium heat and sauté the garlic, green chilli, ginger, salad onion, mushrooms, courgette and asparagus for 3–5 minutes until the mixture has reduced to about half the volume; gradually add the sesame oil and liquid aminos as the mixture cools. Don't overcook or the vegetables will get mushy. Stir in the coriander and the pine nut booster.

To assemble, scoop 50 g (1¾ oz) of the filling into each lettuce leaf, drizzle with 1 teaspoon of the lime drench and sprinkle with the gomasio booster. Serve immediately, passing the remaining lime drench at the table. These are fabulous cold, too. Chill the filling and the dressing before assembling.

'Mind-blowing! Gimme the recipe?' That's the chorus every time I serve these. Lime, sesame, ginger, chilli, coriander and a delicious combo of veggies is killer. The finely chopped veggies give a minced meat look and feel. So your cups don't fall apart, use butterhead lettuce or romaine. But, don't stress – your guests will be happy to lick the drench off their hands. To add crunch, top with pine nuts and *gomasio*; for more heat add the chilli flakes. Any way you serve these stars, they'll be a sensation.

NUTRITIONAL FACTS (PER SERVING, BASED ON 16 SERVINGS)

calories 65 kcal | fat 5.3 g | saturated fat 0.7 g | sodium 224.4 mg | carbs 3.9 g | fibre 1.1 g | sugars 1.5 g | protein 1.4 g | calcium 16.1 mg | iron 0.6 mg

Low-carb lovers: this electric, eclectic array of colours, textures and flavours explodes in your mouth and massages your belly, transporting you to Thailand – where you'll forget the chopping it took to get you there! To cut down the prep time, you can pulse the veggies in a food processor. Tweak the dressing, herbs and heat to your preference, and add the leek, tangerine and kaffir lime boosters for a more dimensional tang.

thai slaw

SERVES 8 AS A STARTER, 6 AS A MAIN; DRESSING MAKES 480 ML (17 FL OZ)

dressing

1 tsp finely grated lime zest, plus extra to taste

120 ml (4 fl oz) fresh lime juice

80 ml (2¾ fl oz) extra virgin olive oil

80 ml (2¾ fl oz) rice vinegar

80 ml (2¾ fl oz) toasted sesame oil

37 g (1¼ oz) roasted unsalted cashews

3 tbsp gluten-free soy sauce or tamari

3 tbsp coconut sugar

2 tbsp finely chopped fresh ginger

¼ tsp chilli flakes

¼ tsp natural salt (see page 139)

salad

480 g (17 oz) Chinese cabbage (1 small head), shredded

400 g (14 oz) red cabbage (¼ large head), shredded

160 g (5¾ oz) beansprouts

180 g (6 oz) red pepper (1 large), deseeded and julienned

40 g (1½ oz) finely chopped coriander

150 g (5½ oz) unsalted roasted cashews, roughly chopped

25 g (1 oz) finely chopped Thai basil

20 g (¾ oz) finely chopped mint

25 g (1 oz) salad onion (green parts only), diagonally sliced

Natural salt (see page 139), to taste

Limes wedges, to serve

optional boosters

50 g (1¾ oz) leek (white part only), julienned

2 or 3 medium tangerines or mandarin oranges, peeled and segmented

1 tsp finely chopped kaffir lime leaves, plus extra to taste

To make the dressing, throw all the dressing ingredients into your blender and blast on high for about 60 seconds until smooth and creamy. Tweak the lime zest to taste.

Toss all of the salad ingredients, including the leek, tangerine and kaffir lime boosters, in a large bowl. Fold the dressing into the salad, then chill, covered, for 30–60 minutes to allow the flavours to open and mingle. Season with salt to taste, and serve with lime wedges.

NUTRITIONAL FACTS (PER SERVING, BASED ON 8 SERVINGS)

calories 360 kcal | fat 29.1 g | saturated fat 4.7 g | sodium 514.7 mg | carbs 22.4 g | fibre 3.8 g | sugars 10.7 g | protein 7.3 g | calcium 120.6 mg | iron 3.3 mg

This quick and easy gazpacho comes together in less than 15 minutes but has the flavour of a gourmet soup. It's also flexible and forgiving. Depending on the character of your fresh tomatoes, add more sun-dried to your preference. I use Bragg Liquid Aminos because it's unfermented and alkaline, but gluten-free soy sauce or tamari will bring in that umami flavour, too. Boost with the olive oil for a richer ride, and gussy up with a garnish of olives and basil. Enjoy this soup raw to retain nutrients and live enzymes. But this also gets raves served warm. Omit the ice cubes, and heat gently on the hob or blend longer in a high-speed machine.

tomato-pepper pleasure

SERVES 6 AS A STARTER, 4 AS A MAIN, OR MAKES 25 SHOTS

360 ml (12 fl oz) filtered water, plus extra to taste

580 g (1 lb 4 oz) tomato, roughly chopped

1 medium red pepper, deseeded and roughly chopped

1 medium avocado, stoned and peeled

3 tbsp finely chopped basil leaves, plus extra to garnish

2 tbsp chopped sun-dried tomatoes packed in oil, drained and patted dry, plus extra to taste (see intro)

2 tsp finely chopped garlic (about 2 cloves)

1¾ tsp natural salt, (see page 139), plus extra to taste

½ tsp Bragg Liquid Aminos, gluten-free soy sauce or tamari

¼ tsp chilli flakes, plus more to taste

250 g (9 oz) ice cubes (see intro, optional)

optional boosters

80 g (3 oz) English cucumber, chopped

1 tbsp extra virgin olive oil

43 g (1½ oz) pitted green olives, finely chopped

Throw everything except the ice, but including the cucumber and olive oil boosters, into your blender and blast on high for 30–60 seconds until smooth and creamy. (You may have to blend in batches.) For a chilled soup, add the ice cubes and blend again for a further 10–20 seconds or place in the fridge until cold. For a warm soup, continue blending in a high-speed blender for 4–6 minutes until hot, or transfer to a saucepan and warm over a medium heat. Tweak the salt and chilli flakes to taste, and add more water if you desire a thinner consistency. Garnish with basil and the olive booster.

NUTRITIONAL FACTS (PER SERVING, BASED ON 6 SERVINGS)

calories 82 kcal | fat 5.2 g | saturated fat 0.8 g | sodium 718.4 mg | carbs 8.9 g | fibre 4 g | sugars 4 g | protein 2 g | calcium 24.7 mg | iron 0.7 mg

Omega fatty acids are essential for health, providing energy to our cells, combating inflammation and boosting immunity. Chock-full of the top plant-based sources of those – flaxseeds, walnuts, chia, hemp, açaí, berries, broccoli and cauliflower – this dark-chocolate smoothie-in-a-bowl is an awesome omega overture, and it's high in fibre, too. Sweetened with antioxidant-loaded fruits (add a banana or dates to the base if you're not policing your carbs) and enriched with healthy fats like coconut oil and avocado, this is the ultimate brain food – and a breakfast of real champions.

omega mama

SERVES 2

base

240 ml (8½ fl oz) unsweetened boxed coconut milk

3 tbsp cacao powder or unsweetened cocoa powder

2 tbsp coconut oil (in liquid form)

1 (100 g/3½ oz) packet unsweetened frozen açaí pulp

78 g (2¾ oz) frozen pitted sweet cherries

½ small avocado, stoned and peeled

30 drops alcohol-free chocolate-flavoured (or plain) liquid stevia, plus extra to taste

toppings

80 g (3 oz) fresh raspberries

80 g (3 oz) fresh blueberries

80 g (3 oz) fresh strawberries, sliced

2 tbsp crushed raw walnuts

1 tbsp ground flaxseed

1 tbsp chia seeds (black or white)

1 tbsp shelled hemp seeds

optional boosters

1 tbsp flaxseed oil or chia oil

25 g (1 oz) frozen raw broccoli florets

30 g (1 oz) frozen raw cauliflower florets

To make the base, throw all of the base ingredients into your blender, including any boosters, and blast on high for 20–30 seconds until well combined but still chilled. Tweak the stevia to taste.

Divide the base between two bowls, and top each bowl with berries, walnuts, ground flaxseed, chia seeds and hemp seeds; and enjoy immediately.

NUTRITIONAL FACTS (PER SERVING)

calories 634 kcal | fat 56.3 g | saturated fat 36.5 g | sodium 26.8 mg | carbs 37.6 g | fibre 15.1 g | sugars 13.3 g | protein 9.9 g | calcium 120.2 mg | iron 7.2 mg

From top: Lick-your-plate Lasagne (page 16), Really Good Ricotta (opposite)

This took me quite a few rounds to get just right. Once I did, I wondered how I'd ever lived without it. This ricotta is light, fluffy and absolutely amazing in Lick-your-plate Lasagne (shown here, recipe on page 16). For use in that dish, I've kept it a little soupy to help hydrate the lasagne sheets. If you want a firmer ricotta to slather on sandwiches, dip veggies into or fill other pasta, reduce the water and the lemon juice to 2 tablespoons each. You can also make sweet ricotta: reduce the water and lemon juice as described above, reduce the oil to 1 tablespoon, omit the onion and garlic and add maple syrup and vanilla extract to taste. That version makes an awesome filling for cannoli or other desserts.

really good ricotta

MAKES 720 G (1 LB 9 OZ)

3 tbsp extra virgin olive oil

150 g (5½ oz) yellow onion, diced

Natural salt (see page 139)

4 tbsp filtered water

60 g (2¼ oz) hulled tahini

2½ tbsp fresh lemon juice, plus extra to taste

1½ tbsp white miso paste

1 tsp finely chopped garlic (about 1 clove)

1 (396 g/14 oz) packet firm tofu, drained and crumbled

optional boosters

1 tbsp finely chopped fresh basil

1 tbsp finely chopped fresh oregano

1 tbsp finely chopped fresh thyme

In a large frying pan over a medium heat, warm 1 tablespoon of the olive oil and sauté the onion and a pinch of salt for about 5 minutes until the onion is soft and translucent. Allow to cool slightly, then transfer to your blender. Add the remaining 2 tablespoons of olive oil, the water, tahini, lemon juice, miso paste, garlic and ¾ teaspoon of salt and blast on high for about 30 seconds until smooth. Transfer to a bowl and stir in the crumbled tofu. Tweak the salt and lemon juice to taste. Stir in the boosters.

NUTRITIONAL FACTS (PER SERVING, BASED ON 6 SERVINGS)

calories 186 kcal | fat 15.2 g | saturated fat 2.3 g | sodium 474.3 mg | carbs 7.3 g | fibre 2.2 g | sugars 1.9 g | protein 8 g | calcium 185.5 mg | iron 2.2 mg

High in health-promoting fats and low in carbs, these tantalizing treats are hard to quit gobbling. And if you can't, no worries – they're cleansing! The heart-healthy, medium-chain fatty acids in coconut oil are easily assimilated and readily metabolized for energy instead of being stored as fat. Promoting the effective utilization of blood glucose and enhancing the secretion of insulin, they also help regulate blood sugar. The maple syrup delivers a nice sweetness, but if you want even fewer carbs, go with stevia. To get that classic chocolate-and-chilli combination, I always add the cayenne – not just for fabulous flavour, but also to stimulate the lymphatic system and encourage detox. If you're tempted to skip the salt, don't! Savoury and spicy flavours enhance sweetness. Boost with Blue Majik for antioxidant-avenging potential, and walnuts for a healthy dose of anti-inflammatory omega-3 fatty acids, plus a crunchy texture. Whichever way you make these, they'll hit the sweet spot.

detox chocs

MAKES ABOUT 10 SMALL CHOCOLATES

120 ml (4 fl oz) coconut oil (in liquid form)

18 g (¾ oz) cacao powder or unsweetened cocoa powder

65 g (2¼ oz) raw almond butter

2 tbsp pure maple syrup or 20 drops alcohol-free liquid stevia

¼ tsp natural salt (see page 139)

optional boosters

½ tsp E3Live Blue Majik (see page 211) or spirulina

⅛ tsp cayenne pepper

30 g (1 oz) crushed raw walnuts

Throw the coconut oil, cacao, almond butter, maple syrup, salt and the Blue Majik and cayenne boosters into the blender. Blast on high for 10–20 seconds until well combined.

Transfer the mixture to a liquid measuring jug. Stir in the walnuts. Pour the mixture into small silicone chocolate moulds or tiny paper baking cases set out on a tray. Chill in the freezer for 20–30 minutes until solidified. Gently release the chocolates from the moulds and transfer to a container. Store, well sealed, in the fridge or freezer, and serve chilled.

Note: Because of the coconut oil, the chocolates will melt if left out at room temperature.

NUTRITIONAL FACTS (PER SERVING, BASED ON 10 SERVINGS)

calories 147 kcal | fat 14.7 g | saturated fat 9.8 g | sodium 59.5 mg | carbs 4.9 g | fibre 1.3 g | sugars 2.7 g | protein 1.7 g | calcium 29 mg | iron 0.5 mg

alkaline forming

alkaline forming

The balance between acidity and alkalinity – our internal pH – is critical for health. Every physiological process yields acidic waste products; and stress, drugs and pollutants dump more acids into the mix. To keep this balance working in our favour, our systems need to maintain a store of 'alkaline buffer' minerals – sodium, calcium, manganese, copper, potassium, iron and magnesium. They neutralize acids and tame the toxic build-up. By reducing acidifying foods, particularly sugars, in our diets and upping our intake of alkaline-forming foods that provide the buffers – lemons, limes, leafy greens, avocado and others, particularly those listed below – we can avoid the harm that comes when the body has to leach these minerals from tissues and organs.

cucumber

Advancing the alkaline agenda, this hydrating hero provides vitamin-mineral-enzyme-electrolyte-rich water to fortify our cells and skin. Naturally diuretic, cukes flush out the kidneys, liver and colon. Botanically a fruit but eaten like a veggie, cucumber combines well with everything. Along with alkaline buffers, these waterborne warriors deliver antioxidant flavonoids, carotenoids, vitamins C and K and manganese, freezing out free radicals and building healthy blood. With milder skins and seeds, which contain more nutrients than the flesh, English and mini (Persian or Lebanese) varieties are my go-to. In some recipes, so as not to en*cumber* delicate flavours, I'll peel and/or deseed. Toss cucumbers into salads for added hydro and crunch, and into juices and smoothies to temper a high-sugar blend.

chard

Like other leafy greens, chard is loaded with alkalizing chlorophyll and mineral buffers. Unlike others, it has a unique ability to help pancreatic cells regenerate for the production of insulin, and it contains syringic acid, which inhibits carb-digesting enzyme activity so less simple sugar enters the bloodstream. Chomp on chard for those benefits, along with cardio-protective antioxidants like flavonoids, carotenoids and betalains; vitamins A, C, E and K; omega-3s; protein; and fibre. With them, chard delivers anti-inflammatory and detox support for bones, lungs and connective tissue. Most of chard's nutrients are found in the leaves; chiffonade them for soups, stews and stir-fries. When using chard in green smoothies, lift earthiness with sweet fruits, lemon, mint, chilli and ginger.

celery

The hefty load of alkaline buffers and phytonutrients in celery blasts acids, calms the nervous system and regulates blood pressure. Like cucumber, celery is a diuretic dynamo. Celery's unique pectin-based polysaccharides combat bloating and inflammation, especially in the stomach. Low in calories and high in fibre; vitamins A, B, C and K; and folate, the whole plant dials up digestion and loves the liver. Use the leaves and ribs in juices and smoothies; every part of celery is great in salads, soups, stews and stir-fries.

almonds

Abundant calcium, potassium and magnesium buffers, monounsaturated fats, and vitamin E help almonds nourish the skin and detox the liver. The highest source of protein among nuts, and with B vitamins that aid carb metabolism, almonds are a weight-loss-promoting, cholesterol-regulating, high-energy food. They've got your back with anti-inflammatory flavonoids, too. Almonds deliver their utmost whole, with their fibre-and-flavonoid-packed skins, but to add a creamy element to smoothies, drinks, sauces, dressings, dips, soups and desserts, and for beautiful presentation in salads and other savoury dishes, I use them blanched, too. The mild flavour of almond milk makes it my go-to base for drinks, desserts and savoury sauces. Almond butter adds a richness to soups, stews and smoothies, along with a magical creamy consistency. To unlock your almonds' full nutrient potential and increase their digestibility, give them a soothing overnight soak (see page 171).

strawberries

This low-sugar fruit helps neutralize acidic waste and oxidation, reducing the degeneration of cells, tissues and organs. Rich in phytonutrients, vitamin C, mineral buffers and omega-3s, these berries pack an arsenal of antioxidant ammo that crushes inflammation to protect the eyes, muscles, blood and nervous system. Strawbs make your circulatory system and heart happy, too. With loads of fibre and polyphenols that block starch absorption to lower blood sugar, these detox dynamos do double-duty as digestive divas. Throw into smoothies, drinks, salads, cereals, sauces, dressings and desserts.

sunflower seeds

Truckloads of vitamin E, magnesium and phytosterols help these sensational seeds attack acids to calm inflammation for cellular, heart, brain and nerve health, while selenium supports detox. With protein, fibre and B-complex vitamins, sunflower seeds are an energizing addition to salads, soups and other savoury dishes. Their texture and richness makes them a nifty nut substitute in sauces, creams and dressings. (For a creamier consistency, blend with pine nuts.) Roughly chopped, sunflower seeds make a magical mock tuna (see page 144).

natural salt

As our bodily fluids are saline, we all need salt to survive. Yes, the 'table' variety deserves a bad rap. High-quality unprocessed, additive-free natural salts, on the other hand, are a whole 'nother story – and abundant in alkaline buffers. Sea salt in particular keeps us hydrated and provides some sixty minerals to replenish electrolytes, support adrenal, immune and thyroid function, enhance digestion and assist detox. Good salt brings out flavour, too. For maximum nutritional density and superior taste, my go-to is Celtic sea salt (see page 211). Table salt is stronger, so if you're using it in these recipes, halve the amount called for, then up the salt to taste. Tip: a pinch of sea salt in a smoothie moderates fruit sugars' acidifying impact.

stevia

The sweet news: this sucrose-free herb doesn't alter blood sugar, and while it isn't specifically alkaline forming, it isn't acid-forming like other sweeteners. Massively sweeter than sugar, stevia can overwhelm other flavours with a bitter aftertaste; alcohol-free liquids, added drop by drop, let you get the balance right. Granulated stevia is harder to measure with precision. Tip: birch xylitol (see page 155) used with stevia delivers a well-balanced sweetness.

more hero foods

- asparagus
- avocado
- berries (blackberries, blueberries, raspberries)
- broccoli
- cabbage
- cauliflower
- coconut
- courgette
- cultured vegetables
- grains (such as amaranth, buckwheat, millet, quinoa)
- grapefruit
- leafy greens (such as kale, lettuce, pak choi, rocket, spring greens, spinach)
- lemon and lime
- nuts (pecans, walnuts)
- peppers
- sea vegetables
- seeds (such as chia, flax, hemp, pumpkin, sesame)
- sprouts (such as alfalfa, broccoli, pea)
- tomatoes (raw)
- watermelon

Loaded with nutrients and alkaline buffers (the liquid chlorophyll and wheatgrass boosters add more), this zesty and refreshing combination is fantastic for alleviating airborne allergies, thanks to the parsley. Depending on the sweetness of your apples, add stevia to taste and boost with ginger for anti-inflammatory power and a beautiful back-end zing!

lime-aid

SERVES 2

1 tbsp finely grated lime zest, plus extra to taste

120 ml (4 fl oz) fresh lime juice, plus extra to taste

12 g (¼ oz) flat-leaf parsley

½ English cucumber, roughly chopped (do not peel)

2 green apples, cored and chopped (do not peel)

½ tsp probiotic powder (see page 154, optional)

Pinch of natural salt (see page 139)

½ small avocado, stoned and peeled

250 g (9 oz) ice cubes, plus extra to taste

5 drops alcohol-free liquid stevia, plus extra to taste

optional boosters

1 tbsp plain liquid chlorophyll

2 tsp finely chopped fresh ginger, plus extra to taste

1 tsp wheatgrass powder (see page 171)

Throw the lime zest, lime juice, parsley and cucumber into your blender, followed by the apples, probiotic powder, salt and the boosters. Blast on high for 30–60 seconds until the ingredients are completely pulverized. Add the avocado and ice and blast again for 10–20 seconds until smooth and creamy. Tweak the lime, ice, stevia and ginger to taste.

NUTRITIONAL FACTS (PER SERVING)

calories 180 kcal | fat 5.6 g | saturated fat 0.8 g | sodium 165.4 mg | carbs 37.4 g | fibre 7.9 g | sugars 21.6 g | protein 2.1 g | calcium 55.2 mg | iron 1.1 mg

From left: Lime-aid (opposite),
Maca Macaroon (page 150)

This no-bean raw blend, a dead ringer for chickpea-based hummus, is alkalizing and packs a wallop of vitamin C along with awesome anti-inflammatory power. Basically, it ticks all the boxes. Chill the blend in the fridge to thicken, then slather it on sandwiches and wraps, or scoop onto veggie sticks and crackers. This dip (see photo, page 26) disappears quickly, but keeps fresh in the fridge for up to 5 days. In the ground-level recipe I've gone for kid-friendly – but the boosters rocket these flavours into outer space.

raw red hummus

MAKES 352 G (12 OZ)

2 tbsp fresh lemon juice, plus extra to taste

1 tbsp extra virgin olive oil

60 g (2¼ oz) hulled tahini, plus extra to taste

150 g (5½ oz) courgette (about 1 medium), peeled and roughly chopped

140 g (5 oz) red pepper (about 1 medium), deseeded and roughly chopped

22 g (¾ oz) sun-dried tomatoes packed in oil, drained, dried and roughly chopped

1 tsp finely chopped garlic (about 1 clove), plus extra to taste

⅛ tsp Bragg Liquid Aminos, gluten-free soy sauce or tamari, plus extra to taste

¾ tsp natural salt (see page 139), plus extra to taste

optional boosters

¼ tsp smoked paprika

⅛ tsp chilli flakes, plus extra to taste

1 tsp raw sesame seeds

Throw all of the ingredients, including the smoked paprika and red chilli flake boosters, into your blender and blast on high for about 1 minute until smooth and creamy. Tweak the lemon juice, tahini, garlic, liquid aminos, salt and chilli flakes to taste. Chill in the fridge for a few hours to thicken. Serve garnished with the sesame seed booster.

NUTRITIONAL FACTS (PER SERVING, BASED ON 12 SERVINGS)

calories 63 kcal | fat 4.8 g | saturated fat 0.7 g | sodium 162.4 mg | carbs 4.4 g | fibre 1.4 g | sugars 2 g | protein 1.8 g | calcium 34.3 mg | iron 0.9 mg

There's always a jar of this protein-rich, alkalizing almond butter in our fridge. Scott makes a batch every few days, and we gobble it with veggie sticks, fruit and raw sprouted crackers. This nutrient-dense treat, loaded with healthy fats and low in sugar, is a satisfying snack that skips the acidic aftermath. We love a batch boosted with almond extract, coconut and cinnamon. But adding cacao powder for a chocolate-almond butter experience is an equally righteous ride.

awesome almond butter

MAKES 350 G (12 OZ)

320 g (11¼ oz) raw whole almonds

4 tbsp cold-pressed grapeseed oil or coconut oil (in liquid form), plus extra as needed

¼ tsp alcohol-free natural vanilla extract

⅛ tsp natural salt (see page 139)

4 drops alcohol-free plain or vanilla-flavoured liquid stevia (optional)

optional boosters

3 tbsp desiccated coconut, plus extra to taste

1 tsp ground cinnamon, plus extra to taste

¼ tsp natural almond extract

Throw everything into your high-speed blender, including the boosters, and blast on high, using a tamper to guide the ingredients through the blades, until you reach the desired consistency. You may have to stop the machine and scrape down the sides of the container. Depending on how thirsty your almonds are, you may have to add more oil. Tweak the coconut and cinnamon to taste. Keep in a sealed jar in the fridge for up to 2 weeks.

NUTRITIONAL FACTS (PER SERVING, BASED ON 12 SERVINGS)

calories 206 kcal | fat 19.1 g | saturated fat 1.4 g | sodium 48.7 mg | carbs 5.8 g | fibre 3.3 g | sugars 1.2 g | protein 5.6 g | calcium 71.8 mg | iron 1 mg

mock tuna swooner

SERVES 6 AS A STARTER, 4 AS A MAIN; DRESSING MAKES 227 G (8 OZ)

dressing

180 ml (6 fl oz) filtered water, plus extra as needed

70 g (2½ oz) blanched flaked almonds, soaked (see page 171)

75 g (2¾ oz) raw sunflower seeds, soaked (see page 171)

1 tsp finely chopped garlic (about 1 clove)

2½ tbsp fresh lemon juice, plus extra to taste

1½ tbsp stone-ground mustard

¾ tsp Bragg Liquid Aminos, gluten-free soy sauce or tamari, plus extra to taste

1 tsp natural salt (see page 139), plus extra to taste

'tuna' salad

150 g (5½ oz) raw sunflower seeds, soaked (see page 171)

2 tbsp filtered water

1 tsp finely chopped garlic (about 1 clove)

2 tbsp fresh lemon juice

1 tsp apple cider vinegar

½ tsp Bragg Liquid Aminos, gluten-free soy sauce or tamari

¼ tsp natural salt (see page 139)

Freshly ground black pepper

80 g (3 oz) gherkins, finely diced, plus extra to taste

132 g (4½ oz) celery, diced

37 g (1¼ oz) red onion, diced

2 tbsp finely chopped flat-leaf parsley

2 tbsp chopped dill

3 large romaine lettuce hearts, cut into ribbons

Micro-greens, to garnish

optional boosters

⅛ tsp cayenne pepper

1 tsp dulse flakes (see page 211)

80 g (3 oz) raw almonds, sliced

To make the dressing, throw all of the dressing ingredients into your blender, add the cayenne booster and blast on high for about 1 minute until smooth and creamy.

To make the 'tuna' salad, throw the sunflower seeds, water, garlic, lemon juice, apple cider vinegar, liquid aminos, salt and pepper into a food processor and pulse until the mixture has the consistency of ground flaky tuna. Do not overprocess or you will get mush, but you need to process enough or the sunflower seeds will be too dominant.

Transfer to a large mixing bowl and stir in the gherkins, celery, onion, parsley, dill and the dulse flake booster. Tweak the lemon juice, liquid aminos, salt and gherkins to taste. Mix three-quarters of the dressing into the 'tuna' mixture.

Place equal amounts of the lettuce into individual salad bowls. Toss the 'tuna' mixture with the lettuce and add the remaining dressing. Garnish with the sliced almonds and micro-greens and serve immediately.

NUTRITIONAL FACTS (PER SERVING, BASED ON 6 SERVINGS)

calories 328 kcal | fat 25.3 g | saturated fat 2.5 g | sodium 726.1 mg | carbs 19.9 g | fibre 9.9 g | sugars 4.5 g | protein 12.4 g | calcium 139.3 mg | iron 3.8 mg

I hit the jackpot with this 'tuna' salad utilizing almonds, sunflower seeds and liquid aminos. Loaded with alkaline immune boosters, this nut and seed mixture really has a texture reminiscent of tuna. Add the dulse flakes and you can nail the taste, too. Make the 'tuna' in advance, chill in the fridge for a day and it gets even better. To avoid a soggy salad, toss it with the romaine and additional dressing just before serving. Or, slap it into a sandwich for a slam-dunk snack.

The classic combo of mint and peas rocks the pot! For the ultimate spoonful, boost with the soured cream, parsley and lemon juice. 'Souperb' hot or cold, this blend serves up nicely as a starter, a main or in shot glasses. Full of flavour, fibre and alkalizing power, these pleasing peas and their pals are dressed to impress!

minty peas please!

SERVES 6 AS A STARTER, 4 AS A MAIN

2 tbsp extra virgin olive oil

300 g (10½ oz) yellow onion, diced

1 tsp natural salt (see page 139), plus extra to taste

120 g (4½ oz) cauliflower florets

1.2 litres (2 pints) vegetable stock

200 g (7 oz) iceberg lettuce, chopped

810 g (1 lb 12 oz) frozen green peas, thawed

30 g (1 oz) mint leaves

Freshly ground black pepper

optional boosters

2 tsp fresh lemon juice

60 g (2¼ oz) So Good! Soured Cream (page 183)

2 tbsp finely chopped flat-leaf parsley

In a large pot, heat the olive oil over a medium heat and sauté the onion with a pinch of salt for about 5 minutes until soft and translucent. Add the cauliflower and stock, raise the heat to high and bring to the boil. Reduce the heat to medium and simmer for about 10 minutes until the cauliflower is just tender. Add the lettuce, peas and 1 teaspoon of salt and simmer for about 2 minutes until the peas are just cooked but still vibrant green. Remove the pot from the heat and allow to cool slightly. Add the mint.

Working in batches, pour the soup into your blender and purée on high for 1–2 minutes until smooth and creamy. (For conventional blenders, remove the small centre lid cap and cover the opening with a tea towel so steam can escape while you blend.) Return the soup to the pan, season to taste with salt and pepper and warm it over a low heat. Add the lemon juice booster.

Ladle the soup into bowls, garnish with the soured cream and parsley boosters and serve.

NUTRITIONAL FACTS (PER SERVING, BASED ON 6 SERVINGS)

calories 181 kcal | fat 5.3 g | saturated fat 0.8 g | sodium 435.7 mg | carbs 26.7 g | fibre 8.8 g | sugars 10.7 g | protein 8.6 g | calcium 70.1 mg | iron 2.5 mg

I'm a sucker for stew, and this one is seriously delicious and so quick and easy. The combination of rich, creamy almond butter, sautéed sweet potatoes and spices will make you *mmmm* your delight at every bite. This hearty dish, loaded with protein (the optional greens and seeds add even more), is an alkalizing, immune-boosting, chlorophyll-rich crusader.

sustenance stew

SERVES 6–8

cauliflower rice

2 medium heads cauliflower, cut into florets

4 tbsp extra virgin olive oil

1 tsp natural salt (see page 139)

stew

1 tbsp grapeseed oil or extra virgin olive oil

1 medium yellow onion, roughly chopped

2 tsp finely chopped garlic (about 2 cloves)

Natural salt (see page 139)

720 ml (1¼ pints) vegetable stock

2 (411 g/14 oz) cans whole tomatoes with their juice

1½ tbsp finely chopped fresh ginger

¼ tsp chilli flakes

570 g (1 lb 4 oz) orange-flesh sweet potatoes, peeled and roughly diced

210 g (7 oz) broccoli florets, chopped

120 g (4½ oz) Swiss chard, stalks removed and leaves cut into ribbons

43 g (1½ oz) roasted almond butter

14 g (½ oz) finely chopped coriander

1 medium avocado, stoned, peeled and sliced

80 g (3 oz) raw almonds, sliced

optional boosters

35 g (1¼ oz) shelled hemp seeds

1 tbsp chia seeds (black or white)

10 g (¼ oz) pea shoots

To make the cauliflower rice, preheat the oven to 180°C/350°F/Gas mark 4. Line a large baking sheet with a silicone liner or baking paper.

Put the cauliflower florets in a food processor and pulse about 5 times until the cauliflower has the texture of couscous. You may have to process in two batches. Transfer the cauliflower to a large bowl and stir in the oil and 1 teaspoon of salt until well combined.

Transfer the 'rice' to the prepared baking sheet and bake for 15 minutes. Stir with a spatula or wooden spoon and continue to roast for another 15 minutes until the 'rice' begins to brown. Set aside until ready to serve.

To make the stew, in a large pot over a medium heat, warm the oil and sauté the onion and garlic with a pinch of salt for about 5 minutes until the onion is soft and translucent.

Meanwhile, add the stock, tomatoes, ginger and chilli flakes to your blender and pulse a few times on low until rustically chopped and combined but not blended. Stir the sweet potatoes and stock mixture into the sautéed onion. Increase the heat to high and bring the mixture to the boil. Reduce the heat to medium, add ½ teaspoon of salt, and simmer, uncovered and stirring occasionally, for about 15 minutes until the sweet potato is just tender. Add the broccoli and simmer for a further 5 minutes. Stir in the chard and almond butter and simmer for a further 5 minutes until the chard is just wilted. The stock should be absorbed and you should have a creamy vegetable dish. Stir in the coriander and tweak the salt to taste.

To serve, spoon equal amounts of the cauliflower rice into bowls and spoon the stew next to or over the 'rice'. Top with the avocado and sliced almonds and sprinkle with the hemp seed and chia seed boosters. Finish by topping with the pea shoots booster.

NUTRITIONAL FACTS (PER SERVING, BASED ON 6 SERVINGS)

calories 126 kcal | fat 9.6 g | saturated fat 1.4 g | sodium 324.8 mg | carbs 8.8 g | fibre 2.8 g | sugars 4 g | protein 3.6 g | calcium 68.6 mg | iron 1.8 mg

When Jay of the Jingslingers taught me the tricks to this restorative tonic (see photo, page 141), I thought I'd been beamed up to Planet Genius. Minutes after my first sip, it felt as if my cells were firing on all cylinders. This warm, creamy elixir balances your hormones and boosts the brain with essential fats from the coconut; amino acids from the maca (which increases circulation and boosts libido); and iron and anabolic vitamin B in the lucuma. The ginger booster increases blood flow. If you want to supercharge your brain, add the mucuna – that ayurvedic herb is renowned for being the highest food source of L-DOPA, a precursor to the critical neurotransmitter dopamine. The L-theanine booster is a precursor to the calming neurotransmitter GABA. If all this technotalk is putting you on Planet Geek, focus on two key facts: this one's sugar-free and tastes like a melted macaroon.

maca macaroon

SERVES 2

600 ml (20 fl oz) warm filtered water

120 ml (4 fl oz) full-fat canned coconut milk (shake, then pour)

135 g (4½ oz) raw young coconut meat (see page 210)

2 tbsp lucuma powder (see page 211)

1 tbsp maca powder (see page 7)

2 tsp powdered birch xylitol (see page 155)

½ tsp alcohol-free almond flavour or natural almond extract

⅛ tsp natural salt (see page 139)

45 drops Sweet Leaf English Toffee stevia (see page 211)

15 drops Sweet Leaf Vanilla Crème stevia (see page 211)

optional boosters

1 tsp ground ginger

1 tsp mucuna powder (see page 211)

¼ tsp L-theanine powder (see page 211)

Throw everything into your blender, including the boosters, and blast on high for 30–60 seconds until smooth and creamy. If using a high-speed blender, continue blending until warm or at your desired temperature. Or, transfer to a saucepan and gently warm over a low heat.

NUTRITIONAL FACTS (PER SERVING)

calories 383 kcal | fat 8.7 g | saturated fat 7.7 g | sodium 44.5 mg | carbs 6.4 g | fibre 2.2 g | sugars 1.6 g | protein 0.9 g | calcium 7.2 mg | iron 0.9 mg

Here's a healthy dessert (or snack) you can throw together fast in a high-speed blender or food processor. Omit the cayenne for an alkalizing frozen treat that will win points with the kids. For a more nuanced flavour, add the pepper and lemon zest; the goji powder ups immunity. This has a soft consistency like a frozen yogurt. For a firmer fix, freeze for an hour or so. Since the mixture isn't churned in an ice-cream maker, too much time below zero and ice crystals will spoil your scoop.

spicy strawberry sorbet

SERVES 4–6

240 g (8½ oz) watermelon, deseeded, peeled and cubed

20 drops alcohol-free liquid stevia

Pinch of cayenne pepper

480 g (17 oz) frozen strawberries

optional boosters

1 tsp goji powder (see page 23)

35 g (1¼ oz) red pepper, deseeded and diced

⅛ tsp finely grated lemon zest

Throw the watermelon, stevia, cayenne pepper and any boosters into your high-speed blender and blast on high for about 30 seconds until the ingredients are completely pulverized and combined. Scrape down the sides of the blender container and inside the lid and add the strawberries. Blast on high for 10–20 seconds, using the tamper to guide the fruit through the blades, until pulverized but still frozen. Scoop out and serve immediately like frozen yogurt, or chill in the freezer for about 1 hour to firm up to a harder sorbet consistency.

NUTRITIONAL FACTS (PER SERVING, BASED ON 6 SERVINGS)

calories 33 kcal | fat 0.1 g | saturated fat 0 g | sodium 1.6 mg | carbs 8.7 g | fibre 1.4 g | sugars 5.2 g | protein 0.5 g | calcium 12.5 mg | iron 0.6 mg

CHAPTER 10

probiotic promoting

probiotic promoting

Our inner ecosystems are — if we're healthy — home to billions of beneficial micro-organisms (the most common being lactobacillus and bifidus). These friendly critters wage an ongoing war against hostile invaders. Stress, pollutants, pesticides, preservatives and drugs (antibiotics in particular) wipe out our buddies, giving the bad guys a happy hunting ground. Nasty bacteria, yeast, fungi and parasites then take over the town. Eating probiotic-rich (chiefly fermented) foods and prebiotic agents (especially fibre-rich foods that feed probiotics and alkaline formers that support them) helps build and sustain healthy digestive flora, strengthening immunity.

kefir

Turn milks, coconut water or plain water into kefir by adding a culture starter or kefir grains, and a sugar to feed the probiotic organisms. Coconut water kefir (my pick) is loaded with potassium and other mineral buffers, protein and vitamin B_{12}, and is a brilliant blood builder and immune booster. Alkaline forming, too, it dials up digestion and detox. Tart, fizzy and potent, this medicinal mama cleans you out! I drink 120 ml (4 fl oz) each morning and before bed. Commercial kefirs often contain excessive sugar; those that do are acid-forming and work against your probiotic-proliferation plan. Kombucha (fermented tea) and rejuvelac (made from sprouted grains) are also fantastic probiotic pilots. Kombucha, though, can exacerbate candida. Use any of the three beverages — kefir, kombucha or rejuvelac — to culture cheeze (see page 161), puddings and raw desserts, and to punch up the probiotics in smoothies and drinks.

live-cultured vegetables

Cabbage, carrots, beetroot and other raw veggies tossed with natural salt and fermented (see page 164) turn into mineral- and probiotic-rich powerhouse foods, with live enzymes to aid digestion. Alkaline-forming, these cultured condiments eliminate toxins to protect cells, tissues and organs. They combine well with starches and proteins; I eat a portion with every meal. With commercial products, go with sauerkraut, pickles and kimchi; make sure they're unpasteurized and vinegar-free.

yogurt

A convenient thickener, yogurt adds tang as well as creaminess to smoothies, desserts, dips, dressings and sauces, and its live cultures are great for the gut. My fave: coconut (for my recipe see page 166). At the supermarket, go for natural yogurts without sugar-based sweeteners. (See my picks of coconut, non-GMO soya and almond yogurts on page 211.)

miso

This probiotic-rich paste, traditionally made from soya, also comes in varieties made from chickpea, brown rice and other grains. Colour and flavour vary with base ingredient and fermentation time. Full of phytonutrient antioxidants, vitamins, minerals, protein and fibre, miso is a pre-digested anti-inflammatory agent that supports intestinal microflora and boosts immunity. To preserve the probiotics, use it raw or slightly warmed. Red or white miso adds richness to soups; white lends a cheezy quality to pesto, dressings and marinades.

probiotic powder

Supplementing your quota of live, raw prebiotic- and probiotic-rich foods with high-quality probiotic powder is a proactive strategy for health. Add ½ teaspoon (roughly the contents of a capsule) to smoothies, raw desserts, dressings and sauces. Go for the potent probiotics that require refrigeration (my picks are listed on page 211). To ease digestion, break gel capsules open and release the powder.

sea vegetables

Grown in marine and fresh waters, these powerful prebiotics are the most mineral-rich foods on the planet. While sea veggies contain regular anti-inflammatory polyphenols like carotenoids and flavonoids, they offer unique alkaloid antioxidants, and sulfated polysaccharides (fucoidans) serving as antivirals that work with vitamins C and E to promote cell integrity and immunity. Seaweeds also cleanse heavy metals and environmental wastes. Among the thousands of sea veggies, each with its own colour, shape, taste and texture, the most readily available are nori, hijiki, wakame, arame, dulse and kombu. Purchase organic sea veg sourced from clean waters, in sheets, flakes or powder. Most in whole form need a soak. Rehydrated seaweed swings in salads and soups; dulse and kelp flakes make great condiments for soups, grains and other savoury dishes; dry nori sheets are a staple for sushi rolls. Tip: dulse flakes bring an anchovy flavour to a Caesar salad (see page 13).

inulin powder

This unique carbohydrate, called chicory root fibre, and also found in asparagus, artichoke, Jerusalem artichoke, dandelion root, banana, onion, leek and garlic, provides primo digestive-tract support as a prebiotic. Inulin passes intact to the colon, where beneficial micro-organisms feast on it. Fortify the digestive power of smoothies and raw dishes with 1 teaspoon of powder (see page 211); it slips in a slight sweetness while elevating the effects of probiotic foods and supplements.

asparagus

A sensational source of prebiotic inulin (see above), these sexy stalks seduce friendly bacteria while their antifungal and antiviral agents, plus alkalizing vitamins and minerals, aid digestion and immunity. In these recipes, I use green asparagus, which is delicious lightly steamed, blanched or roasted, slipped into a stir-fry or tossed raw into a salad.

cayenne pepper

Powering probiotic potential as a prebiotic, this hot pepper is dynamite for digestion and weight loss, boosting the secretion of hydrochloric acid to foster the friendly bugs, while amping up enzyme production, stimulating the colon, firing metabolism and burning fat. High in capsaicin, cayenne is a pain reliever, too – as long as you haven't overdone it and scorched your taste buds. For mega-medicinal magic and brilliant back-end kick, I add a pinch to almost everything.

birch xylitol

A unique five-carbon sugar structure (regular sugar has six) makes this polyalcohol largely indigestible, for a low-GI sweetener that feeds probiotics, reduces acetaldehyde, a toxic by-product of candida, and doesn't alter blood sugar. Many plants produce xylitol, and the body makes its own. I skip xylitol derived from corn and opt for the superior birch variety. (For my picks, see page 211.)

more hero foods

- algae (chlorella, spirulina)
- apples (raw)
- apple cider vinegar
- artichokes
- bananas (raw)
- burdock root
- cabbage (raw)
- celeriac
- chicory (raw)
- dandelion greens (raw)
- garlic (raw)
- Jerusalem artichoke (raw)
- leafy greens (raw)
- leek (raw)
- natto
- natural salt
- onions (raw and cooked)
- tempeh
- wheatgrass
- yacon syrup

This blend's flavour, reminiscent of an Orange Julius *sans* refined sugar, is addictive. Depending on the size and ripeness of your fruits, add more banana to achieve the sweetness you like. But use a light hand or that 'nana flavour gets overpowering. Loaded with probiotic- and prebiotic-rich foods (add the boosters for even more), this one's an immunity and detox agent working undercover as a dessert.

orange greensicle

SERVES 2

260 g (9 oz) dairy-free yogurt (almond, coconut, soya)

1½ tsp finely grated orange zest, plus extra to taste

2 medium oranges, peeled, deseeded and quartered

132 g (4½ oz) baby spinach

150 g (5½ oz) fresh strawberries, hulled and halved

1 tbsp flaxseed oil or chia seed oil

½ tsp natural vanilla extract

½ tsp probiotic powder (see page 154, optional)

⅛ tsp ground turmeric, plus extra to taste

⅛ tsp natural salt (see page 139)

160 g (5¾ oz) frozen sliced bananas, plus extra to taste (see intro)

optional boosters

1 tbsp yacon syrup (see page 211)

1 tsp inulin powder (see page 155)

1 tsp wheatgrass powder (see page 171)

Throw everything into your blender, including any boosters, and blast on high for 30–60 seconds until smooth and creamy.

NUTRITIONAL FACTS (PER SERVING)

calories 572 kcal | fat 16.6 g | saturated fat 0.8 g | sodium 619 mg | carbs 97.5 g | fibre 23 g | sugars 57.6 g | protein 18.3 g | calcium 159.5 mg | iron 2.6 mg

My pals Joy and Jay, aka the Jingslingers, are masters of medicinal magic and what they do takes functional food to the next level. We had fun creating this uplifting elixir. The probiotics in the coconut water kefir promote digestion, boost immunity and help the old bean produce feel-good neurotransmitters like serotonin. Fresh strawberries bring in collagen-supporting compounds like vitamin C (add the camu powder for more) and pelagic acid for radiant skin. Rose expands your heart and soothing orange oil expands the mind, improves mood and relaxes irritations in the body. Three Sisters, a Chinese tincture of tonic berries, builds blood and regulates hormones.

rose-berry radiance

SERVES 2

240 ml (8½ fl oz) coconut water kefir

450 g (1 lb) fresh strawberries (not frozen), hulled and halved

1 tbsp full-fat canned coconut milk (shake, then pour)

2 tsp powdered birch xylitol (see page 155)

½ tsp pure rosewater

½ tsp probiotic powder (see page 154)

Pinch of natural salt (see page 139)

2 drops sweet orange essential oil

62 g (2¼ oz) ice cubes

optional boosters

1 tbsp coconut oil (in liquid form)

1 tsp camu powder (see page 23)

¾ tsp Jing Herbs Three Sisters Tincture (see page 211)

Throw everything into your blender, including the boosters, and blast on high for 30–60 seconds until smooth. Serve immediately.

NUTRITIONAL FACTS (PER SERVING)

calories 161 kcal | fat 6.3 g | saturated fat 4 g | sodium 206.2 mg | carbs 23.2 g | fibre 4.5 g | sugars 16.7 g | protein 5.9 g | calcium 186.6 mg | iron 1.2 mg

The tasty trick of using fermented tofu to make a probiotic-rich creamy salad dressing is one I picked up in a cooking class KitchenAid hosted in Chicago. Fermented tofu (also sold as 'preserved' tofu) is available at Asian grocers and online. The flavour varies considerably. In this recipe, I use the kind most commonly available, which comes seasoned with sesame oil, chilli and salt. You'll find fresh kelp noodles in the refrigerated sections of health food stores. The combination of fermented ingredients in the dressing and mineral-rich, alkalizing sea-vegetable noodles, along with other premier prebiotic veggies, supercharges nutrients (add the boosters for even more) and punches up probiotic proliferation.

fermented kelp help

SERVES 6 AS A STARTER, 4 AS A MAIN; DRESSING MAKES 540 ML (19 FL OZ)

dressing

180 ml (6 fl oz) rice bran oil

105 g (3½ oz) mashed fermented tofu (drain liquid before mashing)

80 ml (2¾ fl oz) rice vinegar

2 tbsp toasted sesame oil

½ tsp finely grated lime zest

1 tbsp fresh lime juice

1 tsp probiotic powder (see page 154)

120 ml (4 fl oz) filtered water

salad

1 (340 g/12 oz) packet kelp noodles, rinsed and drained

70 g (2½ oz) Chinese cabbage, finely shredded

3 heads baby pak choi, julienned

1 medium red pepper, deseeded and julienned

1 carrot, shaved or julienned

25 g (1 oz) salad onion (green parts only), diagonally sliced

20 g (¾ oz) finely chopped coriander leaves

Lime wedges, to serve

optional boosters

80 g (3 oz) beansprouts

160 g (5¾ oz) shelled raw edamame

1 tsp black sesame seeds

To make the dressing, throw the rice bran oil, mashed tofu, rice vinegar, sesame oil, lime zest, lime juice and probiotic powder into your blender and blast on high for 10–20 seconds until smooth and creamy. Add the water and process on low for just a few seconds to thin out the dressing. (If you blend longer, it will thicken again.)

To assemble the salad, in a large bowl, toss the kelp noodles, cabbage, pak choi, pepper, carrot, salad onion and coriander, along with the beansprout and edamame boosters. Add the dressing to taste and toss.

Garnish with the black sesame seed booster and serve with lime wedges. Pass remaining dressing around the table.

NUTRITIONAL FACTS (PER SERVING, BASED ON 6 SERVINGS)

calories 341 kcal | fat 33.6 g | saturated fat 6.3 g | sodium 577.5 mg | carbs 8.5 g | fibre 3 g | sugars 3.3 g | protein 3.4 g | calcium 120.2 mg | iron 1 mg

Ron Russell, owner of SunCafe in Los Angeles, makes amazing fermented cheeses. I invited Ron to experiment in my kitchen and we made a game-changing discovery: kombucha and probiotic powder, used together to culture cheese, gives a taste and texture really close to dairy. Ferment your cheeze in a very warm space in the house or in a dehydrator. I prefer fermenting outside the dehydrator because the result is a milder cheeze with a more subtle character. Once you've cultured your cheeze, serve it with a buffet of veggies and crackers or slather it on sandwiches and wraps.

cultured cheeze

SERVES 8

280 g (10 oz) raw unsalted cashews, soaked (see page 171)

120 ml (4 fl oz) plain kombucha or rejuvelac

2 tbsp fresh lemon juice

2 tbsp finely chopped shallot

1½ tbsp nutritional yeast flakes

1 tsp natural salt (see page 139)

½ tsp garlic powder

½ tsp probiotic powder (see page 154)

optional boosters

½ tsp sweet paprika

Pinch of cayenne pepper

2 tbsp finely chopped chives

Throw the cashews, kombucha, lemon juice, shallot, nutritional yeast, salt, garlic powder and paprika and cayenne boosters into your blender, and blast on high for about 60 seconds until smooth and creamy. With a spatula, scrape the contents into a glass or ceramic bowl. With a non-reactive spoon (I use plastic or wood) gently stir in the probiotic powder and the chive booster. Line a small bowl or ceramic container with muslin or clingfilm and press in the cheeze mixture. Cover the bowl with a flour-sack cloth or other breathable cloth and put in a warm place (about 43°C/110°F). The cheeze will take about 24 hours to culture, depending on the strength of your probiotics and the temperature. The cheeze is ready when it is tangy.

Cover the cheeze and chill in the fridge for 6–8 hours to firm up further. (The cheeze will still have the consistency of soft cream cheese.) The cheeze will keep in the fridge for up to a week.

NUTRITIONAL FACTS (PER SERVING)

calories 211 kcal | fat 15.4 g | saturated fat 2.7 g | sodium 297 mg | carbs 13.3 g | fibre 2 g | sugars 3.5 g | protein 8 g | calcium 14.4 mg | iron 2.5 mg

Loaded with alkaline-rich vegetables, this seaweed salad is great for your gut. Wakame and hijiki rehydrate in minutes and, as sea veg go, are mild mannered. The aquarium aroma that may make you gag is smothered by the orange-miso dressing, which makes any salad seriously sexy. (At least my pals Mika and Toshiko said so!) If you're still wary of these weeds, assemble the rest of the salad with the familiar ingredients, dress it, *then* sea-son to taste.

sea the probiotic potential

SERVES 6 AS A STARTER, 4 AS A MEAL; DRESSING MAKES 300 ML (10 FL OZ)

dressing

1¼ tsp finely grated orange zest

120 ml (4 fl oz) fresh orange juice

95 g (3½ oz) white miso paste

2 tbsp apple cider vinegar

1 tbsp extra virgin olive oil

1 tbsp gluten-free soy sauce or tamari

1 tbsp finely chopped fresh ginger

2 tsp coconut nectar or other liquid sweetener

1 tsp toasted sesame oil

1 tsp finely chopped garlic (about 1 clove)

Pinch of cayenne pepper

salad

18 g (½ oz) dried hijiki

10 g (¼ oz) dried wakame

70 g (2½ oz) curly kale, stalks removed, leaves cut into ribbons

200 g (7 oz) red cabbage, shredded

60 g (2¼ oz) carrots, peeled and shaved (I use a vegetable peeler)

70 g (2½ oz) English cucumber (do not peel), julienned

27 g (1 oz) mooli, peeled and julienned

Natural salt (see page 139) and freshly ground black pepper

25 g (1 oz) Love Your Gut (page 164) or other cultured vegetables

optional boosters

32 g (1 oz) salad onion (green part only), diagonally sliced

35 g (1¼ oz) blanched flaked almonds

1 avocado, stoned, peeled and sliced

Make the dressing first to allow the flavours to develop. Throw the dressing ingredients into your blender and blast on high for 30–60 seconds until smooth and creamy. Chill in the fridge while you soak the seaweeds.

Place the hijiki and wakame into two separate bowls and soak in room-temperature filtered water for 5–15 minutes until soft and expanded. Drain and squeeze out excess water. Set aside.

In a large bowl, toss together the kale, cabbage, carrot, cucumber, mooli and the salad onion booster. Add the dressing and toss to evenly coat. Toss in the almond booster and season to taste with salt and pepper. Serve topped with the cultured vegetables and the avocado booster.

NUTRITIONAL FACTS (PER SERVING, BASED ON 6 SERVINGS)

calories 101 kcal | fat 4.3 g | saturated fat 0.6 g | sodium 798.2 mg | carbs 13.6 g | fibre 2.5 g | sugars 6.1 g | protein 3.5 g | calcium 53.8 mg | iron 1.1 mg

Miso's probiotic potential is primo, and its taste, blended up in this soup with carrot, ginger and coriander, is dy-no-mite. Brands of white miso vary in strength and flavour, so if your carrots cry out for more, add to taste, in half teaspoon increments. Since miso's medicinal magic diminishes and soon dies with high heat, to reap all the rewards, blend in the paste only once the soup has cooled a bit.

crazy-amazing carrot

SERVES 8 AS A STARTER, 6 AS A MAIN

soup

2 tbsp grapeseed oil
or extra virgin olive oil

300 g (10½ oz) yellow onion, diced

33 g (1 oz) celery, diced

1 tbsp finely chopped garlic (about 3 cloves)

Natural salt (see page 139)

1.3 kg (3 lb) carrots, diced

1.9 litres (3⅓ pints) vegetable stock, plus extra as needed

21 g (¾ oz) finely chopped coriander root (or stems)

2 tbsp finely chopped fresh ginger

71 g (2½ oz) white miso paste, plus extra to taste (see intro)

green beans

2 tsp toasted sesame oil

140 g (5 oz) green beans, chopped into 1 cm (½ in) pieces

¼ tsp natural salt (see page 139)

optional boosters

⅛ tsp ground turmeric

Pinch of cayenne pepper

Fresh lemon juice, to serve

To make the soup, in a large pot, heat the oil over a medium heat and sauté the onion, celery, garlic and a pinch of salt for about 5 minutes until the vegetables are soft and translucent. Add the carrots, stock, coriander root, ginger, ¼ teaspoon of salt and the turmeric and cayenne boosters. Bring to the boil, then simmer, partially covered, stirring occasionally, for about 30 minutes until the carrots are tender. Remove the pot from the heat and allow to cool for about 5 minutes. Stir in the miso and purée the soup in batches in your blender on high until smooth and creamy. (For conventional blenders, remove the small centre lid cap and cover the opening with a tea towel so steam can escape while you blend.) Add more vegetable stock for a thinner consistency, if desired. Tweak the salt to taste and warm gently over a low heat.

To make the green beans, heat the sesame oil over a medium heat and sauté the green beans with the salt for about 3 minutes until the beans are al dente. Drain on a kitchen paper-lined plate to soak up the excess oil. Ladle the soup into bowls and top each with green beans and a tiny splash of the lemon juice booster.

NUTRITIONAL FACTS (PER SERVING, BASED ON 8 SERVINGS)

calories 147 kcal | fat 7.4 g | saturated fat 2.3 g | sodium 584.2 mg | carbs 19.3 g | fibre 5.4 g | sugars 8.4 g | protein 3.2 g | calcium 70.7 mg | iron 1.1 mg

For optimal health, we need to support and maintain the gut's bacterial buddies. One of the best ways (if not the best) is eating live-cultured vegetables. To replenish friendly intestinal flora, aid digestion, boost immunity and cleanse, I enjoy a healthy scoop of fermented vegetables, pickles or sauerkraut with every meal. This blend is a simple one, and a great way to get into the probiotic practice. To fire up flavour and detox potential, add the wakame, apple cider vinegar and mooli.

love your gut

MAKES APPROXIMATELY 880 G (1 LB 15 OZ) CULTURED VEGETABLES

2 heads green cabbage

2 medium leeks
(white parts only)

1 carrot

1 green apple

25 g (1 oz) finely chopped flat-leaf parsley

3 tbsp natural salt (see page 139), plus extra to taste

1½ tsp finely grated lemon zest

4 tbsp fresh lemon juice

2 tbsp finely chopped fresh ginger

1½ tbsp finely chopped garlic (about 4 cloves)

⅛ tsp cayenne pepper, plus extra to taste

optional boosters

2 tbsp dried wakame, soaked for 5 minutes in filtered water, then drained and chopped

2 tbsp grated mooli

2 tsp apple cider vinegar

Remove the outer leaves from the cabbages. Wash these leaves and set them aside. (You will use these leaves when packing the jars.) Using a mandoline or a food processor, shred the cabbage. You should have 1.1 kg (2 lb 7 oz) cabbage. Then wash and shred the leeks; you should have 178 g (6 oz). Grate the carrot; you should have 110 g (4 oz). Finally, core and shred the apple; you should have about 125 g (4½ oz).

In a large mixing bowl, combine the shredded veggies, the parsley and the salt. Using your hands, massage the salt into the vegetables for about 5 minutes. This will begin to draw out the liquid from the vegetables; the mixture will reduce significantly in volume. Add the lemon zest, lemon juice, ginger, garlic and cayenne. Add the wakame and the mooli and apple cider vinegar boosters. Tweak the salt and cayenne to taste. (The mixture makes a delicious salad at this point.)

Measure out 440 g (15½ oz) of the vegetables along with some of the juices and put it into your blender. Pulse just a few times, until you have a coarse, soupy pulp (you may have to add a tiny bit of water). Return the pulsed veggies to the shredded mixture and stir well.

Pack the vegetables as tightly as possible into canning jars or stainless steel canisters using a potato masher or heavy spoon to push the vegetables down. Get as much of the air out as possible but leave about 6 cm (2½ in) at the top of each container for expansion. Roll 2 or 3 of the reserved cabbage leaves into tight 'cigars' and place them on top of the vegetables

to fill the remaining space. Seal the containers and leave them to sit at room temperature (21°C/70°F) or slightly warmer (to accelerate fermentation) for at least 4 days, but preferably 7 days. The key is to have a stable temperature, so if you don't have an area that offers that, wrap the jars in towels and place them in a cooler. Don't let the jars sit in direct sunlight. In warm weather, the vegetables will take 3 to 4 days to culture. If you're using jars with screw-top lids, open the jars halfway through fermentation to let gas escape. You may also have to pour out a bit of the liquid if it rises above the level of the shredded vegetables.

After 3 or 4 days, when you hear the vegetables bubbling, taste them and keep tasting every day until they have the right tanginess for you. Once the veggies are ready, place the containers in the fridge to slow the fermentation. The cultured vegetables will keep in the fridge for up to 8 months.

NUTRITIONAL FACTS (PER SERVING, BASED ON 32 SERVINGS)

calories 21 kcal | fat 0.1 g | saturated fat 0.03 g | sodium 373.7 mg | carbs 5 g | fibre 1.7 g | sugars 2.7 g | protein 0.9 g | calcium 27.5 mg | iron 0.4 mg

cultured coconut & mango parfait

SERVES 4; MAKES ABOUT 460 G (16 OZ) YOGURT

yogurt

180 ml (6 fl oz) full-fat
canned coconut milk
(shake, then pour)

360 g (12 oz) young
coconut meat

½ tsp probiotic powder (see
page 154)

1 tbsp fresh lemon juice

½ tsp natural vanilla extract

2 ripe fresh mangoes, peeled,
stoned and diced

10 g (¼ oz) unsweetened
coconut flakes

35 g (1¼ oz) blanched
flaked almonds

1 tsp finely grated
lime zest

optional boosters

1 tbsp yacon syrup
(see page 211)

1 tbsp coconut oil
(in liquid form)

1 tbsp inulin powder
(see page 155)

To make the yogurt, throw the coconut milk and coconut meat into your blender and blast on high for about 1 minute until smooth and creamy. The mixture will be very thick. Transfer this mixture to a glass or ceramic bowl. With a non-reactive wooden or plastic implement (not stainless steel), stir in the probiotic powder. Cover the bowl and place it in a dehydrator at 46°C (115°F) for 8–10 hours until cultured and tangy. (Depending on the strength of your probiotic powder, fermenting times will vary.) If you don't have a dehydrator, place the covered bowl in a warm place with good airflow for about 24 hours. Your yogurt may develop a thin skin. This is edible and can be stirred into the yogurt. But if you prefer not to consume it, gently skim it off the top and discard. Once the yogurt is cultured to your liking, add the lemon juice, vanilla and the yacon booster to taste. Stir in the coconut oil and inulin powder boosters.

To assemble the yogurt parfaits, spoon 115 g (4 oz) of the yogurt into each of four short glasses. Top each with 110 g (4 oz) of the diced mango and 1 tablespoon of the coconut flakes, 1 tablespoon of the blanched almonds and ¼ teaspoon of the lime zest.

NUTRITIONAL FACTS (PER SERVING)

calories 555 kcal | fat 44.3 g | saturated fat 36.5 g | sodium 26.3 mg | carbs 42.3 g | fibre 12 g | sugars 29.2 g | protein 6.6 g | calcium 55.8 mg | iron 4.2 mg

This extra-thick coconut yogurt tastes pretty darn close to the Greek kind. I make a batch every few days and top it with seasonal fruit, nuts and seeds for a probiotic-rich breakfast, snack or dessert. Add the inulin powder booster to encourage probiotic proliferation. Like any yogurt, it's delicious with berries. This combo of coconut, almond and lime zest is my personal favourite. The tang of plain yogurt works in sweet or savoury dishes. Add a splash of yacon syrup (a prebiotic) or stevia for sweet applications. But hold back on adding any flavourings until the yogurt has fully cultured, or the fermentation may be disrupted. Once the culturing's done, add lemon juice to get the balance you like, then add the sweetener. This yogurt gets tangier as it chills and will keep – and develop – in the fridge for up to a week.

CHAPTER 11

well combined

well combined

Food combining works by the premise that the body can digest just one concentrated food (starch or protein) at a time. Starch digestion calls for alkaline conditions; protein-digesting enzymes thrive in an acidic environment. Tackling starch and protein at once, digestive processes have to work at cross-purposes – among other things, taxing the liver and leading to fatigue. Well-combined meals match foods for optimal digestion, so increasing assimilation of nutrients. While food combining practice anchors only some of my recipes, I do employ it in my daily life, and many people tell me this works for them, too. Making things easier, the foods here combine well with everything, so they're my go-to heroes.

lemon and lime

These citrus superstars, low in sugar and loaded with nutrients, play well with all foods. Chemically acidic, but triggering an alkaline-forming response once they've moved out of the stomach, these fruits help neutralize acids to balance pH levels in the lower digestive tract. Citric acid stimulates enzymes and dissolves oxalates, aiding digestion, while ascorbic acid fights free radicals. Bursting with antioxidant phytonutrients (carotenoids and flavonols) that act as antibiotics, these immunity aces are a splendid source of vitamin C. Their alkaline buffers and B vitamins strengthen fat-metabolizing enzymes in the liver, flush toxins from the blood, calm inflammation, build collagen, maintain healthy mucus membranes and block abnormal cell division. The peels are particularly rich in antioxidants, so zest for added nutrition and flavour. Whole (peeled), juiced or zested, lemon and lime lift the pungency of leafy greens, green powders and earthy roots in smoothies. Enhancing the flavour of sweet and savoury dishes, they counterbalance sugars, too.

spinach

Leafy greens are like dream guests at a dinner party – they enliven the table and get along with everyone. In combining fats with proteins or starches, adding leafy greens counteracts fats' inhibiting effects on gastric secretion, so digestion isn't impaired. Mild but not meek, spinach energizes – with folate to calm inflammation and reduce stress and fatigue. Spinach buddies up folate and other B vitamins with antioxidant and anti-inflammatory agents vitamins A, C and K; omega-3s; chlorophyll; and alkaline buffer minerals (see page 138). It also provides protein to boost brain activity, build and oyxgenate blood, strengthen cells and promote respiratory, heart, bone, skin and eye health. Packed with fibre, this leafy legend is prebiotic, too, feeding friendly bacteria. Throw some raw into a smoothie, salad, dip, sauce or dressing, or cook lightly in soups, stews, stir-fries and pastas.

avocado

A non-starchy vege-fruit, full of fabulous fats, this green goddess loves to be worshipped on her own, and with everything edible. A medium avo contains a whopping 30 g of fat – mostly heart-healthy monounsaturates that (drum roll, please): absorb acids; tame toxins; balance hormones and blood sugar; metabolize fats; regulate cholesterol; lubricate the skin, tissues and joints; and energize and support the adrenals. Combining avocado with low-fat foods like sweet potato, tomato and leafy greens ups the absorption of carotenoids. Another key combo: avo and tomato – the absorption of lutein and lycopene both surge (awesome for prostate health). Commanding an army of antioxidants – vitamins A, C, E and K and glutathione, as well as protein, fibre, alkalizing chlorophyll, potassium and B vitamins – this anti-inflammatory amazon delivers the detox. Add her to smoothies, salads, dressings, sauces, soups, stews, dips and sandwiches.

tomatoes

Low in calories and sugar, tomatoes are phytonutrient phenoms, providing antioxidant, anti-inflammatory aid to the liver, kidneys, bones, blood and heart, purifying the blood and flushing toxins from the liver and gallbladder. High in lycopene (heavy in the skins), they combat abnormal cell growth and regulate fat metabolism and cholesterol. Beta-carotene, flavonoids, fibre and vitamins A, C and E also help fight infection, while vitamin

K and potassium regulate heart rate and blood pressure and help iron build blood. Tomatoes neutralize acidity (especially when eaten raw). A nightshade, tomato can aggravate inflammation associated with certain health conditions, but calms inflammation for most of us. Cooking tomato increases its acidity, but ups the availability of lycopene. To get all of fresh tomatoes' benefits, include them raw in salsa, dips, salads, smoothies and gazpacho; cook them in sauces, stews and soups. Blended with fresh, sun-dried and canned tomatoes punch up flavour for a terrific tomato trip.

courgette and other summer squash

Summer squashes calm inflammation and are excellent sources of copper and manganese, helping build blood cells, connective tissue and collagen for brain, bone and nerve health. Courgette, rich in antioxidant flavonols, carotenoids, vitamin C, potassium and fibre, combats oxidative damage to cells. With carb-metabolizing B vitamins, alkaline minerals and omega-3s, it's great for weight loss, and its structured polysaccharides (unusually high in pectin) help to stabilize blood sugar. Frozen peeled courgette fortifies and creams smoothies without any funky flavour. That said, most of the antioxidants and fibre are in the skins, so for a low-carb, enzyme-rich, non-starchy pasta, spiralize courgettes into 'courgetti'.

wheatgrass

This green rejuvenating machine is among the most nutrient dense foods. Rich in alkalizing chlorophyll and protein (about 85 per cent by weight), and loaded with vitamins, minerals, live enzymes, antioxidants and anti-inflammatory agents, wheatgrass neutralizes acids and wastes for oxygenated blood and optimal cellular function and immunity. It's a potent booster for smoothies, juices and raw dressings, sauces and desserts. Freeze-dried powder is not only more convenient than fresh juice, it's milder and more versatile. Up to 1 teaspoon of the powder goes unnoticed in a blend containing sweet fruits or lemon juice.

good food combinations

- Fruit + Protein Fats (nuts and seeds)
- Protein + Non-starchy Veg or Sea Veg
- Protein + Fats and Oils
- Protein Fats + Non-starchy Veg or Sea Veg
- Starchy Veg or Grains + Non-starchy Veg or Sea Veg
- Leafy Greens + Anything

soaking

Soak nuts, seeds and grains in filtered water in a glass or non-reactive metal vessel. The easiest way to incorporate long soaking into your lifestyle is to soak right before bed, then rinse, drain and dry upon rising. Alternatively, soak them in the morning to use at night.

nuts, seeds and grains

the quick way: Cover with boiling water; leave to stand for 10 minutes. The downside is heat destroys live enzymes.

the better but slower way: Submerge in filtered water with $1/2$ teaspoon of salt and 1 teaspoon of lemon juice or vinegar per litre ($1^3/4$ pints); wait the recommended time.

either way: Discard the soaking liquid – it contains anti-nutrients – and rinse the food

dried fruits and vegetables

quick: Chop; cover with boiling water; wait 10 minutes.

better: Cover with filtered water or your recipe's base liquid and let stand until the food is soft.

No anti-nutrients here, so no need to rinse. Use the soaking liquid for a fuller flavour.

From left: Rest and Re-treat (page 182),
Taste of Thailand (opposite)

Lemongrass is divine in a smoothie. Blended with coconut, lime, avocado and chilli, it's mystically mind-blowing. Tweak the lemongrass and chilli depending on your preference and the strength of your ingredients. The boosters don't alter flavour, but aid the anti-inflammatory immunity agents, and give you more energy. Really cold, right out of the blender, this puts you on the beach at Phuket.

taste of thailand

SERVES 2

420 ml (15 fl oz) full-fat canned coconut milk (shake, then pour)

½ tsp probiotic powder (see page 154, optional)

1 tsp finely grated lime zest, plus extra to taste

2 tbsp fresh lime juice, plus extra to taste

½ small avocado, stoned and peeled

2 tbsp finely chopped fresh lemongrass, plus extra to taste (see intro and Note, below)

2 tsp deseeded and finely chopped green chilli, plus extra to taste (see intro)

57 g (2 oz) chopped pitted dates, soaked (see page 171), plus extra to taste

Pinch of natural salt (see page 139), plus extra to taste

1 medium banana, sliced (fresh or frozen)

250 g (9 oz) ice cubes

optional boosters

1 tbsp coconut oil (in liquid form)

1 tsp wheatgrass powder (see page 171)

Pinch of ground turmeric, plus extra to taste

Throw the coconut milk, probiotic powder, lime zest, lime juice, avocado, lemongrass, chilli, dates, salt and the boosters into your blender and blast on high for 30–60 seconds until well combined. Add the banana and ice and blast again for 10–20 seconds until smooth and creamy. Tweak the lime zest and juice, lemongrass, chilli, dates, salt and turmeric to taste.

Note: To use fresh lemongrass, remove the tough outer layers and cut off the ends. Slit the stalk lengthways, smash the stalk halves with a heavy knife or meat tenderizer to release the oils and fragrance and then finely chop.

NUTRITIONAL FACTS (PER SERVING)

calories 587 kcal | fat 47.6 g | saturated fat 38.2 g | sodium 180.3 mg | carbs 46.2 g | fibre 6 g | sugars 26.8 g | protein 6.1 g | calcium 71.7 mg | iron 7.6 mg

Cheezy and sinfully scarfable, this dip dumbfounds even devout artichoke-and-spinach aficionados. 'There's *no* dairy!?' Turmeric and chilli flakes spike the flavour fever, and sliced almonds add a crazy kinda crunch.

baked spinach & artichoke dip

SERVES 6–8

4 tbsp extra virgin olive oil

150 g (5½ oz) yellow onion, diced

1 tbsp finely chopped garlic (about 3 cloves)

1½ tsp natural salt (see page 139)

1 (349 g/12 oz) packet firm silken tofu, drained

25 g (1 oz) nutritional yeast flakes

2 tbsp white miso paste

2 tbsp fresh lemon juice

340 g (12 oz) baby spinach, cut into ribbons

340 g (12 oz) frozen artichokes, rinsed, drained and finely chopped

2 tbsp finely chopped flat-leaf parsley

optional boosters

¼ tsp ground turmeric

⅛ tsp chilli flakes

80 g (3 oz) sliced raw almonds

Preheat the oven to 180°C/350°F/Gas mark 4. Lightly grease a small square or round ovenproof serving dish with olive oil.

Heat 1 tablespoon of the olive oil in a large frying pan over a medium-high heat and sauté the onion and garlic with a pinch of the salt for 5 minutes until the onion is soft and translucent. Allow to cool slightly, then transfer this mixture to your blender. Add 2 tablespoons of the olive oil, the remaining salt, the tofu, nutritional yeast, miso, lemon juice and the turmeric and red chilli flake boosters and blast on high for 30–60 seconds until smooth and creamy. Transfer to a large mixing bowl.

In the same pan, heat the remaining 1 tablespoon of olive oil over a medium heat and gradually add the spinach, stirring and cooking until just wilted. This should take less than a minute. Stir in the artichokes and mix thoroughly. Stir the spinach and artichokes into the bowl with the onion mixture until well combined.

Pour the mixture into the prepared serving dish and bake, uncovered, for about 1 hour, or until just cracking on the top and lightly browned. Allow to cool for about 10 minutes (to let the dip solidify a bit), then serve warm, topped with the parsley and the almond booster.

NUTRITIONAL FACTS (PER SERVING, BASED ON 6 SERVINGS)

calories 200 kcal | fat 12.3 g | saturated fat 1.9 g | sodium 924.1 mg | carbs 15.8 g | fibre 7.2 g | sugars 3 g | protein 11.9 g | calcium 230.5 mg | iron 4.3 mg

Decadent desserts present a challenge if you want to follow traditional food-combining principles because sugar and sweeteners don't combine well with anything. But this recipe turns the optimal combo of fruit and nuts into dessert dynamite. Blending nut milk, dates and chia creates a five-minute healthy pudding that you can top with whatever fresh fruit you have on hand. This version with almond extract has gourmet flavour that hints at marzipan. Go with the hemp seed and flax boosters for added antioxidants and anti-inflammatory omega-3s, and garnish with berries for gorgeous presentation. Fully loaded or without the boosters, this one's the ultimate almond joy.

a date with a nut

SERVES 2

480 ml (17 fl oz) unsweetened almond milk (strained if homemade)

57 g (2 oz) chopped pitted dates, soaked (see page 171)

1 tsp natural almond extract

Pinch of natural salt (see page 139)

53 g (1¾ oz) black chia seeds

53 g (1¾ oz) sliced raw almonds, plus extra to garnish

optional boosters

80 g (3 oz) fresh raspberries or strawberries

1 tbsp shelled hemp seeds

1 tbsp ground flaxseeds

Throw the almond milk, dates, almond extract and salt into your blender and blast on high for about 30 seconds until the dates are pulverized.

Transfer this mixture to a mixing bowl and whisk in the chia seeds until well combined. Chill in the fridge for about 2 hours, stirring occasionally to evenly distribute the chia seeds, until chilled and thickened.

Add the almonds and stir to evenly distribute the chia and almonds.

To serve, spoon the pudding into two serving glasses or bowls and garnish with sliced almonds and the berry, hemp seed and ground flaxseed boosters.

NUTRITIONAL FACTS (PER SERVING)

calories 495 kcal | fat 32.4 g | saturated fat 1.9 g | sodium 196 mg | carbs 43.3 g | fibre 17.1 g | sugars 21.3 g | protein 15.2 g | calcium 350.6 mg | iron 4.1 mg

tricked-up tabouli

SERVES 6–8; DRESSING MAKES 180 ML (6 FL OZ)

½ large head cauliflower, cut into florets

200 g (7 oz) finely chopped flat-leaf parsley (about 4 large bunches)

340 g (12 oz) tomato, deseeded and diced

300 g (10½ oz) English cucumber, peeled, deseeded and diced

140 g (5 oz) red pepper, deseeded and diced

80 g (3 oz) salad onion, finely chopped (white and green parts)

75 g (2¾ oz) red onion, diced

20 g (¾ oz) finely chopped mint

2 tbsp finely chopped dill

70 g (2½ oz) shelled hemp seeds

1 tsp natural salt (see page 139), plus extra to taste

¼ tsp freshly ground black pepper, plus extra to taste

dressing

80 ml (2¾ fl oz) extra virgin olive oil

¼ tsp finely grated lemon zest

6 tbsp fresh lemon juice, plus extra to taste

1 tbsp finely chopped garlic (about 3 cloves)

¾ tsp ground allspice, plus extra to taste

optional boosters

270 g (9½ oz) cooked chickpeas or 1 (425 g/15 oz) can chickpeas, rinsed and drained

80 g (3 oz) gherkins, diced

⅛ tsp chilli flakes, plus extra to taste

Put the cauliflower in a food processor and pulse a few times, until the cauliflower has the texture of couscous. You should have about 390 g (13¾ oz) of cauliflower 'rice'.

Transfer the 'rice' to a large mixing bowl and combine well with the parsley, tomato, cucumber, pepper, onions, mint, dill and hemp seeds. Add the chickpea and gherkin boosters.

To make the dressing, throw the olive oil, lemon zest, lemon juice, garlic, allspice and the red chilli flake booster into your blender and blast on high for about 30 seconds until the dressing is emulsified and the garlic has been completely pulverized.

Pour the dressing over the salad and toss well to evenly combine. Add the salt and pepper and tweak the lemon juice, allspice, chilli flakes, salt and pepper to taste. Serve immediately for the best flavour.

NUTRITIONAL FACTS (PER SERVING, BASED ON 6 SERVINGS)

calories 220 kcal | fat 16.5 g | saturated fat 2.5 g | sodium 483.3 mg | carbs 16.2 g | fibre 5.3 g | sugars 6.1 g | protein 6.3 g | calcium 107.7 mg | iron 3.9 mg

With cauliflower rice stepping in for cracked wheat, the classic Middle Eastern salad goes raw and grain-free. Loaded with hydrating, alkaline ingredients, this version is a cleansing superstar. Its aromatic elements – herbs, allspice and lemon zest – enliven the sweet fruits and vegetables. The pickles come in with crunch, tanginess and probiotics; the chilli flakes stimulate digestion and help flush your system. For the most balanced flavour profile, consume the tabouli as soon as it's dressed. If you're not serving it right away, chill the salad and the dressing separately, and combine just when you're ready to serve.

Artichoke addicts: forget the trimming, stemming and steaming to get your fix. This dish gets to the heart of the matter with a fraction of the work. Awesome served hot or cold, this rich, velvety soup doubles as a sauce for grains or cooked veg. Defrosted frozen hearts will deliver the best flavour. If you use canned, make sure they're packed in water (not marinated), rinse thoroughly and squeeze out liquid to avoid a salty-sour blast that mars the bliss. Add lemon juice to taste to complement the character of your 'chokes. For a truly righteous ride, add the thyme and truffle boosters; or, to temper the artichoke element, work in an additional 50–100 g (1³⁄₄–3¹⁄₂ oz) of cauliflower.

artichoke ace

SERVES 6 AS A STARTER, 4 AS A MAIN

2 tbsp grapeseed oil
or extra virgin olive oil

300 g (10½ oz) yellow onion,
diced

2 tsp finely chopped garlic
(about 2 cloves)

Natural salt (see page 139)

100 g (3½ oz) cauliflower
florets, chopped

1.4 litres (2½ pints) vegetable
stock

720 g (1 lb 9 oz) thawed frozen
artichoke hearts or 3
(240 g/8½ oz) cans artichokes
in water (see intro)

Freshly ground black pepper

35 g (1¼ oz) blanched
flaked almonds

1½ tbsp fresh lemon juice,
plus extra to serve

optional boosters

1½ tsp finely chopped fresh
thyme, plus extra to taste

2 tsp truffle oil

1 tbsp finely chopped
flat-leaf parsley

In a large saucepan, heat the oil over a medium heat and sauté the onion and garlic with a pinch of salt for about 5 minutes until the onion is soft and translucent. Add the cauliflower and sauté for another minute. Add the vegetable stock, artichokes, ½ teaspoon of salt and pepper; increase the heat to high and bring just to the boil. Reduce the heat to medium and simmer, uncovered, for about 20 minutes until the cauliflower is just tender. Remove the pan from the heat, stir in the almonds and the thyme booster and allow the soup to cool slightly.

Working in batches, pour the soup into your blender and purée on high for 30–60 seconds until smooth and creamy. (For conventional blenders, remove the small centre lid cap and cover the opening with a tea towel so steam can escape while you blend.) Return the soup to the saucepan, add ½ teaspoon of salt, the lemon juice and truffle oil booster. Tweak the salt, pepper, lemon juice and thyme to taste, and warm the soup over a low heat. (This soup also tastes phenomenal cold.)

Ladle the soup into bowls and garnish each bowl with pepper and the parsley booster. Pass lemon juice, pepper and salt around the table.

NUTRITIONAL FACTS (PER SERVING, BASED ON 6 SERVINGS)

calories 159 kcal | fat 7.8 g | saturated fat 0.7 g | sodium 543.6 mg | carbs 20.3 g | fibre 8.5 g | sugars 4.1 g | protein 6.2 g | calcium 95.1 mg | iron 2 mg

Pasta and cream sauces are all but impossible to combine well for optimal digestion since the nut-, soya-, seed- or dairy-based sauce involves considerable protein and the noodles are high in carbs. This raw, low-carb, grain-free version anchored to courgette noodles is fabulous – rich, creamy, super tasty and surprisingly filling. A sprinkle of Seed Cheeze (see page 13) ups the indulgence, and the turmeric and cayenne boosters spike flavour while adding a warming quality to balance the high-raw experience. This sauce does brilliant work with steamed veggies, and if you're not concerned with food combining, is superb on cooked conventional pasta, too.

pine-macfredo

SERVES 4; SAUCE MAKES 486 G (17 OZ)

sauce

180 ml (6 fl oz) filtered water

5 tbsp fresh lemon juice

2 tbsp extra virgin olive oil

105 g (3½ oz) raw unsalted macadamias, soaked (see page 171)

105 g (3½ oz) raw pine nuts, soaked (see page 171)

2 tsp finely chopped garlic (about 2 cloves)

1½ tbsp white miso paste

1 tbsp finely chopped yellow onion

1 tbsp finely chopped fresh thyme

1 tsp natural salt (see page 139), plus extra to taste

⅛ tsp freshly ground white pepper, plus extra to taste

4 medium green courgettes

90 g (3¼ oz) broccoli florets, finely chopped

40 g (1½ oz) salad onion (white and green parts), finely chopped

70 g (2½ oz) raw pine nuts

12 g (½ oz) finely chopped flat-leaf parsley

optional boosters

¼ tsp ground turmeric

Pinch of cayenne pepper

55 g (2 oz) Seed Cheeze (see page 13)

To make the sauce, throw all of the ingredients into your blender, including the turmeric and cayenne boosters, and blast on high for about 1 minute until smooth and creamy. Tweak salt and pepper to taste.

Cut the ends off the courgettes and use a spiralizer to create long spaghetti-style noodles. Or use a vegetable peeler to shave thin fettucine-style noodles. You should have 800 g (1 lb 12 oz).

In a large bowl, toss the 'noodles', the broccoli and salad onion with about 364 g (13 oz) of the sauce, adding more sauce as needed. Stir in the pine nuts and parsley. Season to taste with salt and white pepper. Swirl portions onto plates or into bowls, and pass extra sauce and the Seed Cheeze booster around the table.

NUTRITIONAL FACTS (PER SERVING)

calories 609 kcal | fat 57.8 g | saturated fat 6.5 g | sodium 858 mg | carbs 21.8 g | fibre 7.5 g | sugars 9.3 g | protein 12.4 g | calcium 99.2 mg | iron 5.2 mg

At our cleanse retreats, Karen Kipp shares two sleep-aid secrets: rub a few drops of lavender oil on the soles of your feet at bedtime, and drink this blueberry-lavender milk (see photo on page 172). Lavender is potent, so start with an eighth of a teaspoon, and resist the urge to add more blueberries, as their gelatinous quality thickens the blend. Overdo that blue and your luxurious lavender tonic turns to slimy sludge. The drink separates with chilling, and loses its vibrant colour, so if you want to store it, seal in a glass jar and then shake to revive the prize. For purple perfection, add the coconut oil, maqui and açaí. They'll elevate the healing potential and boost your blend into a divine dimension.

rest and re-treat

SERVES 2

160 g (5¾ oz) raw whole almonds, soaked (see page 171)

720 ml (1¼ pints) filtered water

43 g (1½ oz) chopped pitted dates, soaked (see page 171), plus extra to taste

80 g (3 oz) fresh blueberries

½ tsp probiotic powder (see page 154)

½ tsp natural vanilla extract, plus extra to taste

⅛ tsp edible fresh lavender (leaves), plus extra to taste

¼ tsp ground cinnamon, plus extra to taste

Pinch of natural salt (see page 139)

optional boosters

1 tbsp coconut oil (in liquid form)

1 tsp maqui powder (see page 107)

1 tsp açaí powder (see page 122)

Throw the almonds, water and dates into your blender and blast on high for 30–60 seconds until the ingredients are pulverized. Strain with a filtration bag, nut milk bag or sheer piece of clean nylon hosiery and pour the strained liquid back into the blender. Add the blueberries, probiotic powder, vanilla, lavender, cinnamon, salt and the boosters, and blast for another 60 seconds until smooth and creamy. Tweak the dates, vanilla, lavender and cinnamon to taste and enjoy chilled or gently warmed.

NUTRITIONAL FACTS (PER SERVING)

calories 84 kcal | fat 0.2 g | saturated fat 0 g | sodium 160.3 mg | carbs 21.9 g | fibre 2.5 g | sugars 18.1 g | protein 0.7 g | calcium 30 mg | iron 0.3 mg

Because I slather gobs of this on just about anything, I had to put myself in handcuffs so I wouldn't work it into every recipe. For a creamy texture, you just gotta soak those cashews. Chill the cream in the fridge for a few hours, preferably overnight, so the flavours mingle and the blend thickens. Boost with cauliflower to ramp up nutrition, and with onion powder and chives for a magical middle note. I use this on Nosh-on-'em-nachos (page 10), Punched-up Potato & Leek (page 190), Gentle Lentils (page 59) and Minty Peas Please! (page 147). It keeps in the fridge for about 5 days, but never lasts that long.

so good! soured cream

MAKES 385 G (13½ OZ)

80 ml (2¾ fl oz) filtered water

2½ tbsp fresh lime juice, plus extra to taste

1½ tbsp apple cider vinegar, plus extra to taste

140 g (5 oz) raw unsalted cashews, soaked (see page 171)

2 tsp Dijon mustard

1 tsp finely chopped garlic (about 1 clove)

¾ tsp natural salt (see page 139), plus extra to taste

optional boosters

30 g (1 oz) raw cauliflower florets

1 tsp onion powder

1 tbsp finely chopped chives

Pour the water, lime juice and apple cider vinegar into the blender. Then add the cashews, mustard, garlic, salt and the cauliflower and onion powder boosters. Blast on high for about 1 minute until smooth and creamy. You may have to stop the machine periodically and scrape down the sides of the container. Tweak the lime juice, vinegar and salt to taste. Stir in the chive booster. Transfer to a container and chill in the fridge for a few hours to thicken.

NUTRITIONAL FACTS (PER SERVING, BASED ON 8 SERVINGS)

calories 99.5 kcal | fat 7.7 g | saturated fat 1.4 g | sodium 205.1 mg | carbs 5.9 g | fibre 0.7 g | sugars 1.2 g | protein 3.3 g | calcium 9.2 mg | iron 1.2 mg

CHAPTER 12

feed the soul

feed the soul

Food is one of the great pleasures of life, and healthy food can be fun, decadent and delicious. Here are some of my favourite foods that deliver fabulous flavour with powerful health-promoting benefits.

cacao

Loaded with live enzymes, anti-inflammatory agents and more nutrients and antioxidants than its roasted counterpart, raw cacao is the best chocolate fix going. Feel-good gratification extends way beyond the flavour and aroma. Cacao contains neurotransmitters that increase serotonin in the brain, and so elevate mood; its polyphenols, iron and magnesium oxygenate the body for energy; and the calcium, iron, zinc and potassium in cacao have got your heart, muscles and bones covered. Go easy though, as cacao contains the stimulant theobromine (similar in effect to caffeine) and can put a strain on the adrenals. Use raw cacao anywhere cocoa powder is called for. Add a tablespoon or more to home-made nut and seed milks, and mask the brown, sludgy look and earthy flavour of experimental green smoothies by going chocolate! Cacao goes crazy with a cutter like cayenne, and is thrown into euphoria with a splash of vanilla, almond, peppermint or orange extract.

aubergine

High in water and fibre and almost fat-free, aubergine is a heart-healthy fruit. It's a rich source of fabulous phenolic compounds – the predominant ones being chlorogenic acid and nasunin, two of the most potent antimicrobial and antiviral antioxidants known. Aubergine rages at free radicals, fighting proliferation of abnormal cells, cholesterol build-up and bacterial infections. Yes, aubergine is a nightshade and can aggravate arthritis; for most of us, though, this is delicious food with incredible versatility. Slice thinly for a low-carb alternative to conventional lasagne sheets, bake in slices or squares slathered with miso (see page 193), or sauté with oil and herbs for divine dining delights.

mint

Fresh flavour and medicinal magic make me a maniac for mint. Volatile oils in the leaves and stems (among them pain-relieving menthol) cool the body and banish bacteria to ease sore throats, clear respiratory congestion and relieve headaches. These oils are also dynamite for digestion and nifty for the nervous system. Rich in alkalizing minerals, fibre and antioxidant vitamins, mint cleanses the blood and bowels and supports strong bones and teeth. This herb adds a refreshing note to drinks, salads, dressings, sauces, soups and grains, and elevates a gross green smoothie up from the depths of undrinkable despair.

mango

An abundance of antioxidant vitamins A (beta-carotene), C and E, and phytonutrients in mangoes combat free radicals. With B vitamins, too, alkaline buffers and loads of pectin, mangoes enhance digestive, heart, eye and brain function, and promote gorgeous skin and hair. Mango's glutamine acid megaboosts mental power as well. Low in saturated fat, with a sensational sweetness and decadent buttery texture, mango is marvellous at bringing lush richness to smoothies and desserts.

onion

Like garlic, this polyphenol-filled, heart-healthy allium infuses foods with fantastic flavour. Cross the colour lines with yellow, white, red and green onions. With antiseptic, antibacterial and anti-inflammatory powers, onions relieve colds, gastrointestinal distress, arthritis and asthma. The combination of health-promoting sulfur compounds like allicin and flavonoids like quercetin stimulate production of antioxidant glutathione, one of the strongest allies of the liver and skin. Sulfuric oils stimulate mucus in the respiratory and digestive tracts, help to oxygenate blood by eliminating excess fat and protein deposits and build bone and connective tissue. The flavonoids are more concentrated in the outer layers, so discard only the papery skin (or the external sheath of a spring onion). The best news: cooking doesn't impair onions' powers, so sauté with reckless abandon!

watermelon

With succulent flesh that's over ninety per cent energizing vitamin- and mineral-rich water and loaded with sodium and potassium, this sweet melon hydrates to fight fatigue and replenish electrolytes. Packing in lycopene and glutathione antioxidants, watermelon is an anti-inflammatory ace, too, protecting the heart, bones, skin, respiratory system and prostate in men. It eases the symptoms of asthma and arthritis. Our kidneys convert the citrulline in watermelon to the amino acid arginine, which is a detox detonator. Watermelon's combo of vitamins A (through beta-carotene) and C ups immunity ammunition. Hop into the dried seeds — they're chock-full of protein, iron and zinc and have a buttery texture and flavour that falls somewhere between cashew and sunflower seeds. Watermelon seeds are sensational in salads and as a topping for desserts.

orange

Full of antioxidant phytonutrients, oranges are anti-inflammatory and antiviral warriors with abundant vitamins A (in the form of beta-carotene) and C, plus citrus limonoids to stimulate white blood cells, fend off free radicals and maintain mucus membranes for healthy skin and eyes. Calcium, potassium and copper chip in to protect our heart and bones. Despite its sweetness, orange rates as a low-GI food, its B vitamins helping convert food into fuel for energy and combating stress to aid brain and nerve function. The pectin in orange flesh clears toxins in the colon, aiding digestive regularity. And it's not just the juice and pulp that are beneficial: the flavonoid hesperidin, in the rind, is heart healthy, so zest away, and don't overlook the white pith! Orange, juice and flesh, adds sweetness to drinks, smoothies, dressings, sauces and desserts. To boost orange flavour, add zest — with caution, as it readily gets a bit bitter.

nutritional yeast flakes

This supplement is a gift from the vegan gods, adding umami and a cheesy flavour to sauces, dips, spreads, soups, veggie bakes and (of course) dairy-free cheeze. Far from *Candida albicans*, the yeast that feeds bacteria and fungus, nutritional yeast (or savoury yeast flakes) is the deactivated form of a primary yeast grown from a mixture of cane sugar and molasses. With a load of nourishing minerals and B vitamins, including B_{12} and 3 g of complete protein per tablespoon, this is the perfect blend of function and flavour.

more hero foods

- avocado

- banana

- berries (blackberries, blueberries, raspberries, strawberries)

- Bragg Liquid Aminos

- broccoli

- cauliflower

- chillies (fresh and dried)

- coconut

- courgette

- garlic

- herbs (such as basil, coriander, dill, oregano, parsley, rosemary, tarragon, thyme)

- miso

- natural salt

- nuts (such as almonds, cashews, macadamias, pecans, pistachios, walnuts)

- oils (such as coconut, flax, grapeseed, olive, sesame)

- pineapple

- seeds (such as chia, flax, hemp, poppy, pumpkin, sesame, sunflower)

- spices (such as cardamom, cinnamon, coriander, cumin, paprika, turmeric)

- sweeteners (dates, coconut nectar, coconut sugar, maple syrup, yacon syrup)

- tamari (wheat-free)

Frozen peeled courgette adds a fantastic frosty element to smoothies without changing the flavours! And the inclusion makes this sweet sip come off a tad less cheeky. Dates, maple syrup and cashews conjure up a caramel-like flavour. To heighten the effect, add the lucuma booster. The salted-caramel experience is sensational, but if you boost with the apple sauce, you may want to increase the salt to half a teaspoon, to nail that salted-caramel-apple taste. Whichever way you make it, this is dessert in a glass.

caramel cravings

SERVES 2

480 ml (17 fl oz) unsweetened almond milk (strained if homemade)

70 g (2½ oz) raw unsalted cashews, soaked (see page 171)

43 g (1½ oz) chopped pitted dates, soaked (see page 171), plus extra to taste

3 tbsp pure maple syrup, plus extra to taste

2 tbsp chia seeds (black or white)

1 tsp natural vanilla extract

½ tsp probiotic powder (see page 154, optional)

¼ tsp ground cinnamon, plus extra to taste

¼ tsp natural salt (see page 139), plus extra to taste (see intro, optional)

145 g (5 oz) frozen peeled and chopped courgette

62 g (2¼ oz) ice cubes

optional boosters

90 g (3¼ oz) unsweetened apple sauce

30 g (1 oz) frozen raw cauliflower florets

1 tsp lucuma powder (see page 211), plus extra to taste

Add the almond milk, cashews, dates, maple syrup, chia seeds, vanilla, probiotic powder, cinnamon and salt to your blender and blast on high for about 30 seconds until the ingredients are completely pulverized. Add the frozen courgette, ice and any boosters and blast again for a further 30 seconds until smooth and creamy. Tweak the dates, maple syrup, cinnamon, salt and lucuma to taste and enjoy immediately for the most balanced flavour.

NUTRITIONAL FACTS (PER SERVING)

calories 521 kcal | fat 29.4 g | saturated fat 3.1 g | sodium 353.1 mg | carbs 58.1 g | fibre 9.3 g | sugars 37.5 g | protein 13.8 g | calcium 223.8 mg | iron 4.4 mg

If you've got 30 minutes, you can whip up this sauce to throw over pasta, grains or cooked vegetables. I use it in Lick-your-plate Lasagne (page 16). It's great, too, as a base for tomato soup. Combining canned and sun-dried tomatoes delivers a depth of flavour while keeping this an inexpensive staple. Use fresh herbs, as they liven up the canned components, and boost with the carrot, celery and chilli flakes for even more flavour.

terrific tomato sauce

MAKES ABOUT 1.75 KG (3 LB 14 OZ)

2 tbsp grapeseed or extra virgin olive oil

300 g (10½ oz) onion, diced

1 tbsp finely chopped garlic (about 3 cloves)

1 tsp natural salt (see page 139), plus extra to taste

4 (400 g/14 oz) cans diced tomatoes with their juice

35 g (1¼ oz) sun-dried tomatoes packed in oil, drained, dried and roughly chopped

25 g (1 oz) finely chopped fresh basil leaves

25 g (1 oz) finely chopped flat-leaf parsley

2 tbsp finely chopped fresh thyme

2 tbsp finely chopped fresh oregano

360 ml (12 fl oz) vegetable stock

⅛ tsp freshly ground black pepper, plus extra to taste

1 tsp pure maple syrup (optional)

optional boosters

80 g (3 oz) carrots, diced

33 g (1¼ oz) celery, diced

¼ tsp chilli flakes

In a large pot over a medium heat, warm the oil and sauté the onion, garlic and ¼ teaspoon of salt for about 5 minutes until the onion is soft and translucent. Add the carrot, celery and chilli flake boosters and sauté for another 5 minutes until the carrot starts to soften. Add the canned tomatoes with their juice, sun-dried tomatoes, basil, parsley, thyme and oregano and stir to combine. Add the vegetable stock, black pepper and ½ teaspoon of the salt and bring to the boil. Reduce the heat to medium and simmer, partially covered and stirring occasionally, for about 15 minutes until slightly thickened. You don't want the liquid to reduce too much or you won't have sufficient sauce for the lasagne (see page 16). Allow to cool slightly, add the remaining ¼ teaspoon of salt, maple syrup, if liked, and tweak the salt and black pepper to taste. Purée in batches in your blender at medium speed for about 10 seconds, so the sauce is still rustic and somewhat chunky.

NUTRITIONAL FACTS (PER SERVING, BASED ON 14 SERVINGS)

calories 52 kcal | fat 2.4 g | saturated fat 0.4 g | sodium 189.6 mg | carbs 8 g | fibre 3.2 g | sugars 4.8 g | protein 1.6 g | calcium 61.2 mg | iron 1.2 mg

punched-up potato & leek

SERVES 8 AS A STARTER, 6 AS A MAIN

1 medium head garlic

1 tsp plus 2 tbsp extra virgin olive oil or grapeseed oil

1 kg (2 lb 4 oz) yellow potatoes (6 medium), peeled and diced

2 large leeks, roughly chopped (white and pale green parts)

33 g (1¼ oz) celery, diced

¾ tsp natural salt (see page 139), plus extra to taste

150 g (5½ oz) cauliflower florets, chopped

1.9 litres (3⅓ pints) vegetable stock

1 tsp mild yellow curry powder

70 g (2½ oz) raw unsalted cashews

1 tbsp fresh lemon juice, plus extra to serve

44 g (1½ oz) baby spinach, cut into ribbons

So Good! Soured Cream (page 183), to garnish

2 tbsp finely chopped chives

optional boosters

¼ tsp ground turmeric

Extra virgin olive oil

75 g (2¾ oz) raw unsalted cashews, roughly chopped

Preheat the oven to 180°C/350°F/Gas mark 4.

Remove the papery outer layers from the head of garlic, leaving it whole, with all cloves connected. Trim 6 mm (¼ in) off the top of the head to expose the cloves. Drizzle with the 1 teaspoon of olive oil. Wrap the head in baking paper, then in foil (to allow the garlic to steam and not burn, and to reduce aluminium transfer), and roast for 40–60 minutes until tender. Allow to cool, then squeeze the garlic pulp out of the skins and set aside. You should have 2–3 tablespoons of roasted garlic.

Rinse the diced potatoes to wash off some of the starch.

In a large saucepan, heat the remaining 2 tablespoons of olive oil over a medium heat and sauté the leeks and celery with ¼ teaspoon of salt for about 5 minutes until soft and translucent. Add the potatoes, the cauliflower, roasted garlic pulp and 1.65 litres (3 pints) of the vegetable stock. Increase the heat to high and bring just to the boil. Reduce the heat to medium-low and simmer for 10–15 minutes until the potato and cauliflower are just tender. Immediately remove the saucepan from the heat and allow the soup to cool slightly; stir in the curry powder, the turmeric booster and cashews, and allow to cool for a few more minutes.

Working in batches, pour the soup into your blender with the remaining vegetable stock and purée on high for 30–60 seconds until smooth and creamy. (For conventional blenders, remove the small centre lid cap and cover the opening with a tea towel so steam can escape while you blend.) Return the soup to the saucepan and warm it over a low heat. Stir in the lemon juice and the remaining ½ teaspoon salt, then tweak the lemon juice and salt to taste. Stir in the spinach for 30 seconds just to wilt it.

Ladle the soup into bowls and swirl 1 teaspoon of soured cream through each serving. Garnish with ¼ teaspoon of the olive oil booster, a sprinkle of the cashew booster and ¼ teaspoon of the chives. Serve with more soured cream, lemon juice, olive oil and the remaining chives.

Roasted garlic and a touch of curry pull the classic potato-and-leek combo up to a new level. Resist the urge to overcommit to curry, because this soup sings when it's subtle. (The turmeric boost will up colour, flavour and anti-inflammatory ammo.) Lemon juice brightens the blend, a dollop of soured cream adds a beautiful tang and creaminess and chives chime in with bite. Depending on the character of your potatoes, stir in more soured cream, and for a richer texture go with that drizzle of olive oil. For crunch, top with the crushed cashews.

NUTRITIONAL FACTS (PER SERVING, BASED ON 8 SERVINGS)

calories 208 kcal | fat 8.3 g | saturated fat 1.1 g | sodium 281.2 mg | carbs 30.3 g | fibre 4.2 g | sugars 2.7 g | protein 5.4 g | calcium 60.8 mg | iron 2.3 mg

Inspired by the *gomadofu* (sesame tofu) in *The Blender Girl* cookbook, my friend Susan Stitt suggested we cut the aubergine in squares instead of the slices or halves. When we topped each roasted square with batons of salad onions, we declared smugly, 'We have elevated the aubergine.' If you're after even more impressive visuals, serve with the chiffonade of spinach, cucumber and a drizzle of sesame oil, for pure plate porn.

miso-glazed aubergine

SERVES 8; GLAZE MAKES 125 G (4½ OZ)

2 large aubergines

80 ml (2¾ fl oz) extra virgin olive oil

¼ tsp natural salt (see page 139)

glaze

2 tbsp filtered water

71 g (2½ oz) red miso paste

1½ tbsp pure maple syrup

1 tbsp tomato purée

2 salad onions, cut into long, thin batons (green parts only)

1 tsp gomasio (ground sesame seeds and sea salt, see page 210) or sesame seeds

optional boosters

44 g (1½ oz) baby spinach, cut into ribbons

1 tsp toasted sesame oil

2 tbsp peeled and finely diced cucumber

Preheat the oven to 180°C/350°F/Gas mark 4.

Cut the ends off each aubergine and cut each into four equally thick rounds. Lay one slice flat, and cut off the rounded edges to make a skinless square piece. Use your first square as a guide to cut the remaining squares. In a baking dish, coat the squares with the olive oil, sprinkle with the salt and set aside to allow the oil to seep into the aubergine.

To make the glaze, add the water, miso, maple syrup and tomato purée to your blender and blast on high for about 30 seconds until well combined. Line a shallow roasting tin with baking paper or a silicone liner. Measure out about 1 tablespoon of the glaze and, using an icing knife or butter knife, coat each aubergine square on all sides. Place the coated squares in the prepared tin and roast, uncovered, for about 40 minutes until the aubergine is cooked through and tender. Some excess oil may seep out of the aubergine. Transfer the aubergine squares to sheets of kitchen paper for a minute to soak up excess oil. Place the salad onion batons in a bowl of iced water for a minute until they curl up.

To serve, place 2 tablespoons of the spinach booster on the centre of each plate, then place a warm aubergine square on top to wilt it. Top with salad onion curls, a drizzle of the sesame oil booster, a sprinkle of the diced cucumber booster and a sprinkling of gomasio.

NUTRITIONAL FACTS (PER SERVING)

calories 156 kcal | fat 10.1 g | saturated fat 1.4 g | sodium 423.5 mg | carbs 16.1 g | fibre 6 g | sugars 9.4 g | protein 3 g | calcium 32.2 mg | iron 0.9 mg

When pal and salad sommelier Geoffrey threw this refreshing dish together on a hot summer night – in under 15 minutes – I knew I had to smuggle it to the blendaholic world, tweak it a bit and spread the love! You *do* need the ponzu citrus marinade to get the dressing just right. Ponzu sauce has a very different character, and lacks the essential zesty quality. From the tangy citrus and the aromatic herbs to the creamy and crunchy fruits and vegetables, this offering showers you with sensations in every bite.

citrus sunshine

SERVES 4; DRESSING MAKES 360 G (12 OZ)

dressing

120 ml (4 fl oz) expeller-pressed safflower oil

120 ml (4 fl oz) Marukan ponzu citrus marinade (not ponzu sauce, see page 210)

4 tbsp grapefruit juice

15 g (½ oz) mint leaves

15 g (½ oz) chopped chives

10 g (¼ oz) finely grated lime zest (about 5 limes)

3 tbsp fresh tarragon leaves

1 tsp natural salt (see page 139)

½ small avocado, stoned peeled and sliced

salad

1 large head butterhead lettuce, leaves pulled apart but kept whole

2 ruby red grapefruits, peeled and segmented

2 red radishes, thinly sliced (I use a mandoline)

1 avocado, stoned, peeled and sliced

optional boosters

1 tbsp raw sprouted watermelon seeds or shelled hemp seeds

1 tbsp finely chopped chives

¼ tsp finely grated lime zest

To make the dressing, throw everything into your blender and blast on high for 30–60 seconds until smooth and creamy.

Assemble the salad on four large plates. Place one-quarter of the lettuce leaves on each plate, arranging them like cups. Then divide the grapefruit segments among the four plates. Top with the radish slices and avocado slices. Drizzle 4 tablespoons of dressing over each lettuce cup and sprinkle the salads with the watermelon seed, chive and lime zest boosters. Serve immediately and pass the remaining dressing around the table.

NUTRITIONAL FACTS (PER SERVING)

calories 426 kcal | fat 37.4 g | saturated fat 3.2 g | sodium 594.8 mg | carbs 23.5 g | fibre 7.9 g | sugars 11.3 g | protein 3.7 g | calcium 88 mg | iron 2.2 mg

This healthy homage to a family fave tastes like it's swimming in mature Cheddar. For kids, omit the mushrooms and herbs. For grown-ups, max out the flavour with the cayenne, chives and salad onion boosters. Mac 'n' cheeze *just* got interesting!

cauliflower mac 'n' cheeze

SERVES 4; CHEEZE SAUCE MAKES 517 G (1 LB 2 OZ)

454 g (1 lb) gluten-free elbow macaroni

6 tbsp extra virgin olive oil

Natural salt (see page 139)

220 g (7¾ oz) shiitake or chestnut mushrooms, diced

1 tbsp gluten-free soy sauce or tamari

1 tbsp finely chopped fresh thyme

150 g (5½ oz) onion, diced

1 tbsp finely chopped garlic (about 3 cloves)

4 tbsp vegetable stock

2 tbsp fresh lemon juice

140 g (5 oz) raw unsalted cashews, soaked (see page 171)

140 g (5 oz) cauliflower florets, steamed

44 g (1½ oz) nutritional yeast flakes, plus extra to taste

1 tbsp white miso paste

⅛ tsp ground turmeric

2 tbsp finely chopped flat-leaf parsley, plus extra to taste

Freshly ground black pepper

optional boosters

⅛ tsp cayenne pepper

2 tbsp finely chopped chives, plus extra to taste

2 tbsp finely chopped salad onion (green parts only), plus extra to taste

Bring a large pot of water to the boil with 1 tablespoon of the olive oil and pinch of salt. Cook the pasta according to the instructions on the packet until al dente, and drain thoroughly.

While the pasta is cooking, in a large frying pan over a medium heat, warm 3 tablespoons of the olive oil and sauté the mushrooms with the soy sauce and thyme for about 5 minutes until the mushrooms are tender. Transfer to a large bowl.

In the same frying pan, heat 1 tablespoon of olive oil over a medium heat and sauté the onion and garlic for about 5 minutes until soft and translucent. Allow to cool slightly.

To make the sauce, throw the onion mixture, 1½ teaspoons of salt, the stock, lemon juice, cashews, cauliflower, nutritional yeast, miso paste, turmeric and the cayenne pepper booster into your blender and blast on high for 30–60 seconds until smooth and creamy.

Transfer the pasta to a large pot, and stir in the remaining 1 tablespoon of olive oil. Stir the sauce into the pasta along with the mushrooms and gently warm over a low heat. Stir in the parsley and the chive and salad onion boosters. Tweak the salt, nutritional yeast, parsley, chives and salad onion to taste, and season with black pepper.

NUTRITIONAL FACTS (PER SERVING)

calories 913 kcal | fat 35.6 g | saturated fat 5.5 g | sodium 1296.3 mg | carbs 117.1 g | fibre 16 g | sugars 11.1 g | protein 40.6 g | calcium 69.1 mg | iron 6.3 mg

If you make just one recipe in this book, let it be this one! Thousands of wows from fans of The World Is Not Right Without Pizza recipe from *The Blender Girl* cookbook put the pressure on when I set out to conjure up a worthy encore to that prize pie. Rather than go solo, I called in my tasters, the pizza-loving supremes: soul sister Stacey and kitchen wing-woman Denise. The garlic-infused base, herbed pesto, spice blend, roasted vegetables, crunchy kale chip topping and pine nut, lemon and red chilli flake boosters rolled out in a rhythm that got this a standing ovation. You'll be on your feet for this pizza, too.

mind-blowing moroccan pizza

SERVES 4–8 AS A STARTER, 2 AS A MAIN; PESTO MAKES 195 G (7 OZ)

vegetables

2 medium heads garlic

5 tbsp extra virgin olive oil

Natural salt (see page 139)

½ tsp ground cumin

½ tsp ground coriander

½ tsp smoked paprika

½ tsp ground nutmeg

¼ tsp ground cinnamon

Pinch of ground allspice

½ yellow onion, cut into 8 wedges

1 medium sweet potato, peeled and sliced into 3 mm (⅛ in) rounds (I use a mandoline)

1 medium courgette, sliced into 3 mm (⅛ in) rounds (I use a mandoline)

50 g (1¾ oz) whole curly green kale leaves (with stalks removed)

¼ tsp freshly ground black pepper

pesto

4 tbsp extra virgin olive oil

1½ tbsp fresh lemon juice, plus extra to taste

50 g (1¾ oz) flat-leaf parsley leaves (about 1 large bunch)

40 g (1½ oz) coriander leaves (about 1 large bunch)

10 g (¼ oz) mint leaves

35 g (1¼ oz) dry-toasted pine nuts

1 tsp white miso paste, plus extra to taste

1 tsp deseeded and finely chopped green chilli, plus extra to taste

1 tsp finely chopped garlic (about 1 clove), plus extra to taste

¼ tsp natural salt (see page 139), plus extra to taste

Pinch of freshly ground black pepper, plus extra to taste

1 tbsp extra virgin olive oil

2 thin, gluten-free, vegan or regular pizza crusts (20–25 cm/8–10 in each), prebaked if packet instructs to do so

1 tbsp finely chopped flat-leaf parsley

optional boosters

3 tbsp dry-toasted pine nuts

¼ tsp finely grated lemon zest, plus extra to taste

¼ tsp chilli flakes, plus extra to taste

Preheat the oven to 200°C/400°F/Gas mark 6. Remove the papery outer layers from the heads of garlic, leaving them whole, with the cloves connected. Trim 6 mm (¼ in) off the top of the heads to expose the cloves. Drizzle each head with 1 teaspoon of the olive oil and sprinkle with

continued

a pinch of salt. Wrap the heads separately in baking paper, then in foil and roast for 40–60 minutes until tender. Allow to cool, then squeeze the garlic pulp out of the skins. You should have 3–4 tablespoons of roasted garlic. Set aside.

To prepare the vegetables, in a large bowl, mix together ½ teaspoon of salt and the spices, then stir in 3 tablespoons of the olive oil. Add the onion, sweet potato and courgette and massage the spiced oil into the vegetables until evenly coated. Lay the vegetables in a single layer on a prepared baking sheet and roast for about 25 minutes until tender and starting to brown. Remove from the oven and allow to cool.

Meanwhile, toss the kale in a bowl with 4 teaspoons of the olive oil, the black pepper and ⅛ teaspoon of salt. Lay the kale leaves in a single layer on a second prepared baking sheet and roast for 10–12 minutes until crispy. Remove from the oven and allow to cool.

While the vegetables are roasting, make the pesto. Throw all of the pesto ingredients into your blender and blast on high for 30–60 seconds until well combined. For conventional blenders you may have to stop the machine, scrape down the sides of the container and add 1 table-spoon of water (or more) to get the mixture to blend. Tweak the miso paste, chilli, garlic, salt and black pepper to taste. Set aside.

Reduce the oven temperature to 190°C/375°F/Gas mark 5.

To assemble the pizzas, use a pastry brush to smear 1½ teaspoons of the olive oil onto each pizza crust. Then spread half of the roasted garlic (about 2 tablespoons) on each. Spread 6 tablespoons of the pesto onto each crust, leaving a 1 cm (½ in) border around the edge. Arrange half of the courgette slices, sweet potato slices and onions over the pesto on each pizza. Sprinkle 1½ tablespoons of the pine nut booster over each.

Bake the pizzas for 10–20 minutes until the crust is fully cooked and the vegetables are slightly browner. Remove from the oven and allow the pizzas to cool slightly. Sprinkle 1½ teaspoons of the parsley on each pizza, along with ⅛ teaspoon each of the lemon zest and chilli flake boosters. Scatter half of the kale chips on top of each pizza, slice and serve.

NUTRITIONAL FACTS (PER SERVING, BASED ON 4 SERVINGS)

calories 794 kcal | fat 44.6 g | saturated fat 6.3 g | sodium 954.4 mg | carbs 86.2 g | fibre 8.1 g | sugars 6.8 g | protein 15.8 g | calcium 208.6 mg | iron 6 mg

For a decadent breakfast, brunch, dessert or (dare I say it?) snack, you can't beat this phenomenal French toast. So simple, so delicious, so creamy, so crispy you may never blend your batter using dairy milk and eggs again. The coconut and nut boosters increase the indulgence, and the rum lobs the flavour into 'to-die-for' territory. Caramelized bananas are always a hit, but this fried bread will get cosy with any fruit. *Bon appetit*!

NUTRITIONAL FACTS (PER SERVING)

calories 476 kcal | fat 26.4 g | saturated fat 16.4 g | sodium 414.3 mg | carbs 60.5 g | fibre 6.1 g | sugars 29.4 g | protein 6.5 g | calcium 78.6 mg | iron 1 mg

french toast with caramelized bananas

SERVES 4

french toast

240 ml (8½ fl oz) unsweetened almond or macadamia milk (strained if homemade)

1 ripe medium banana

2 tbsp pure maple syrup, plus extra to serve

1 tsp natural vanilla extract

1 tbsp white (or black) chia seeds

1 tsp ground cinnamon

¼ tsp natural salt (see page 139)

8 slices gluten-free sandwich bread

4 tbsp coconut oil (in liquid form), plus extra as needed

caramelized bananas

2 medium bananas, thickly sliced on the diagonal

37 g (1¼ oz) coconut sugar

1–2 tbsp coconut oil (in liquid form)

optional boosters

4 tbsp bourbon or rum

2 tbsp crushed raw pecans or walnuts

1 tbsp desiccated coconut

Set the oven to its lowest temperature or the 'warm' setting.

To make the French toast, pour the milk, banana, maple syrup, vanilla, chia seeds, cinnamon and salt into your blender and blast on high for about 30 seconds until well combined. Pour the mixture into a large shallow baking dish and leave to rest for about 5 minutes to thicken slightly. In batches, place slices of the bread in the baking dish and leave to soak on one side for 8–10 seconds. Flip the slices and soak for a further 8–10 seconds until evenly moistened.

In a medium frying pan (that fits two slices of bread) or on a large griddle (that holds all of the slices) over a medium heat, warm 1–2 tablespoons of coconut oil per two slices of bread. (Resist the urge to use less coconut oil, or the bread won't get crispy.) Add the bread and fry for 4–6 minutes on each side until golden brown and crispy on the edges; you may need to add more coconut oil after you flip the bread. If cooking in batches, transfer the French toast to a lined baking sheet and place in the oven to keep warm, and repeat to fry the remaining bread, adding more coconut oil to cook each batch.

While the last pieces of toast are cooking, make the caramelized bananas. Combine the banana slices and the coconut sugar in a zipper-lock bag, seal and shake to coat evenly. In a frying pan over a medium-high heat, warm the coconut oil, add the coated bananas and the bourbon booster and fry for about 2 minutes on each side until nicely caramelized.

Serve two slices of French toast on each plate, topped with one-quarter of the caramelized bananas, one-quarter of the crushed nut boosters and one-quarter of the coconut booster. Pass maple syrup around the table.

choc-mint mania

MAKES ABOUT 20 SQUARES

crust

110 g (4 oz) raw walnuts

170 g (6 oz) chopped pitted dates, plus extra as needed

18 g (½ oz) cacao powder or unsweetened cocoa powder

filling

120 ml (4 fl oz) unsweetened almond milk (strained if homemade)

80 ml (2¾ fl oz) coconut oil (in liquid form)

35 g (1¼ oz) cacao powder or unsweetened cocoa powder

120 ml (4 fl oz) pure maple syrup

210 g (7½ oz) raw unsalted cashews, soaked (see page 171)

¾ tsp peppermint extract

Pinch of natural salt (see page 139)

optional boosters

130 g (4½ oz) courgette, peeled and diced

1 tbsp açaí powder (see page 122)

½ tsp spirulina or chlorella powder (see page 39)

Cut a piece of baking paper to fit in the bottom of a 20 cm (8 in) square tin. Cut two long strips of baking paper to fit along the base of the tin and up and over the sides and place them criss-crossed in the tin; this will help with removal of the chocolate slab after it's frozen. Place the square piece on top.

To make the crust, throw the walnuts, dates and cacao powder into a food processor and process until well combined. Form the mixture into a ball; if it doesn't hold together, add more dates and process again. But add more dates gradually – you don't want the crust to be too sticky. Press the mixture into the base of the prepared tin and set aside.

To make the filling, throw all of the ingredients into your blender in the order listed, including the boosters, and blend for 1–2 minutes until rich and creamy. To achieve the smoothest filling, stop the machine periodically and scrape down the sides of the container. Pour the filling into the crust. Cover the tin with foil and freeze for 4–6 hours until solidified.

To serve, transfer the tin from the freezer to the fridge and leave to thaw for about 30 minutes. Use the baking paper tabs to lift the slab out of the tin. Using a sharp knife, cut it into equal-sized squares. Keeping the squares together, return the slab to the fridge until ready to serve or for up to 7 days.

Note: Because of the coconut oil, this filling will melt if left out at room temperature. If you add the courgette booster, store the dessert in the freezer to keep it for more than 5 days.

NUTRITIONAL FACTS (PER SERVING, BASED ON 20 SERVINGS)

calories 186 kcal | fat 12.5 g | saturated fat 4.5 g | sodium 18.7 mg | carbs 19.3 g | fibre 2.5 g | sugars 13.1 g | protein 3.6 g | calcium 30.3 mg | iron 1.4 mg

This insanely delicious treat is so quick and easy, it's hard not to make it every week! One rich, creamy square is never enough. Suppress any urge to reduce the measure of peppermint extract. It may seem like it'll be overpowering, but trust me – you'll get a perfect balance. The courgette and the superfood powders sneak in the side door without getting in the flavour's way, and put a great boost of goodness into your indulgence. Is there anything chocolate can't cover up?

These gluten-free babes are the bomb, and they have the look, feel, taste and pliability of wheaty ones. Don't be alarmed if your crêpes are a tad crisp when you first flip them out – they soften up fast. But enjoy them quickly or they'll get dry. Blueberries, cinnamon and lemon cashew cream pair beautifully with these (even more so with the ginger, nutmeg and walnut boosters). Simpler: splash with lemon juice and dust with sugar, or drizzle with maple syrup. Filled with anything, these pancakes are delish.

blueberry & lemon cashew cream crêpes

MAKES 8 CRÊPES, 630 ML (JUST UNDER 1¼ PINTS) BATTER, 305 G (10½ OZ) LEMON CASHEW CREAM, 375 G (13 OZ) FILLING

lemon cashew cream

4 tbsp filtered water

2 tbsp pure maple syrup

1 tsp finely grated lemon zest

1 tbsp fresh lemon juice

140 g (5 oz) raw unsalted cashews, soaked (see page 171)

Pinch of natural salt (see page 139)

crêpe batter

420 ml (14¾ fl oz) unsweetened almond milk (strained if homemade)

4 tbsp grapeseed oil

1 tbsp pure maple syrup

¾ tsp natural vanilla extract

70 g (2½ oz) sweet sorghum flour

70 g (2½ oz) garbanzo and fava bean flour blend (see note)

55 g (2 oz) potato starch

½ tsp gluten-free baking powder

¼ tsp natural salt (see page 139)

filling

4 tbsp filtered apple juice

320 g (11¼ oz) blueberries

2 tbsp pure maple syrup

1 tbsp fresh lemon juice

½ tsp natural vanilla extract

½ tsp ground cinnamon

½ tsp finely grated lemon zest

Pinch of natural salt (see page 139)

2 tsp arrowroot

to serve

Coconut flour

Finely grated lemon zest

optional boosters

½ tsp ground ginger

¼ tsp ground nutmeg

55 g (2 oz) raw walnuts, roughly chopped

To make the lemon cashew cream, throw the ingredients into your blender and blast on high for 1 minute until smooth and creamy.

To make the batter, pour the milk, grapeseed oil, maple syrup and vanilla into your blender and process on medium speed for a few seconds until combined. Sift together the flours, potato starch, baking powder and salt and add to your blender. Blend on medium speed for 10–15 seconds until well combined with no lumps.

Using kitchen paper, very lightly coat a 20 cm (8 in) non-stick crêpe pan or frying pan with grapeseed oil. Heat the pan over a low–medium-low heat, depending on your hob. Lift the pan off the heat and pour in 80 ml (2¾ fl oz) of the batter, quickly swirling the pan to allow the mixture to evenly coat the base of the pan. (I swirl the batter twice over the edges so that they don't get too thin and crispy.) Return the pan to the heat and cook the crêpe for about 2 minutes until bubbles form on the top and the sides lift easily from the pan. Gently flip the crêpe with a spatula and cook for about a further 1 minute until lightly browned. Transfer the crêpe to a plate. Repeat with the remaining batter, lightly greasing the pan as needed. Stack the finished crêpes on top of each other so that they soften.

To make the filling, combine the apple juice, blueberries, maple syrup, lemon juice, vanilla, cinnamon, lemon zest, salt, arrowroot and the ginger and nutmeg boosters in a small pot over a medium-high heat and stir gently for about 5 minutes until the berries break down slightly and release some of their juices but the mixture is still chunky. Remove from the heat and allow to cool slightly and thicken.

To serve, use a butter knife to spread 2 tablespoons of the cashew cream over the surface of each crêpe, leaving a 1 cm (½ in) border. Over the cashew cream, spread 2 tablespoons of the blueberry filling. Sprinkle with 1 tablespoon of the walnut booster. Carefully fold the crêpes into quarters and dust with coconut flour and a couple of pinches of lemon zest. Serve immediately.

Note: If you can't find the garbanzo/fava bean flour mix, substitute 175 g (6 oz) gluten-free plain flour in place of the garbanzo and fava bean flour, sorghum flour and potato starch. The taste and texture will vary slightly.

NUTRITIONAL FACTS (PER SERVING, BASED ON 8 SERVINGS)

calories 341 kcal | fat 17.4 g | saturated fat 2.1 g | sodium 185.7 mg | carbs 42.3 g | fibre 3.2 g | sugars 13.8 g | protein 6.5 g | calcium 69.6 mg | iron 1.8 mg

Bread pudding is my dad's default dessert, and he goes for humble flavours like apple and cinnamon. So this one's for you, Dad, and it's deeelicious! The amounts of cinnamon and vanilla may look insane, but don't hold back – the bread needs them for flavour. Be sure to let the pudding rest after it comes out of the oven so that it cuts beautifully and stands up in gorgeous squares. If you want to go nut-free, leave out the walnuts, but the bananas do love the brandy. Serve topped with a big old scoop of vanilla ice cream, to melt and ooze all over the pudding, and gorge yourself senseless.

apple, cinnamon & raisin bread pudding

SERVES 8–12

cream
480 ml (17 fl oz) full-fat coconut milk (shake, then pour)

405 g (14 oz) unsweetened apple sauce

120 ml (4 fl oz) pure maple syrup

2 tbsp grapeseed oil

2 semi-ripe bananas (not fully ripe)

2½ tbsp ground cinnamon

2 tbsp natural vanilla extract

½ tsp natural salt (see page 139)

bread mixture
560 g (1 lb 3 oz) 2.5 cm (1 in) gluten-free sandwich bread cubes (not wholemeal or glutinous bread)

110 g (4 oz) raisins

apples
4 tbsp pure maple syrup

2 tbsp filtered water

2 green apples, peeled, cored and sliced

¾ tsp ground cinnamon

Pinch of natural salt (see page 139)

2 tbsp maple sugar or coconut sugar

optional boosters
4 tbsp brandy

60 g (2¼ oz) raw walnuts, roughly chopped

1 tbsp coconut flour, for dusting

Preheat the oven to 180°C/350°F/Gas mark 4. Lightly grease a 23 x 33 cm (9 x 13 in) tin with coconut oil.

To make the cream, throw the coconut milk, apple sauce, maple syrup, grapeseed oil, bananas, cinnamon, vanilla, salt and the brandy booster into your blender and blast on high for 30–60 seconds until smooth and creamy.

In a large mixing bowl, combine the bread cubes and raisins. Pour the cream over the bread and toss with a spoon to evenly coat. Allow to stand for about 15 minutes to let the bread soak in the liquid.

While the bread is soaking, prepare the apples. In a saucepan over a high heat, bring the maple syrup and water to the boil (this should take less than a minute). As soon as the mixture bubbles, reduce the heat to medium and stir in the apples, cinnamon and salt. Cook the apples for 10–15 minutes, stirring occasionally, until the liquid is absorbed and the apples are lightly caramelized and softened slightly but remain mostly firm. Allow to cool slightly, then add the apples and the walnut booster to the bread mixture. Toss to evenly distribute the ingredients. Transfer the mixture to the prepared tin, then lightly press it down with the back of a spoon so that the bread is evenly covered with liquid. Sprinkle the maple sugar over the top, to help the pudding caramelize on the surface and edges.

Bake, uncovered, for about 1 hour until golden brown and a skewer inserted into the centre comes out relatively clean. Remove from the oven and allow to cool and firm up for 15 minutes. Cut into 8–12 equal-sized squares, dust with the coconut flour booster and serve warm.

Note: This recipe was developed with liquid ratios to work with standard gluten-free sandwich bread. Substituting wheat, rye or other gluten-grain bread will alter the consistency of the pudding.

NUTRITIONAL FACTS (PER SERVING, BASED ON 8 SERVINGS)

calories 540 kcal | fat 21.4 g | saturated fat 11.1 g | sodium 560.6 mg | carbs 87.5 g | fibre 7.1 g | sugars 46.9 g | protein 7.8 g | calcium 108.9 mg | iron 3.1 mg

This elegant sangria is exquisite, and so refreshing in hot weather. A full 24-hour chill lets the flavours *really* mingle. The ginger, lime zest and mint boosters further elevate the elation. Now, this sweet sip tastes deceptively tame, so if it knocks you on your . . . well, don't say I didn't warn you. Go easy and keep things peachy.

peach sangria

SERVES 6

5 ripe peaches

480 ml (17 fl oz) unsweetened white grape juice

1 (750ml) bottle Sauvignon Blanc

120 ml (4 fl oz) apricot brandy

1 vanilla pod, sliced lengthways (seeds intact)

250 g (9 oz) ice cubes (optional)

optional boosters

1 tsp finely chopped fresh ginger

½ tsp finely grated lime zest

5 g (⅛ oz) mint

Peel and stone the peaches. Roughly chop 3 of the peaches to make 380 g (13½ oz). Cut the remaining 2 peaches into 16 slices.

Throw the grape juice and the chopped peaches, plus the ginger and lime zest boosters, into your blender and blast on high for 30–60 seconds until smooth. In a glass jug or punch bowl, combine the wine and brandy. Stir the blended mixture into the wine mixture. (Don't be concerned about the frothiness; it settles.)

Add the peach slices, vanilla pod and the mint booster to the sangria. Stir to combine and leave to sit at room temperature for about 2 hours to allow the fruit flavours to infuse the mix. Chill in the fridge for at least 12 hours, and preferably 24 hours for the best flavour.

Remove the vanilla pod and mint leaves. If serving all of the sangria at once, add the ice to the jug. Otherwise, drop ice into individual glasses. The sangria will keep in the fridge for up to 3 days.

NUTRITIONAL FACTS (PER SERVING)

calories 252 kcal | fat 0.3 g | saturated fat 0 g | sodium 7.7 mg | carbs 26.6 g | fibre 2 g | sugars 22.3 g | protein 1.2 g | calcium 13.4 mg | iron 0.4 mg

resources

appliances

Excalibur
amazon.co.uk
Dehydrators

KitchenAid
kitchenaid.co.uk
Blenders, other appliances

Omega
juicers.co.uk
Juicers

coconut products

Raw Living
rawliving.eu
Coconut aminos, coconut crystals, coconut flour, coconut nectar

Dang
amazon.co.uk
Toasted coconut chips

Coconutty
coconutty.co.uk
Coconut cream, coconut sugar, raw coconut meat and water

Tiana
amazon.co.uk
Coconut water

Let's Do . . . Organic
amazon.co.uk
Creamed coconut, coconut flour, raw and toasted dried coconut flakes, sweetened and unsweetened coconut chips, reduced-fat shredded coconut

Biona
amazon.co.uk
Full-fat classic canned coconut milk

Nutiva
nutiva.com
Coconut butter, coconut flour, coconut oil, coconut sugar

gluten-free flours, grains and pasta

Ancient Harvest Quinoa
amazon.co.uk
Quinoa, quinoa pasta

Arrowhead Mills
amazon.co.uk
Gluten-free flours and grains

Bob's Red Mill
bobsredmill.com
Gluten-free flours and grains

Goodness Direct
goodnessdirect.co.uk
Quinoa, millet, buckwheat, buckwheat soba noodles

King Soba
kingsoba.com
Buckwheat soba, rice noodles

Goodness Direct
goodnessdirect.co.uk
Brown rice, brown-rice pasta

Tinkyáda
amazon.co.uk
Brown-rice pasta and lasagne sheets

herbs, spices, flavourings and seasonings

Goodness Direct
goodnessdirect.co.uk
Ketchup, mustard, Worcestershire sauce, other condiments

Bragg
bragg.com
Liquid aminos

Cortas
amazon.com
Rose water

Biona
biona.co.uk
Gomasio

Floracopeia
amazon.co.uk
Orange essential oil

Steenbergs
steenbergs.co.uk
Alcohol-free flavours and extracts, herbs, spices

The Wasabi Company
thewasabicompany.co.uk
Ponzu sauces

Clearspring
clearspring.co.uk
Miso pastes

Goodness Direct
goodnessdirect.co.uk
Wheat-free tamari

juices

Lakewood
amazon.co.uk
Juices

Santa Cruz Organics
amazon.co.uk
Juices

kitchenware

Amco Houseworks
amazon.co.uk
Citrus squeezers

Cutco
cutco.co.uk
Knives

Dreamfarm
formahouse.co.uk
Kitchen tools

Eco Jarz
amazon.co.uk
Jars, lids, stainless-steel straws

Global
Globalknives.uk
Knives

KitchenAid
kitchenaid.co.uk
Cookware, kitchen tools

KitchenIQ
amazon.co.uk
Citrus zesters, ginger tools, knife sharpeners, spice graters, other tools

Klean Kanteen
international.
kleankanteen.com/eu
Stainless-steel drink bottles and mugs

Le Creuset
lecreuset.co.uk
Cookware, tools

Life Factory
formahouse.co.uk
Glass drink bottles

Knives For Chefs
knivesforchefs.co.uk
Knives

Williams-Sonoma
williams-sonoma.com/
customer-service/
international-orders
Cookware, kitchen tools and appliances

milks

Goodness Direct
goodnessdirect.co.uk
Almond, cashew and coconut milks

Alpro
alpro.com/uk
Almond, cashew and coconut milks

Suncoast Gold
suncoastgold.com.au
Macadamia milk

Good Hemp
amazon.co.uk
Hemp milk

nuts and seeds

Artisana Organics
amazon.co.uk
Tahini, other organic nut and seed butters

Goodness Direct
goodnessdirect.co.uk
frontiercoop.com
Flax, pumpkin, sesame and sunflower seeds

Go Raw
amazon.co.uk
Sprouted pumpkin, sunflower and watermelon seeds

Biovea
biovea.com/uk
Raw cashews, chia and hemp seeds

Nutiva
nutivauk.com
Chia (white and black) and hemp seeds

Goodness Direct
goodnessdirect.co.uk
Nuts, nut butters, seeds

Suncoast Gold
suncoastgold.com.au
Macadamias

oils and vinegars

Barlean's
amazon.co.uk
Flaxseed oil

Olivado
waitrose.com
Avocado oil

Bragg
amazon.co.uk
Apple cider vinegar and extra-virgin olive oil

Bulletproof
uk.bulletproof.com
Brain Octane MCT oil, XCT oil, coconut charcoal, other supplements

Mediterranean Direct
mediterraneandirect.
co.uk
Truffle-infused extra-virgin olive oil

Goodness Direct
goodnessdirect.co.uk
Brown rice vinegar

Biona
amazon.co.uk
Organic flaxseed oil

Alfa One
waitrose.com
Rice bran oil

Marukan
thespiceshop.co.uk
Seasoned rice vinegar

Napa Valley Naturals
amazon.co.uk
Balsamic vinegar, extra-virgin olive oil, grapeseed oil, toasted sesame oil

Nutiva
amazon.co.uk
Coconut oil, hemp oil

Omega Nutrition
omeganutrition.co.uk
Avocado, olive, sesame and sunflower seed oils

Panaseeda
activationeurope.com
*Medicinal black cumin
seed oil, chia seed oil,
coriander seed oil, five-oil
blend*

Spectrum Organics
amazon.co.uk
*Coconut, flaxseed,
grapeseed, olive and
toasted sesame oil*

Styrian Gold
styriangold.ca
Styrian pumpkin seed oil

Suncoast Gold
suncoastgold.com.au
Macadamia oil

probiotics

Body Ecology
bodyecology.com/
international
*Culture starters, probiotic
beverages, supplements*

Cultured Cellar
the culturedcellar.co.uk
*Sauerkraut (without
vinegar), other pickles*

Cultures for Health
happykombucha.co.uk
*Starters and supplies
for kefir, kombucha
and other ferments*

Biocare
biocare.co.uk
*Probiotic powder
and supplements*

Raw Living
rawliving.eu
*Fermented vegetables
and beverages*

GO!
gokombucha.co.uk
Kombucha

Nourish Kefir
nourishkefir.co.uk
*Kefir including grains to
make your own*

Kevita
amazon.co.uk
Probiotic beverages

Rejuvenation Company
amazon.co.uk
Rejuvelac

Rhythm Health
rhythmhealth.co.uk
Coconut kefir

produce, organic and conventional

Driscoll's
driscolls.eu
Berries

Abel & Cole
abelandcole.co.uk
Fruits, vegetables, tofu

produce, organic and frozen

Goodness Direct
goodnessdirect.co.uk
Frozen vegetables

protein powders and green powders

Indigo Herbs
indigo-herbs.co.uk
*Brown rice, hemp, raw
and pea protein powders*

PlantFusion
amazon.co.uk
Fermented protein powder

Sprout Living
amazon.co.uk
*Raw and sprouted
protein powders*

Sun Warrior
evolutionorganics.co.uk
*Protein powder,
Ormus Supergreens*

Vega
evolutionorganics.co.uk
Protein powders

salt

The Natural Salt Seller
naturalsaltseller.co.uk
Celtic sea salt

sea vegetables

**The Cornish Seaweed
Company**
cornishseaweed.co.uk
Different types of seaweed

Maine Coast
amazon.co.uk
*Dulse and kelp flakes,
kelp, nori, wakame*

Sea Tangle
rawliving.eu
Kelp noodles

superfood boosters

Biovea
biovea.com
Pomegranate powder

Pulpa Store
pulpastore.co.uk
*Unsweetened frozen
açaí puree, plus superfood
boosters and supplements*

E3 Live
detoxyourworld.com
Frozen algae supplement

Jarrow Formulas
amazon.co.uk
L-theanine capsules

Jing Herbs
aggressivehealth
shop.com
*Three Sisters tincture,
various herbal tonics
and powders*

Lily of the Desert
amazon.co.uk
Organic aloe vera juice

Miracle Clay
amazon.co.uk
Edible clay

Indigo Herbs
indigo-herbs.co.uk
*Superfood powders: açaí,
baobab, cacao, camu,
chaga mushroom,
chlorella, goji, maca,
lucuma, maqui, mucuna,
spirulina and wheatgrass*

Sambazon
synergy-health.co.uk
*Unsweetened organic
frozen açaí puree*

Swanson Health Products
healthmonthly.co.uk
Inulin powder

World Organic
amazon.co.uk
Liquid chlorophyll

sweeteners

Raw Living
rawliving.eu
*Coconut crystals,
coconut nectar*

Meridian
amazon.co.uk
Organic maple syrup

Biovea
biovea.com
*Coconut sugar, lucuma
powder, yacon syrup*

Nu Naturals
amazon.co.uk
*Alcohol-free liquid stevia,
plain and flavoured*

Nutiva
nutivauk.com
Coconut sugar

Smart Sweet
amazon.co.uk
Birch xylitol

SweetLeaf
amazon.co.uk
*Alcohol-free liquid stevia,
plain and flavoured*

Xyla
amazon.co.uk
Birch xylitol

tea

Goodness Direct
goodnessdirect.co.uk
*Organic and
fair-trade teas*

Numi Tea
amazon.co.uk
*Plain rooibos, other
organic teas*

Traditional Medicinals
amazon.co.uk
*Herbal and
medicinal teas*

vegan and speciality ingredients

AFC Soy Foods
afcsoyfoods.com
*Hot chilli fermented
beancurd (tofu) cubes*

Bragg
amazon.co.uk
Nutritional yeast

Clearspot
clearspottofu.co.uk
Organic tofu

Enjoy Life
amazon.co.uk
Vegan chocolate chips

Goodness Direct
goodnessdirect.co.uk
Organic silken tofu

Green Giant
amazon.co.uk
canned hearts of palm

Heera
amazon.co.uk
*Organic canned young
jackfruit*

Seapoint Farms
amazon.co.uk
Frozen shelled edamame

The Wasabi Company
thewasabicompany.co.uk
*Mirin, wasabi powder and
other Japanese products*

Tiger Tiger
gluten-freeshop.co.uk
*Gluten-free
Worcestershire sauce*

Veggie Stuff
veggiestuff.com
Gluten-free tempeh

Westbrae
amazon.co.uk
*Organic unsweetened
ketchup, various canned
beans*

vegetable stock

Massel
amazon.co.uk
*Bouillon cubes and
liquid stock*

water

AlkaViva
amazon.co.uk
Alkaline water machines

Icelandic glacial water
amazon.co.uk
Alkaline glacial water

Nikken PiMag Waterfall
nikkenwellbeing.co.uk
Water-filtration systems

yogurt, dairy-free alternatives

Alpro
alpro.com/uk
Soya and almond yogurt

Coyo
coyo.com/gb
Coconut yogurt

acknowledgements

I couldn't do what I do without the talent, support and guidance of the remarkable Sharon Bowers, Jess Taylor, Hugh Marks, Beverley Flower, Joe Stallone and Stephen Digby. Thank you for your honesty, good humour, business savvy and for always having my back.

The stars aligned to create the perfect storm for aesthetic ascendance when Jody Scott teamed up the creative genius of Anson Smart, Deborah Kaloper, Russell Horton, Maxwell Adey, Samantha Powell, Inez Garcia, Xanthe Wetzler, Louella Adey, Maria Esztergalyos, Vlad Ivanovic, Randy Jackson and Mervat Fanous to bring these recipes and their contexts to life. I am humbled, blessed and grateful beyond words to have collaborated with such extraordinary talent.

Ten Speed Press makes the best cookbooks in the world, and I'm honoured to have a seat at the premier table. Thanks to the incomparable Kelly Snowden for steering this project with grace and ease, and to Aaron Wehner, Julie Bennett, Hannah Rahill, Emma Campion, Betsy Stromberg, Mari Gill, Michele Crim, Kristin Casemore, Allison Renzulli, Erin Welke, Daniel Wikey, Ashley Matuszak, Andrea Chesman and Dawn Yanagihara for adding your talent and publishing prowess to create the perfect blend. And to the magnificent David Drake, Ranjana Armstrong, Carisa Hays, Henri Clinch, Emily Pollack, Candice Chaplin, Pam Roman, Daryl Mattson, Liisa McCloy-Kelley and the rest of the teams at the Crown Publishing Group and Penguin Random House – thank you for your tenacious support and enthusiasm for The Blender Girl message.

I am fortunate to work with some of the world's best food and lifestyle brands. Thank you to the brilliant teams at KitchenAid, Massel, Suncoast Gold, Earthbound Farm, Silk, So Delicious, Vega, Driscoll's, Navitas Naturals, Frontier Co-op, Selina Naturally, Nutiva, Kitchen IQ, Dreamfarm, Temple Turmeric, Edward & Sons, Let's Do . . . Organic, Native Forest, Enjoy Life, Nu Naturals, SweetLeaf, Vivapura, Nuts.com, Sprout Living, Harmless Harvest, Barlean's, Sunlighten and a special mention to the extraordinary Robert Schueller and Nick Quintero from Melissa's Produce.

For generously providing items to help with production and photography, I extend my gratitude to: KitchenAid Australia, Le Creuset Australia, Dreamfarm, Nutribullet, Jac + Jack, Lee Mathews, Levi's, Rationale, Sodashi, The FortyNine Studio, M.H. Ceramics and the incredible David Morgan. And immeasurable thanks go to Georgie and Merrick Watts, for opening their gorgeous home.

To my righteous recipe testers: your constructive feedback pushed me towards excellence at every turn. I share the success of this book with: Karen Kipp and Bobby Herman; Rachel and Joe Fulginiti; Karen, Sean, Tahlia and Harvey Kirke; Marie-Guy Maynard, and Louis, Tomas, Jacob and Lucas Subirana; Robin and Jay Eller; Sharon Geake and Scott Henderson; Andrea Libretti, Jaclyn and Jade DiDonato, and Ed Halvorsen; Dawn Agran and Chris Woolley; John and Sandra Hanes; Pola, Dave and Mark Snell; Elaine and Kathleen Morales; Hillary Huber Wilson and Steven Wilson; Jennifer, Scott, Catherine and Benjamin Ward; Judith and Peter Lewis; Kate Lewis and Devin Echle; Annette and John Beck; Chuck Constant; Lori Robin Wilson; Magali, Alessia and Andreas Pès Schmid; Richard Parsons; and Wendi, Scott, Ava and Danny Higginbotham.

Nothing in my life works without some pretty serious hand-holding from the unstoppable Hanna Lundgren and Gina Smith. Ladies, I raise a glass to you. Ashley Koff, dietician dynamo, I bow to you for your unending knowledge, friendship and prudent guidance; all helped shape this book. I lie at the feet of the remarkable Joy Coelho and Jay Denman of the Jingslingers who've taught me so much about bio-hacking health and nutrition and have been unbelievably generous and unfailingly kind. And, I thank my performance agents at AVO Talent, KMR Talent and EM Voices, as well as Melissa Rose and Annette Robinson, for your continued patience and support as I go on blowing off my real job to blend!

With Scott recording numerous books in our home studio, right below the kitchen, my sacred circle of friends opened their houses yet again, shared their culinary creativity and rolled up their sleeves to chop, dice and blend with me. To Trent and Melissa Lanz; Stacey Aswad and Chuck Duran; Geoffrey Rodriguez and Bernhard Punzet; Ron Russell; Danielle Jean-François, Michelle Smith; Eda Benjakul; Olivia MacKenzie-Smith and Kitch Membery; Susan Stitt; Alicia Buszczak; Katy Townsend; Toshiko Mohr; my best friend of twenty years, Mika Hara; and my unfailing kitchen companion and soul sister, Denise Chamberlain, who walked, trudged and crawled every step of this latest journey with me: I love you all and am so fortunate to have you as my chosen family. Your generosity of spirit boosts my blend and replenishes my heart, giving constant reminders of the power of human connection.

I struck gold with the best blendaholic family in the world: Mum and Dad, who bought me my first blender and stocked all the right ingredients; Scott Brick, who strives alongside me for the perfect blend every day; Kara, sister and consigliere; Leigh, cocktail cohort; and star ice lolly and chocolate slice models Alexandra and Sullivan. The joy of my life is wrapped up in my memories with you.

Finally, to my readers: your stories and interaction are my greatest inspiration and reward.

index

Quarto is the authority on a wide range of topics.

Quarto educates, entertains and enriches the lives of our readers – enthusiasts and lovers of hands-on living.

www.QuartoKnows.com

First published in 2017 by
Jacqui Small LLP
74-77 White Lion Street
London N1 9PF

A catalogue record for this book is available from the British Library.

Design by Betsy Stomberg

ISBN: 978 1 911127 20 8

2019 2018 2017

10 9 8 7 6 5 4 3 2 1

Printed in China